W. B. Yeats
Interviews and Recollections
Volume 2

Also by E. H. Mikhail

The Social and Cultural Setting of the 1890s
John Galsworthy the Dramatist
Comedy and Tragedy
Sean O'Casey: A Bibliography of Criticism
A Bibliography of Modern Irish Drama 1899–1970
Dissertations on Anglo-Irish Drama
The Sting and the Twinkle: Conversations with Sean O'Casey
(co-editor with John O'Riordan)
J. M. Synge: A Bibliography of Criticism
J. M. Synge: Interviews and Recollections *(editor)*
British Drama 1900–1950
Contemporary British Drama 1950–1976
W. B. Yeats: Interviews and Recollections, Vol. I *(editor)*

W. B. YEATS

Interviews and Recollections

Volume 2

Edited by

E. H. Mikhail

M

First published 1977 by
THE MACMILLAN PRESS LTD
London and Basingstoke
Associated companies in New York
Dublin Melbourne Johannesburg and Madras

SBN 333 19712 7

Printed in Great Britain by
BILLING AND SONS LTD
Guildford, Worcester and London

C C

To my wife

Contents

Acknowledgements

The editor and publishers wish to thank the following who have kindly given permission for the use of copyright material:

Earnán P. de Blaghd for the extract 'The Yeats I Knew' by Earnán de Blaghd Snr from *The Yeats We Knew*, ed. Francis MacManus, published by Mercier Press, 1965.
British Broadcasting Corporation for 'As Yeats Was Going Down Grafton Street' by Diarmuid Brennan from the *Listener*, LXXI, Feb 1964.
Curtis Brown Ltd for the extract 'W. B. Yeats' from *All for Hecuba: An Irish Theatrical History* by Micheál MacLiammóir. Published by Methuen & Co. Ltd 1946.
Chatto & Windus Ltd for the article 'W. B. Yeats' from *Writers at Work* by Louise Morgan.
R. Dardis Clarke for the extract 'The Yeats I Knew' by Austin Clarke from *The Yeats We Knew*, ed. Francis MacManus, published by Mercier Press, 1965.
Edmund Dulac for 'Without the Twilight' from *Scattering Branches*, ed. Stephen Gwynn.
Monk Gibbon for 'The Yeats I Knew' from *The Yeats We Knew*, ed. Francis MacManus, published by Mercier Press, 1965.
Emmet M. Greene for the extract 'The Yeats I Knew' from *Life and the Dream* by Mary M. Colum published by Dolmen Press, Dublin, 1964 and Doubleday & Co. Inc., New York, 1947.
Guardian Newspapers Ltd for the extract from 'De Valera as Play Censor' from the *Manchester Guardian Weekly*, 13 Apr 1934.
Mrs F. R. Higgins for 'Yeats as Irish Poet' by F. R. Higgins from *Scattering Branches*, ed. Stephen Gwynn.
David Higham Associates Ltd for 'W. B. Yeats: Chameleon of Genius' by Clifford Bax from *Some I Knew Well* published by Phoenix House/J. M. Dent & Sons Ltd, and for the extract 'Yeats *Smelt* the Spirits' by Louis MacNeice from *The Strings are False*, published by Faber and Faber Ltd.
The Hokuseido Press for 'An Interview with W. B. Yeats' by Shotaro Oshima from *W. B. Yeats and Japan*, 1965.

Irish Independent Newspapers Ltd for the extract 'Mr Yeats Explains Play' from the *Irish Independent*, 13 Aug 1938.

The Irish Press Ltd for the extracts 'W. B. Yeats Looks Back; Poet Celebrates his Seventieth Birthday' from the *Irish Press*, 14 June 1935 and 'W. B. Yeats Looks Back; Ireland in the Early Days of Abbey Theatre' from the *Irish Press*, 14 Oct 1935.

The *Irish Times* for the extracts 'Reminiscences of "W. B." by E. R. Walsh from the *Irish Times*, 10 Feb 1940 and 'May Craig Recalls the Abbey Days' from the *Irish Times*, 10 June 1965.

Macmillan Publishing Co. Inc., New York, for the extract from *Rose and Crown (Autobiographies)* by Sean O'Casey.

Ethel Mannin for the extract 'No Shore Beyond' from *Privileged Spectator*.

The *New York Times* for the extract from Book Review, Speaking of Books: 'Visions of Yeats' by Walter Starkie, © 1965 by the *New York Times*. Reprinted by permission.

A. D. Peters & Co. for extracts 'Quarrelling with Yeats: A Friendly Recollection' by Frank O'Connor, published in *Esquire*, and 'Reminiscences of Yeats' by Frank O'Connor from *Leinster, Munster & Connaught*, published by Robert Hale Ltd, 1950.

Lennox Robinson for 'The Man and the Dramatist' from *Scattering Branches*, ed. Stephen Gwynn.

Marianne Helweg Rodgers for the extract from the script of W. R. Rodgers on 'W. B. Yeats', broadcast in June 1949. Reprinted in *Irish Literary Portraits*, BBC, 1972.

William Rothenstein for 'Yeats as a Painter Saw Him' from *Scattering Branches*, ed. Stephen Gwynn.

Saturday Review for the article 'Memories of Yeats' by Mary M. Colum from the *Saturday Review of Literature*, XIX, 25 Feb 1939.

Shenandoah, The Washington & Lee University Review, for 'Glimpses of W. B. Yeats' by Austin Clarke from *Shenandoah*, XVI, No. 4. Copyright 1963 by *Shenandoah*. Reprinted by permission of the editor.

The Society of Authors as the literary representative of the Estate of James Stephens for the extract 'W. B. Yeats' from *James, Seumas & Jacques: Unpublished Writings of James Stephens*.

The Statesman & Nation Publishing Co. Ltd for 'Meetings with Yeats' by Hugh Kingsmill from the *New Statesman*, 4 Jan 1941, and 'Encounters with Yeats' by V. S. Pritchett from the *New Statesman*, 4 June 1965.

Francis Stuart for 'The Yeats I Knew' from *The Yeats We Knew*, ed. Francis MacManus, published by Mercier Press, 1965.

The *Texas Quarterly* for the article 'Some Memories of W. B. Yeats' by Brigit Patmore from the *Texas Quarterly*, Vol. VIII, Winter 1965.

University College Dublin for 'W. B. Yeats—A Generation Later' by Thomas MacGreevy, from the *University Review*, III, No. 8.

George Weidenfeld & Nicolson Ltd and Harvard University Press Ltd for 'W. B. Yeats' from *Memories 1898–1939* by C. M. Bowra. Reprinted by permission of the publishers; © 1966 by C. M. Bowra and M. B. Yeats and Miss Anne Yeats for the letter and poem sent to C. M. Bowra by W. B. Yeats.

The *Yale Review* for 'Yeats's Phantasmagoria' by Frank O'Connor from *Two Friends: Yeats and A. E.* from *The Yale Review*, Sep 1939.

The publishers have made every effort to trace the copyright holders but if they have inadvertently overlooked any they will be pleased to make the necessary arrangements at the first opportunity.

W. B. Yeats*

LOUISE MORGAN

Unless you are one of his old friends, it is almost impossible to arrange a talk with W. B. Yeats. For more than a year I had been writing him letters in the attempt to fix an appointment. Each of the letters had been duly answered, from Ireland or Italy, but only after such long delay (the first letter after an interval of three months) that I had missed his passing through London. But at last I managed to reach him on the telephone at his London club, and we fixed a time and place for the following morning.

Even then, it was only by an act of God that we met.

The rendezvous was (or so I understood it) at Hatchard's, the famous bookshop in Piccadilly, at eleven. I was there ten minutes before the hour turning over the pages of the newest books. At 11.25 I was still turning over pages. Had he forgotten? A minute or two later a man walked in who dwarfed all the other people in the shop.

He was surprised when I greeted him. 'It is due to the interference of Providence that I came here at all,' he said in a quiet, slow, hesitant voice, looking at me with grave eyes that saw everything and nothing at the same time. 'I went to Hatchett's, at Dover Street I think it is, where I thought we'd have a cup of tea. I meet people there sometimes. But it was closed. And then when you didn't come I thought perhaps I'd said 11.30, and I would just have time to walk down here and get a book I had ordered. That's the only reason in the world you see me here at all.'

For me, the reasons, whatever they were, had at the moment not the least significance. The only thing that mattered was the fact that he was there. *Vates aderat.*[1]

We went to a little café next door which smells deliciously of ground coffee and bales of tea, and sat in a corner downstairs. Some astonishingly everyday people were drinking coffee all about, and talking probably about everything under the sun but poetry. I thought how rarely satisfying it was to see a great poet who looks the great poet—though in not a detail of dress or appearance did he differ from the average man. I had often heard from people who knew him rumours of a magnificent presence, a warmth of human understanding, and an endless power of talk. Echoes of gargantuan talks in Rapallo[2] and Dublin had reverberated excitingly in my ears even at their faintest diminuendo. And now with the living voice

* *Writers at Work* (London: Chatto and Windus, 1931) pp. 1–9.

beginning to weave a pattern of thought and sound across the glass-topped table of a tea-shop, and the noble head and shoulders bending over the blessed banality of a cup of tea, I was not disappointed.

His voice has almost a separate life of its own. It is charged with the thousands of overtones of story, argument, song, anecdote, comment, and fable which have so richly freighted it. It is an intimate, quiet voice, with a touch of brogue and more than a touch of humour. It goes along swiftly, in grave sweeps of eloquence, and then hesitates, gropes—as if seeking the right word or waiting to be sure how his listener is following him. The hour was already sadly reduced by the misunderstanding over the place of meeting, and he had some things to do before going to Hampstead for lunch, but the brief minutes left us he stuffed full of odds and ends of glory.

I asked him what he thought of the present and future state of poetry.

'Technically we are in a state corresponding to the time of Dryden,' he said. 'The position of the young poet to-day is not unlike that of the young Swift in the library of Sir William Temple. At that time, they were moving away from the Elizabethans and on towards Pope. To-day, we are moving away from the Victorians and on towards the modern equivalent of Pope. We are developing a poetry of statement as against the old metaphor. The poetry of to-morrow will be finely articulated fact. T. S. Eliot fascinates us all because he is further on towards this consummation than any other writer.'

'Do you think it a good consummation?'

'It isn't a question of good or bad, but of what is before us. I myself am inclined to think it's not so good as the old song.'

'Then you don't think too highly of modern poetry?'

'It is very ungracious of the old, as well as exceedingly unwise, to criticize the younger generation!'

'Could you define the period we are going through?'

'We are in our Hellenistic Age. I think we have seen the best of European literature. We may have a Virgil ahead of us, but certainly not a Homer. The romantic age is over—and by romantic I mean the expression of personality and passion. All recent movements have been away from it. People are everywhere conscious of change, but they haven't yet got hold of the new thing. There is a great deal of manufactured literature to-day. Romance is extinct, with its stress on personality; so people are artificially making up a personality for themselves.'

'But so many are saying that we are on the verge of a romantic revival.'

'The immediate past never returns. We are gradually developing towards a literature of spiritual belief. Perhaps it would be better to say *philosophical* belief. Some people might misunderstand my use of the word *spiritual*. There is an inexhaustible mass of philosophical material from the past that is deeply imbedded in us emotionally, an incredible accumulation of material about nature and the supernatural that has as deep associations emotionally as the spade or any other ancient symbol. Some of it is Platonic, and some of it is older than Plato, going as far back as the Vedas. I think there will be a revival of that kind of philosophy. It will become vital again. We shall have next a literature of spiritual conviction.'

'Meantime, do you think the machine the proper subject for poetry?'

'Nothing new is good as a subject for poetry. The spade is ancient; it has become a symbol. But the sewing-machine has not had time to become a symbol. Certainly a few prosaic elements are good in poetry, to give it a touch of reality. But the substance of poetry is a mass of symbol which has been passed on from age to age, slightly enlarged, but only slightly, as time goes on. It is a slow process because human experience is capable of taking in only a little at a time. In three or four generations perhaps, the machine may be a proper subject for poetry—and then for a long time only in factories. Of course any amount of poetry can be written now about the machine if you take it superficially, but that poetry will be merely rhetoric. You can always write rhetorical poetry about any subject under the sun if you have an exciting conviction on the matter.'

'Will you tell me some things about your own writing of poetry? It somehow seems absurd to ask, but do you *work* over your poetry?'

'Of course I work. My poetry costs me endless labour. I begin every day at 11, and work steadily until lunch at 1.30. After that I may or may not write. But mornings without work would be unthinkable. I sit down to it, as some French poet has said, like the galley-slave to his oars. But it comes more easily now. Inspiration can be as automatic as the clock. I begin with great difficulty. The thing that gets you over the horrible business of beginning is the momentum of the subconscious. The subconscious is always there lying behind the mind, ready to leap out. The weight of its momentum grows with experience. The whole aim of consciousness is to make the subconscious its obedient servant. That I think is why as one grows older one gets happier.'

'Has your speed quickened?'

'Yes. My pace is now seven or eight lines a day. It used to be that many a week.'

'Do you remember the time it took you to write any particular poems?'

'There's a little poem[3] in *The Wind in the Willows* [sic] that describes the beloved as a fish. It's not a particularly good poem. But I spent a whole week over it, and several sleepless nights. There is another poem, quite a good one, called *The Impetuous Heart* [sic], only six lines long. I spent nine unbroken hours on that, and I wrote it in a rage. I was in a rage because a woman editor badgered me to write it, and she wouldn't let me off. I timed it by the clock. Mind, I am not saying that my poetry is the better because I labour over it. Other men write fine poetry with no trouble to themselves at all. It's a matter of temperament.'

'Do you enjoy writing?'

'Writing poisoned my youth! I could have been a happier man if I had stopped writing.'

'How early did you begin?'

'I began by accident. A school-fellow wrote a long poem, and I wanted to see if I could do as well. I never thought of writing before that. I had all the usual preposterous ambitions of youth. Piracy wasn't practicable when I was a boy, but there were equivalent things! I wrote my first poetry when I was seventeen.'

'What gives you the initial impulse for a poem?'

'Some situation in life—a sudden emotion. My poems all originate like that. The idea for a poem comes in moments of personal excitement. I sometimes jot down a few prose lines in a notebook, leaving them purposely vague. Then begins the process of gradually giving the poem rhythmical form. Rhythm produces a faint hypnosis. I always work with regular metres. If I were writing an intimate love-song I couldn't use *vers libre*.[4] In fact, the more intimate the poem is, the more obvious is the metre I choose. I like to think of it as everybody's song, to think that thousands of men all over the world have felt the same thing. That frees me from indiscretion. I try to think of myself perhaps as a camel driver. I choose the camel driver because he represents something very ancient. But it must be myself and it must be also the camel driver. The camel driver is the subconscious. The poem is prosaic and useless unless it is the song of the subconscious, the camel driver's song, which is everybody's song. The eighteenth-century philosopher Vico[5] said, "Do not believe in any philosophy that does not begin in myth." So I would say, "Do not believe in the depth of any emotion that has not a similar ancestry." '

'Does your emphasis on *everybody's song* mean that you believe in international literature?'

'I hate international literature. The core of a thing must be national or local. But at the same time it ought to be a fundamental piece of human life, which is the same everywhere. I used to turn bad plays into good ones when I was working at the Abbey Theatre by saying to the author, "Put that play into Japan." If the plot survived that treatment I would say, "Now put it back into Ireland." I'd like to make Agamemnon[6] a publican who comes home from America to Patrick Street, Dublin, and finds his wife has been carrying on with the bartender, and I'd like to turn Cassandra into an old char prophesying in a tea-cup. Any great play can be put into any other nation or age, but at the same time it is essentially local. A great piece of literature is entirely of its own locality and yet infinitely translatable.'

'What novelist would you say was local and universal at the same time?'

'Balzac, without any hesitation.'

'Would you put Stendhal in the same class?'

'Stendhal is the beginning of what I hate. He says a novel should be like a mirror dawdling down a lane. Stendhal began the collapse of the human soul.'

'What novelists do you enjoy reading?'

'I love Jane Austen and her perilous pursuit of good breeding. With Pickwick the democratic movement began, because he offers qualities which everybody can possess. I love Henry James also. With him the perilous pursuit of good breeding begins once more!'

'What Victorian poet do you admire?'

'Browning, of course, and if I live another ten years I shall admire Tennyson again. I am entirely devoted to William Morris. He is a magnificent story-teller. There you have all the great stories of the world greatly told.'

We had spent the last ten minutes alternately looking at our watches. It was almost time for him to go.

'I'd like to ask you one or two more questions about your own writing,' I said. 'Is there any mood or object or image that you associate with the writing of poetry?'

'I often think of a man in a little inn in the West of Ireland. There's a stormy sea and a ship. I think he's going into exile, but I'm not certain of it.'

'Is it a visual impression?'

'I have an image of him. I could describe the room to you.'

'Do you write the poem in your head?'

'It grows on paper. I couldn't work without paper in front of me.'

'Do you mind where you write?'

'Not in the least. The more inaccessible I am, and the less of the telephone there is, the better. Not that I am annoyed by it. I like being interrupted. But I have an indolent nature that has to be protected against its own instincts!'

'What are you writing now?'

'I've just finished the *de luxe* edition of my works that Macmillan is bringing out. I deposited on his floor the other day six of the seven volumes. I'm now going back to Ireland to get the seventh. The seventh volume is entirely philosophical, with a small amount of fantastic romance. Then I want to feel free for a little. After that, I don't know what I shall begin. One thing I never want to happen again. When I was ill a while ago, I was haunted by the thought of an unfinished work which I felt I might never be able to complete. It's horrifying to think of leaving unfinished work of any importance. I shall write short things, nothing that might agonize me when I am ill.'

It is difficult to think of his being ill, for he is browned by the Italian sun, and there is not the remotest suggestion of age about him, in spite of his grey hair. He looks fifteen or twenty years younger than his sixty-five years—a much more vigorous person than he was in his slenderer days, when the black lock hung down over his forehead.

But he came back to the subject of illness and death once more.

'If you don't express yourself,' he said, 'you walk after you're dead. The great thing is to go empty to your grave.'

It would be impossible to describe the charm with which he said it. He spoke in his characteristic manner, with a tentative pause between the sentences, and with gravity behind which humour hid, a gnome behind a great forest tree.

When we left the tea-shop there was a taxi moored in a traffic jam in front of the door. He hailed the taxi. I saw him stoop to crowd himself into it, and had an instant's vision of Deirdre and Oisin, and the Celtic Twilight, and the Secret Rose, and the Shadowy Waters, and the Wind Among the Reeds all sweeping into that Piccadilly taxi with him in a flash of glory before the stream of traffic blotted it out.

NOTES

Louise Morgan was onetime lecturer in English in the United States; editor of the London *Everyman* (1930–3); and staff reporter for the London *News Chronicle* (1933–53). Her writings include *Ten Point Way to Health* (1938) and *Inside Yourself* (1954)

1. The seer was there.
2. Yeats moved to Rapallo, Italy, in the middle of February 1928. He had been advised by his doctors to spend his winters out of Dublin and to avoid public life.
3. W. B. Yeats, 'The Fish'; *The Wind among the Reeds* (1899).
4. Free verse.
5. Giovanni Battista Vico (1668–1744), Italian philosopher who is known especially for his attempt to discover and organise laws common to the evolution of all society.
6. Agamemnon was King of Mycenae and Commander-in-Chief of the Greeks in the war with the Trojans to recover Helen. Upon the capture of Troy, Cassandra, daughter of Priam, became his prize. Returned home he was murdered by his wife Clytemnestra and her paramour Aegisthus but later avenged by his son Orestes. He is the subject of the dramatic trilogy by Aeschylus.

Yeats *Smelt* the Spirits*

LOUIS MACNEICE

Dodds[1] and I went to tea with W. B. Yeats in Rathfarnham. Yeats in spite of his paunch was elegant in a smooth light suit and a just sufficiently crooked bow tie. His manner was hierophantic, even when he said: 'This afternoon I have been playing croquet with my daughter.'[2] We were hoping he would talk poetry and gossip, but knowing that Dodds was a professor of Greek he confined the conversation to spiritualism and the phases of the moon, retailing much that he had already printed. Burnet, Yeats said, was all wrong; the Ionian physicists had of course not been physicists at all. The Ionian physicists were spiritualists.

* Extracted from *The Strings Are False: An Unfinished Autobiography* (London: Faber and Faber, 1965) pp. 147–8.

He talked a great deal about the spirits to whom his wife, being a medium, had introduced him. 'Have you ever seen them?' Dodds asked (Dodds could never keep back such questions). Yeats was a little piqued. No, he said grudgingly, he had never actually seen them . . . but—with a flash of triumph—he had often *smelt* them. [As he saw us out at the gate he was urging Dodds to remember that Julius Caesar was killed at a full moon.]

NOTES

Louis MacNeice (1907–63) was a poet and classical scholar. From 1930 to 1936 he was Lecturer in Classics at Birmingham, then became Lecturer in Bedford College, London. At this time he went on a trip to Iceland with W. H. Auden, and collaborated with him in *Letters from Iceland* (1937), which he followed with *I Crossed the Minch* (1938). As a poet he belonged to the school of Auden and Spender, exhibiting the same irony and satire. His books of verse include *Blind Fireworks* (1929), *The Earth Compels* (1938), *Autumn Journal* (1939), *Plant and Phantom* (1941), *Springboard* (1944), *The Dark Tower* (1946), *Holes in the Sky* (1948) and *The Burnt Offerings* (1952). He also translated the *Agamemnon of Aeschylus* and Goethe's *Faust*. His critical writings include *Modern Poetry* (1938), *The Poetry of W. B. Yeats* (1941) and several articles on Yeats. In 1958 he was made a C.B.E.

   1. E. R. Dodds (1893–1974), Professor of Greek. He had gone to Dublin to collect reminiscences for his *Journal and Letters of Stephen MacKenna* (London: Constable, 1936).
   2. Anne Butler Yeats (1919–   ), for whom Yeats wrote 'A Prayer for My Daughter', *Michael Robartes and the Dancer* (1921). A distinguished artist and associate of the Royal Hibernian Academy, she lives in Dublin.

Reminiscences of Yeats[*]

PADRAIC COLUM

My first meeting with William Butler Yeats was on the night of the last performance of A.E.'s *Deirdre* and Yeats's *Kathleen Ni Houlihan*,[1] the plays that were the first offerings of the National Theatre Society which eventually became the Abbey Theatre. I was the youth[2] who, in *Deirdre*, carried a spear and had a speech about Fergus whom Deirdre accused of 'Bartering his honour for a feast'. I was a player and so was Maud Gonne who played Kathleen ni Houlihan, and who was a party to Yeats's invitation to come to a hotel—his or hers—to discuss the draft of a play of mine. 'My first meeting' I say, but I had seen the poet at rehearsals and had more distant glimpses of him on platforms and on streets. A.E. and Yeats had furnished the initial plays of the theatre, but no other playwrights had shown themselves, and so Yeats was interested when Fay told him I was

* *The Yeats We Knew*, ed. Francis MacManus (Cork: The Mercier Press, 1965) pp. 13–24. Reprinted, with slight variations, from *Tri-Quarterly* (Evanston, Illinois: Northwestern University) W. B. Yeats Centenary Issue, no 4 (Fall 1965) 71–6.

trying to write a play. I need not say how exciting it was for a beginner to have himself put in the rank of a possible dramatist for a National Theatre.

The Yeats whom I now met as a man of the theatre was getting on to his fortieth year. He had written *The Wind Amongst the Reeds*, and it was known that he was eager to pass from such tremulous kind of poetry to the more public kind that he would have to grapple with in the theatre. Therefore, it was at a developing period in his life that I was fortunate enough to meet the great poet. He was preparing himself for a new career—indeed I might say for a new sort of being. He was reading all the dramatists, including the dramatists of the day, Ibsen and Maeterlinck. I remember I spoke of these two dramatists with fervour. Yeats spoke a word of warning in that voice of his that had something oracular in it. 'We are obsessed with the translation . . .' He meant that the personal style that all great writers have was blurred in translation and that we mustn't give a complete adherence to the text. This is one of the illuminating things I remember from early conversations with one who said most revealing things about literature. That night, in a hotel whose name I have forgotten, I read to him and to Maud Gonne the little play I had shown our school-master, Willie Fay. Yeats noted that there were too many people, too many motives in the opening. He made me aware that there was exposition in a play, and that the exposition had to be clear. He gave me a watchword—'Clear the decks for action.' That was the first real directive I had been given for the writing of a play.

At this time, Yeats was still the youngish man of the velvet jacket and the flowing tie. To the Catholic intelligentsia who had, a few years before, picketted his play '*The Countess Cathleen*', he was subversive. But that did not recommend him to the other side, the Ascendency side, the side of his father's friend, Professor Dowden.[3] They had seen him from the site of the projected Wolfe Tone[4] monument make a speech that was not at all in the spirit of Queen Victoria's Jubilee and denouncing that eminent lady in letters to the press. Percy French[5] had Victoria, on her visit to Ireland, retort in words that a head waiter committed to memory.

> There must be a slate, sez she,
> Off Willie Yeats, said she,
> Denouncing me crimes, sez she,
> In the *Irish Times*, sez she.

But the fact that two sides of the Irish public were hostile to him made this thirty-year old man interesting, and to be interesting, Yeats would probably have said, was the first duty of a public man. And Yeats wanted to be a public man. I fancy that if, at this stage, someone had said to him 'But you are a poet. Why want to be a public man?' Yeats would have told him that the entry into public life would give what he thought the entry into the theatre would give a poet, 'more manful energy'.

It was not his opinions alone that made him a marked man in the Dublin of the early 1900's. The tall, lank figure in black clothes, with the blue-black hair coming over his forehead, his frequent gestures and deliberate utterance, challenged and discomfited people. 'Pose' was a word that was often used about him. With reference to this word 'pose' I should like to say a word.

Yeats was a man who believed in style—or manner, if you like to call it that. 'Art is art because it is not Nature', said Goethe, and Yeats often repeated that saying. This insistence on art, style, manner, infuriated Dubliners, all except the sophisticated and certain members of the rising generation. People whose literary tradition went back to Thomas Moore and the poets of 'The Nation' felt affronted by his dismissal of 'The Minstrel Boy' kind of verse and by his downgrading Thomas Davis to the category of oratory rather than poetry. Speaking of verse in the Davis style, he said to me, 'I am leaving "The Spirit of the Nation" for my old age.' When I repeated this saying to an intelligent young man, he said furiously, 'The Spirit of the Nation will leave Yeats for its old age.' This aloofness of his may have been deliberate and due to the vocation that he felt in himself. But it may have been due to something in his character. His father once said to me, 'Willie is like his mother. She seldom if ever showed any sign of affection. I could be six months in Africa, and when I came back all she would say would be "Did you have your dinner?"' 'But' the old reflective painter added, 'there's a Yeats side to Willie, too. He is expansive and he loves discourse.' At the time, he was comparing Willie the poet with his other son, Jack the painter—Willie's aloofness, Jack's liking for the commonality, Willie's discourse with Jack's laconic utterance. Yes, Willie was undemonstrative about everything except art and abstract ideas, and perhaps this contributed to the malice that was in Dubliners' talk about him. The elaborateness of his speech was also a theme for mockery. This elaborateness comes over in an interview reported by Gogarty between the young James Joyce and Yeats—an interview which may never have taken place. 'Joyce, the Japanese have a proverb: be brave in battle, be truthful to your friends, be courteous always. You are not courteous, Joyce. When Arthur Symons mentioned Balzac, you laughed.' But perhaps the way of accounting for the malice directed against a man whose gifts were known and whose purpose was enriching is the saying that is in the Bible—'My heritage is to me as a speckled bird—all the birds of the air are against it.' Still, this discussion about the ways of one who was admitted to be a poet with the sacredness and mystery that has always surrounded the poet in Ireland, had another effect. His personality, his plans, his ideas were made current. And there was something about Yeats that rarely goes with the poet—the successful public-relations man, the one who made a theatre of amateurs playing in a hall that held only a hundred or so people into an institution, into what one never had before, an Irish theatre.

He was a great poet partly through his realisation that poetry should be personal but that it should also be related to some public effort. A poet whose life he admired, William Morris, had spoken sadly of the poet of his time as 'the idle singer of an empty day'. Yeats was determined to be not that sort of a singer. Poets are well served, he knew, when they have a cause, an ideal that brings them on the stage as spokesmen. He once said to me that the Catholic poets in England, Coventry Patmore and Francis Thompson, were fortunate in having a definite public. From his beginning he asked a public to recognise him as an Irish poet.—

> Know that I would accounted be
> True brother of that company
> Who sang to sweeten Ireland's wrong
> Ballad and story, rann and song.

But he also wanted to be a power in Irish public life. Remember that if the Irish coinage is stamped with creditable designs it is through Yeats the Senator working in committee. He was a capable man of affairs and was resolved to have his way in them. I remember that, during a dispute in the formative theatre group, a letter he wrote to A.E. which A.E. showed to me. Speaking of his own intention about the theatre, he left no doubt as to who was to be in control. 'The tools to him who can use them.'

He recognised in the theatre, whose nucleus was Fay's company, a real form of national expression. Quoting Victor Hugo, he used to say, 'In the theatre the mob becomes the people.' I am not here telling the story of the early days of the theatre, but my impressions of the Yeats who was taking over the theatre. He was able to fill with enthusiasm the members of this semi-amateur group. I remember the occasion of the re-organisation of that group. The great affirmation in that speech came through a poem he repeated—the poem of Lionel Johnson's that is dedicated to John O'Leary and begins, 'A terrible and splendid trust/Heartens the host of Innisfail' and, as you will remember ends with.—

> A dream, a dream, an ancient dream—
> Yet ere peace comes to Innisfail,
> Some weapon on some field must gleam,
> Some burning glory fire the Gael.

He made our enterprise seem equal to Robert Emmet's[6] and Wolfe Tone's when he repeated, the last, the significant verses.—

> That field may lie beneath the sun,
> Fair for the treading of an host,
> That field in realms of thought be won,
> Where armed minds do their uttermost.
>
> Some way, to faithful Innisfail
> Shall come the majesty and awe
> Of martial truth, that must prevail
> To lay on all the eternal law.

There and then he enlisted us for the field 'in realms of thought', for the martialness that was of the mind.

At the rehearsals of the Yeats play that we put on after *Kathleen ni Houlihan,*—it was *The King's Threshold,* rehearsals that were held at the back of a grocery shop in Camden Street, Yeats was often amongst us. He would read a poem that someone had sent him and speak to us about it. He was on the watch for the rise of a poet who would help to forward the enterprise—'The Avatar', to use a word of his. And it was there that he brought us evidence of the Avatar's arrival, two short plays by a man none of us had heard of. The plays were 'The Shadow of the Glen' and 'Riders to the Sea' and the writer was J. M. Synge. One or two new players had joined what had been the Fays' company. They, like the older members, had taken lessons from Frank Fay or Willie Fay. I remember the rehearsal at which one of these neophytes came to the platform to say a few lines. Her movement, her gesture, her enunciation were assured and she had extraordinary distinction. Yeats turned to Willie Fay excitedly, 'Fay, you've got an actress.' She was Sara Allgood.

It requires practice to write verse which, spoken from the stage is intelligible to an audience. When Yeats wrote the opening speech for *The King's Threshold,* the King's speech of greeting to the poet's pupils, he did not yet know how to make a speech that has some complicated expression. The climax of that play has been changed since it was first put on, but that opening speech remains unchanged and is still impossible to make intelligible. It is a question of the timing of its delivery. Yeats was discomfited. I knew that the speech couldn't be made clearer no matter how the actor tried. I went to Yeats who was standing ruefully aside and said to him, 'The speech is frankly a public oration. What the audience will know is that the King is making a speech; it does not have to be intelligible line by line.' His head went up and his face cleared. Running across to Fay he said, 'Colum says that the speech is frankly an oration.' It was then given as an oration without any attempt to make it particularly intelligible. I like to think that the unaltered speech that we now read with all that talk about horses that draw the sun and the moon being welcome by someone for some fair woman's sake was due to my intervention.

Synge's plays were produced and also a play of mine which he thought was immature—as it was. But he had faith in me as a dramatist, and when I was finishing my next play, *The Land,*[7] he had Lady Gregory invite me to Coole where we could discuss revisions and developments in the play. By this time Yeats had learned a good deal about the technique of playwriting, and I well remember one or two scenes in *The Land* that profited by his professionalism. But I am speaking of the poet and not of a play. In that beautiful house with its noble woods and lonely lake I saw him without any of the pose that was mocked at in Dublin. He was a good oarsman and we sometimes rowed on the lake. The lake was in a picture he had painted—a golden crown in deep water.—

> The golden crowns that kings had hurled
> Into deep pools when armies fled.

It was a picture that evoked something of the verse in 'The Wind amongst the Reeds' or 'Shadowy Waters'. But that was a stage that he had passed through. He told me that he was trying to get out of his poems 'the reds and yellows that Shelley had brought back from Italy'. Henceforth he was going to try to get into his poems that grey of the West of Ireland—the stones and clouds that belonged to Galway. How well he has done that we know from the later poems of his.—

> The trees are in their autumn beauty,
> The woodland paths are dry,
> Under the October twilight the water
> Mirrors a clear sky.
> Between the brimming water and the stones
> Are nine and fifty swans. [8]

I used to go through the woods with Robert Gregory who shot pigeons there—we often had a grand pigeon-pie for dinner. Or I walked in the walled garden with Lady Gregory while she spoke to me of the guests of hers who had thrown wallflower seeds into the corners of the walls where there were now bunches of wallflowers. What a charming way of memorialising Douglas Hyde and Hugh Lane and many other illustrious visitors. And what can we say of the philistinism of an Irish government that let a house, beautiful in itself and so full of the history of our most creative generation, and woods that were so celebrated, be destroyed!

But William Butler Yeats is my subject. Naturally I was interested in the methods of work of a poet. In the morning he stayed in the large drawing-room, sitting before a table, or pacing about murmuring lines of verse that he had set down or was about to set down. Like many imaginative workers he had to tease himself into getting on with the job. At one time he used to smoke a cigarette between lines, but that gave him too much time off. Now he cut cigarettes into halves. The smoking of a half cigarette was the interval he now allowed himself. I told him that I thought of helping in some newspaper office for a while every day so as to give myself the discipline of a task that had to be done on time. There was no point, he told me, in doing this. The only discipline that mattered to the imaginative worker was the discipline he gave himself through his work.

In the drawing-room where we sat after dinner—Lady Gregory, W. B., Robert Gregory and myself, the conversation was natural and interesting. Yeats no longer made oracular pronouncements but spoke on all kinds of topics, gossiping with some humour on the coteries in London, repeating sayings of painters and writers. The son of a really great conversationalist, John Butler Yeats, he himself was a remarkable conversationalist. In the room across from us, the music room, Lady Gregory's nieces, sometimes played. I discovered that Yeats who was so varied in the music of his verse was absolutely tone deaf. I had heard him say that he liked a harp because it looked well-shaped. Now as we heard the music from outside the drawing-room, he said to me, 'What are they playing? Fiddle or piano?' I left Coole, bearing Lady Gregory's gifts—an enormous barm brack, and a large, well-cooked ham. Yeats was satisfied with what I had produced. Speaking to me as a counsellor, he said, 'Make yourself indispensable.'

There was more than one great moment in Yeats's life. To the honour of Ireland he was selected for the Nobel Prize. As he addressed an audience that included the King of Sweden and the members of the Swedish Academy he must have felt that this was a dazzling moment. And yet I think that the moment of achievement for him was the first night in which plays were performed in the Abbey Theatre. Irish dramatists and Irish players already had an international reputation. Now they were an institution. The audience for the plays that inaugurated the theatre were the elite of Dublin. Then there came on the stage that tall, darkgarbed figure whom they could now recognise for a standard-bearer. They knew he was a man who could make this an occasion they would remember. He raised his hand in the gesture so familiar to all who approached him. There was drama in the way he repeated lines from Spenser, lines over the gate of the Castle. 'Be bold; Be bolder still! Be yet more bold! But not too bold!' I will always remember that appearance and utterance of his as one of the great performances I had ever known.

And now for my last meeting with the poet who gave such greatness to his time. He was then living with his family in Rathfarnham, an ailing man. He consented to receive my wife and myself. We had been away from Ireland for some years. As compared with other times we had seen him, he was subdued. But in spite of the tiredness that he showed now and again he talked as a man with a continuing interest in what was creative in the world. He wanted to know more about certain contemporary poets whom he had seen or heard of, particularly of a German poet whom my wife had read. Stefan George. She was able to repeat some phrases from poems—he listened with much attention and made some comments. We left a stooped, white haired, courteous man, bringing with us a sense of grandeur. Here was one of the rare men in the world who had fully lived the creative, the intellectual life.

NOTES

Pádraic Colum (1881–1972) was an Irish poet and playwright who became one of the group of writers, including Yeats, George Russell, J. M. Synge and Lady Gregory, who are identified with the Irish literary renascence. His play *The Land* (1905) was the Irish Theatre's first success. With James Stephens and Thomas MacDonagh he founded the *Irish Review*. In 1914 he visited the United States, where he later settled. His writings include *The Road Round Ireland* (1926), *Arthur Griffith* (1959) and several articles on Yeats and reviews of his works.
  1. Both George Russell's three-act play *Deirdre* and Yeats's one-act play *Cathleen ni Houlihan*

opened by the Irish National Theatre Society at St Teresa's Hall, Clarendon Street, on 2 April 1902.

2. Pádraic Colum played the part of Buinne, Fergus's son.

3. Professor Edward Dowden (1843–1913), the first holder of the Chair of English at Trinity College Dublin, was an opponent of Irish home rule.

4. Wolfe Tone (1763–98), Irish revolutionary leader and the founder of the United Irishmen. He came to Ireland with the French fleet, was captured and committed suicide in prison.

5. Percy French (1854–1920), Irish poet and singer, who was a great success, hitting off the English taste for stage Irishry without offending his fellow countrymen to too great an extent.

6. Robert Emmet (1778–1803), Irish nationalist who travelled in Europe and met Napoleon and Talleyrand trying to secure their support for Irish independence. He led an abortive revolution and was executed in Dublin after being tried for high treason.

7. *The Land* had its premiere at the Abbey Theatre on 9 June 1905.

8. W. B. Yeats, 'The Wild Swans at Coole', *The Wild Swans at Coole* (1919).

Black Oxen Passing By*

SEAN O'CASEY

Home he [Sean] came from America,[1] very tired and strangely thrilled, to sit and think and recover by an electric fire in a new home formed from a flat in Battersea. There one day a letter came to him from W. B. Yeats. He recognised the writing: from the poet, right enough, the great Yeats. He was bade to come to take dinner with the poet in his lodgings at Lancaster Gate.[2] At last, Yeats had stretched out a hand of friendship; and the heart within Sean rejoiced greatly. Then here's a hand, me trusty frien', an' gi'e's a hand o' thine! Seas between us braid ha'e roared sin' auld lang syne.

At Lancaster Gate, Mrs. G. Yeats was there watching over her famous husband. Pushing death away from him with all the might in her little hands. Anxious that he should not do too much. When dinner was on the table, she left the two men alone to eat it, and Sean felt the lack of her quiet charm and her good looks. Yeats was stuck in the centre of strife, selecting poems for his *Oxford Book of Modern Verse*, and shortly after dinner, he tried to win Sean into an hour's fight with him. The room seemed to be thronged with poem-books from all persons; while on the mantelpiece lay a pile of Western Tales of cowboy and Indian chief, sliced here and there by a detective story, which were there, he told Sean, to ease a mind tired and teased with a long concentration of thought on the imagination of others. Twice, he asked Sean's advice on selections, but Sean shut his ears, saying, with finality in his voice, that he could not suffer himself to give a judgement on a poetical piece. Yeats desisted, sighing and saying, it was

* Extracted from *Rose and Crown* (London: Macmillan, 1952).

hard work, but his ear was true, his ear was sure; the tone of his murmur seeming to indicate that he wasn't so sure as his words declared.

They turned to talking of the Elizabethans, whom Yeats evidently loved, and was glad that Sean shared his delight in the careless splendour of their poets, who made even violent death majestic in a mass of jewelled words. The stern intensity that Tourneur and Webster showed in velveted revenge, plumed murther, and rotten lust that ermine covered grandly. Mighty souls decayed to shivering flesh and chattering teeth. Two minds whose thoughts were phosphorescent lightning, to whom the world became a great revolving skull in which life tried to live, knocking its energy against bony walls; out of whose eyeless sockets life looked out on nothing, to shrivel back, to look, and see the less within. Where the Jew of Malta bows to the Duchess of Malfi, and Vittoria Corombona stands indecently triumphant on the pedestal of Liberty's statue.

And yet, in spite of all their weary boniness, their mire of lacerated flesh, their spilling wildly of the shrill, sad scent of death, a sombre rosiness lights up their caverned despair, and simple blossoms, wild and wanton, steal and wind around their tomby places. Brocaded butchery of power sinks to the tender:

> Call for the robin redbreast and the wren,
> Since o'er shady groves they hover,
> And with leaves and flowers do cover
> The friendless bodies of unburied men.

What better mourners could a dead man have than a robin and a wren, decking his buried dust with animation and broidering it with a song; fluttering over his dense, deep sleep, disturbing gently the everlasting silence of the dead. Finer salute to what was, and is not now, than the cold mumbling of cardinal-bishop or cardinal-deacon, black-robed as a Jesuit or scarlet-clad as a Secularius. A quiet trumpet sounds elation in the chirruping *de profundis* of the birds, for the dead live on in their work left behind with the living.

The teeming thoughts of Yeats turned suddenly into himself as a tremulous stoppage of breath started an outburst of coughing that shook his big, protesting body, stretching his wide chest on a rack of straining effort to rid itself of congestion, or end the effort by ending life. His hands gripped the sides of his chair, his fine eyes began to stare and bulge, showing the storm within, as he leant back and bent forward to sway with the waves of stuffy contortion that were forcing resistant life from his fighting body. The whole stately dignity and courage of the poet was crinkling into a cough. He has caught an everlasting cold, thought Sean. His own black oxen are treading him down.

These Elizabethan poets pulled a bell to tell of criminals, hidden and revealed, hiding in ermine and scarlet taffeta; the horrid things they did, nagging at heaven to get rid of the lot of them; as if the slimiest and most villainous souls of Paradise Lost had come to town to be converted into duke, cardinal, and courtier. Cardinals who 'made more bad faces with their oppressions than Michael Angelo made good ones'; and lords, who, when they laughed, were 'like deadly cannons that lighten ere they smoke'. No worse than Hogarth's later gin-mad men and maids; no more mischievous than those later ones who gambled their estates away in London, Bath, and Tunbridge Wells, impoverishing their tenants, ruining the land over which they claimed an immortal, menacing ownership. And do today.

Sean longed to cross to the coughing Yeats, and lay a warm, sympathetic hand on his heaving shoulders; to say silently so that Yeats could hear, God knows, if power were mine, you would be for ever young; no cough would ever come to warn you that the body withers. But custom held him back; the fear of offending his structured dignity by resting a kindly hand on another's shoulder. Afraid of the outward and visible sign of an inward and invisible sympathy.

—I get this way at times, the creaking voice of Yeats apologised behind his curtain of coughing. I have had congestion of the lungs.

Here, in Elizabethan drama, was not one particular court of Calabria, but all courts caught in a poet's mirror, where kings and dukes, spunned in flatteries, walked; and toadies tumbled in their haste to lick the shoes more costly than their own; where

> The poor rogues
> Pay for 't which have not the means
> To present bribe in fist; the rest o' the band
> Are raz'd out of the knaves' record; or else
> My lord he winks at them with easy will;
> His man grows rich, the knaves are the knaves still . . .
> While divinity wrested by some factious blood,
> Draws swords, swells battles, and o'erthrows all good.

Ay, and you can see the same things today, if you only look out of the window.

There's a man, Sean went on thinking of Yeats, who never saw it; and, if he did, censured the crowd because they came uncultured. But his is more than a bare name; one who will never shake hands to say farewell to reputation; who sought the society of queens and kings over the hilly lands and hollow lands of thought; and thought them brave and precious; never descrying that their careless grandeur and perfumed manners were milled from the sludgy life the people lived; from whose satin-bound laws, but a day ago, came the decisions that he who snatched and ran, who stole two pounds from a dwelling-house, or five shillings from a shop, or picked from a pocket a coin but one farthing over a shilling, must suffer death by hanging; and when a kindlier man brought in a bill to substitute transportation for hanging in cases of theft from dwelling or shop, six bishops voted against it, led by his grace, the Lord Archbishop of Canterbury. Oh, brave old world!

Here is he whose dreams of his loved one were wronged by

The cry of a child by the roadside, the creak of a lumbering cart,
The heavy steps of the ploughman, splashing the wintry mould;

so that he turned away that he might not hear. A buccaneer among shining shadows. So different from Lady Gregory, who would run out to see why the child cried, or why the wheel of the wagon creaked. And yet his poems belie the man, belie him badly; for there was no braver man among the men of Eireann than W. B. Yeats. In every fray of politics, in every fight for freedom in literature and art, in every effort to tempt Dublin's city into the lure of finer things, the voice of Yeats belled out a battle-cry.

Some have said that Yeats was an actor, enjoying himself posing about in trismegistic mask on a painted stage. A charming fellow, they said, wearing his cabbalistic cloak well; but genuine only in making his acting look genuine, though done in a world painted into the panels of his own deceptions. But beneath the masque, under the cloak, was the man of powerful integrity; vain and childlike, fearful of what might be a humiliation; brave before rich or poor; courteous, even to those who lingered to bore him; a truer rebel than truest politician; and eager, like the upsprung husband of Malfi's duchess, to fashion the world right.

—The scene where the echo sounds is fine, said Yeats, when the cough had loosened its grip; where the echo tells the lover-husband, out of his own words, his wife's end and his own. It is beautiful, is it not, O'Casey?

—It is very beautiful, and it is very sad.

—Yes, Webster, murmured Yeats, though not too deep for tears, is far too deep for laughter. Others may bind the brow of life with laurel; Webster binds her brow with crêpe. The incense in his temple's burning brimstone.

—But through the choking mist, said Sean, burn many coloured candles.

—We are afraid of sadness, the poet murmured; we have it in life, but we fear it in the theatre. You mustn't be afraid of it, O'Casey.

—I'm not, if it tinges, or even startles, life, like a discordant note in a lovely symphony. I'm not when it has nobility. But when it comes brazen through hunger, disease, or wretchedness, then I hate it; then I fight against it, for through that suffering there can be no purification. It is villainous, and must be destroyed. Even Webster condemns the sorrow his own imagination created. He, too, was one of those who longed to fashion the world right.

—You're a Communist, O'Casey, aren't you? His face came closer, and his bright eyes peered and pierced, as if he would read Sean's thoughts ere any could be fashioned into words. It is astir in the world today. What is this Communism so many place their hope in, so many fight for, and so many speak about, as if it were a new *lux mundi?* [3]

A shock to Sean. He never imagined that Yeats would smite his mind with such a question; and he wondered if the poet was really interested in any answer to his question. Was the interest in Communism, or was it but Yeatsian curiosity eager to peer into the mind of another? Even were the poet genuine in his question, what was he to say to the white-haired man who so often took up a current question to look at it for an hour, and then let it fall from him when interest faded?

—Communism's no new *lux mundi,* he said. Its bud-ray shone when first a class that had all, or most, of what was going, became opposed by a class that had little or nothing. It has grown in power and intensity till today it floods half of the world's skies. We give it the symbol of a red star. Earlier it was called the sword of light; Prometheus; Lugh of the Long Hand.

—Ah, O'Casey, these things, symbol or myth, do not belong to the crowd. There is danger here: would you set the rabble in power against the finer and fuller things common to great and gracious people?

—No, Mr. Yeats, not against them; but set the rabble, as you call them, down among the finer things of life, and give them the chance and power to help create them.

Yeats shrank back into his chair; shrank into himself, and saw the little streets hurling themselves against the greater ones. So Sean thought, and so he seemed to see that Yeats didn't like the sight entrancing.

—The finer things aren't so common among your great people as you think. There are many of them who have never read a line by Yeats. Some of them know no painting but a few handed to the family hundreds of years ago, hanging on the wall still, not as a graceful glory, but merely as a rich endowment. They journey each year to the Royal Academy Exhibition, where they are rarely puzzled, and can cry Hem! before the pictures. Many of them today do not even know the clock, and are constrained to cry out with Falstaff's What time o' day is it, Hal? Most of your great people, Mr. Yeats, are so ignorant of, and so indifferent to, fine things that Lady Gregory and a few more stand out as remarkable or even unique.

Yeats sat silent for quite a time, staring into the gas-fire, not altogether relishing what Sean had said. He coughed again, then the fine head moved closer towards Sean, and he said, What is this Communism: what is its divinity—if it has any; what is its philosophy? Whatever the State, there must be a governing class placed by wealth far above fear or toil.

The mind of the poet was probing again: what did that mean, now, what does this mean? Why should Sean worry this white-headed man with thoughts alien to his nature; this man who was a warrior among mere fighters,who had given to life more than he got from it? He got to his feet, laughing. Ah, Mr. Yeats, he said, the divinity in our philosophy is but the things the massed energy and individual thought can do. All of us will be above the common fear of life, and work will be a desire in us as strong as hunger or love. Our leaders will be above the rest only in the measure of more vivid minds and more enduring energy; used for the fuller security and higher benefit of all. Communism isn't an invention of Marx; it is a social growth, developing through the ages, since man banded together to fight fear of the unknown, and destroy the danger from mammoth and tiger of the sabre-tooth. All things in science and art are in its ownership, since man painted the images of what he saw on the wall of his cave, and since man put on the wooden share of his plough the more piercing power of iron or of bronze.

—It isn't enough. What I've heard of it, O'Casey, doesn't satisfy me. It fails to answer the questions of What is life. What is man? What is reality? It tells us nothing of invisible things, of vision, or spiritual powers: or preternatural activities and energy beyond and above man's ordinary knowledge and contemplation.

—Aha, said Sean, what philosophy does? Even Christian theology leaves us prostrate and puzzled. You yourself have read many philosophers who failed to answer your questions: failed utterly, or you wouldn't be asking them now. Communism deals with man as man, a glory great enough to begin with. Think deep as you can, think long as you may, life depends on low reality.

—But the Catholic Church, which has a vision, however we may disagree with it, and a divinity, though we may not believe in it, has a social philosophy, O'Casey, just as Communism has.

—Well, said Sean laughingly, the Roman Church builds her social contract on the Rearum Noharmum Harum Scarum Rerum Novarum,[4] but we build ours on the Communist Manifesto: this time it is our philosophy that is built on a rock, theirs on a hill of sand. All the glory that was Greece, the grandeur that was Rome, sprang from corn and oil and wine. We cannot safely go a day without a hug from Demeter. All the poetry of Shakespeare, Milton, Shelley, and Yeats was first embedded in the bosom of Demeter.

They talked about the Abbey and its newer plans; of the new Directors appointed on the Board to broaden its outlook, for Yeats thought the time had come for a braver display of European drama; the poet mentioning Hauptmann's *The Weavers* and Toller's *Hoppla!* He asked Sean to tell him of any new play the Abbey might do.

The cough shook the fine frame of the poet again; the breast ebbed and flowed spasmodically: and the fine hand grasped the arm of the chair with tenseness. Odd that Yeats couldn't see that no divinity, Gaelic or Christian, came with balm to refresh with health the corroding chest of the poet. Sean stood silent, watching the shock of lovely silver hair bounce up and down to the rhythm of the racking cough, and waiting for the hoarse harshness to decline into a deceitful peace. The last mask—a mask of pain.

—It hampers me, this, he said, in little gasps; comes on so often, so often.

—You mustn't let anything disturb you, said Sean, trying to put the affection he felt into his voice, and hoping Yeats would sense it; nothing but the vexing necessity of resting. We need you, sir. Your very presence, without one thing done, one word said, is a shield before us all. I have tired you. I shall go now, and leave you in peace. Goodbye. No, no; don't stir—I can easily let myself out; for the poet was rising to give three steps from the door in courtesy to his guest.

—We shall talk of this again, said Yeats, stretching out a hand in farewell. Thanks for coming to see me, O'Casey.

Sean left him staring at the gasfire, crouching in the big armchair. His greatness is such, thought Sean, that the Ireland which tormented him will be forced to remember him for ever; and as Sean gently closed the door behind him, he heard the poet coughing again: broken by the passing feet of his own black oxen.

NOTES

Sean O'Casey (1880—1964), Irish dramatist.

1. O'Casey had gone to the United States to help in a production of his play *Within the Gates*, which had its American premiere at the National Theatre, New York on 22 October 1934. See 'Irish Playwright Sean O'Casey Here: Author of *Within the Gates* Comes To Be Present at Play's Rehearsal', *New York Times* (18 Sep 1934), p. 23.

2. Yeats was in London at the end of January 1933, having completed an American lecture tour. After a short stay in London he returned to Dublin.

3. Light of the world. The term is used in the Gospel of St John 1. 9 to refer to Christ, the Messiah.

4. *Rerum Novarum* is a major social encyclical of Pope Leo XIII, written in 1891. Although the Pope called for radical social and economic reforms he condemned the principles of Marx and Engels, laid down in the *Communist Manifesto* of 1848. O'Casey's 'pig latin' makes fun of the encyclical because he feels that in comparison with the Manifesto it is too broad and represents the 'harem scarum' policy of the Roman Catholic Church.

As Yeats was Going Down Grafton Street*

DIARMUID BRENNAN

William Butler Yeats was going down Grafton Street that golden August of 'thirty-four and old Tom Boylan, who had the eye of an experienced hawk, nudged my painting arm. The paint we were using for the window-frames of the Bailey[1] bar and restaurant smudged the glass lagoon-blue.

* *Listener* (London) LXXI (6 Feb 1964) 236–8.

There were just the two of us on the job in the side street, [2] a few steps from the corner, and I was so occupied with the rubbing rag I missed Yeats going down the fashionable side of Grafton Street which is the far side.

Old Tom Boylan was at the corner now, peering down towards Trinity College where the Tudor ghosts rub shoulders with the statues of the younger set like Goldsmith, Burke, and Henerry Grattan.

'Ah, you've missed him, begod', he called out, and I knew by his voice that this interruption had something to it. 'Well, thanks be to the Almighty I've been spared to see this day'.

Tom Boylan was nearly sixty and his paint-speckled bowler was about the same age. He was old only because I was nineteen. I joined him at the corner.

'Missed who?'

I tried to follow his gaze down the street; but all I could see was people, strolling singly and in groups, and window-shopping girls.

The old man turned on me, aghast.

'The ould poet', he said. 'The great man himself, William Butler Yeats . . . " *I will arise and go now and go—*" '

I cut him short and ranged over the multitude, a wild boy.

'Where, for God's sake?'

'Down the far side, you thick-you'.

Then, suddenly, in an island of sunlight, I saw the great man plainly: tall as a lance, a plume of white hair, a sort of biscuit-pale suit. Oh, it was him all right—William Butler Yeats.

He crossed Wicklow Street against a post office van and the driver slowed.

'Come on', I said. 'Hurry it up if you want to meet him'.

The old man looked at me, pityingly.

'You're not . . . you're not trying to tell me', he said, 'that you're in a position to stop a man the likes of that in the street'.

'I am', I said. 'I'm a friend of his. And if you put a spurt on I'll stop him'.

He looked a bit stunned at that, but this wasn't the time to study the collapse of an old man's face.

'What about me poor leg?'

I pulled up at the kerb trying to smother my irritation. That leg; that goddam, all-purposes leg.

'To think of all the brave men who fell in Flanders', I said, 'and to think of you and your game leg being spared'.

'Anyway, I've seen him', he said. 'That's all that counts'.

I went back to the Bailey.

'Well, I'm in need of a pint after that. Do you think you can make it?'

He made it all right. I put a two-shilling piece on the counter and got two pints and ten fags and tuppence change. That was the way of the world in that golden August. The old man took off his bowler like in a church.

'It's news to me how a fellow like you got to know a bard as great as that',

he said. 'I suppose you were painting one of the big houses out
Rathfarnham way where he lives'.

'I wasn't even in Dublin. I wrote to him'.

The old man thought about this, and his face showed he was thinking,
'ah yes, that's feasible'.

'Do you know what', he said then. 'If I had an experience the like of that
I'd go to me grave jigging'.

'Oh, I even had tea with him', I said. 'It was nothing . . .'

Nothing?

Well, there's a lie for a start. There's more to it than that.

It started with a group of us, all country boys, book-minded in a home-
made way. I suppose we were scrambling for some kind of a national
toehold when we got the notion of making a collection of all the verse that
had come out of those six revolutionary years in Ireland, 1916–1922. The
shimmering jewel was to be Yeats's 'Easter 1916'.

LETTER FROM WATERFORD

I wrote to Yeats from Waterford in the south, 110 miles from Dublin, and
the letter asked could we use the poem in our anthology. In a few days a
reply came from Yeats: of course you can use 'Easter 1916', it said, but
where is this anthology going to lead you?

Aye, indeed . . . where?

It seemed simpler than writing back to thank Yeats on the telephone. I
put through a trunk call and then, when a woman's voice answered, I was
barely able to hold the telephone still. That was how, from then onwards, I
came to be in communication with Mrs. Yeats.

I must have been delirious after that phone call, I sent her some verses I
had sweated over; crudely constructed quatrains with hardly a line that
was not haunted by the younger Yeats.

Yeats called her George. That, more than anything, was proof that I
had crossed the threshold to a mysterious new world. A world of Georges in
skirts had been hitherto veiled.

George Yeats insisted I should call out and have tea with the poet when I
happened to be in Dublin. The only time I happened to be in Dublin up till
then was when I was fourteen, and that was on an excursion. But I
managed to convey the impression that Dublin was a kind of second home
I nipped in and out of.

I could never imagine George Yeats easily surprised; but she must have
been surprised by the speed in which I happened to be in Dublin, two days
after her invitation. It was August bank holiday and the sky was weepy, so
I wore a heavy jet-black overcoat. If a neighbour hadn't died I would have
had no coat. On the box-carriage train it looked like I was on my way to an
important funeral.

The pockets of that coat were capacious and I put a book into each. One
was called *The Prison Letters of Constance Markieviez* which I was in the

middle of; and the other was Yeats's latest book of poems, *The Winding Stair*, that had cost me three-and-six.

There was a churning of brown water under the mossy-stone bridge along the pathway to Riversdale, the house set among plum and apple orchards. George Yeats, in a lawn-green dress and bright pinny, opened the glass-panelled door smilingly and in the small hallway I took off my mourner's coat, first taking out my two books. I had made up my mind it would look more literary to carry them.

'You're in beautiful time for tea', she said as she led me into a longish room that was a mixture of study and lounge, fire-lit and cosy with easy-chairs, shelves of books, landscapes on the lemon walls, and a tea trolley. This, then, was where the great man wrote his poems.

A SUIT THE COLOUR OF PORRIDGE

Yeats stood up from a sturdily built writing table that had some notepaper and open books on it, and he looked inquiringly at George. His suit was the colour of porridge. He wore a soft butterfly tie.

'Here's our young correspondent, dear', said George, smiling amiably like the mother of a big family showing off one of them. 'He's a poet, too'.

The lavishness of this introduction wilted me. I'll take the agony of it with me to the grave. I had the illusion Yeats towered over me like a column of honey and cream. I didn't know what to do with Con Markieviez's prison letters. I had the book in my right hand and tried to transfer it, fumblingly, but Yeats stretched out a Japanese hand and took the book and sat down. His armchair was beside the tea-things and he gestured me to sit opposite. George surveyed the scene and then said she would get the tea.

Yeats pushed back his soft white plume of hair and began opening the book at random. Now and then he paused to read something. Everything about him had a white coffee glow; everything except his eyes. Since that day I have never seen pools of such lustre repeated in any man's face. Sometimes a medieval painting hints at what I remember. The voice I heard, sometimes unmelodic, sometimes droning, is the kind that is neutral in Ireland but unmistakably Irish anywhere outside of the country.

George reappeared with a tray that was laden with a variety of hillocks: thinly sliced bread; pats of butter; homemade jam; scones with a powdering of flour; iced pastries; and a pot of tea under a cosy.

She was pouring the tea when, with unexpected enthusiasm, he said a thing that devastated me even more so than being labelled a poet.

'George', said Yeats, 'have you seen this book he has written about Constance Gore-Booth's gaol letters?'

Over the steaming cups he held the book aloft.

'Well, now, isn't that commendable', said George, and she encouraged me to eat up and then left the room and stayed away busy elsewhere.

The book had a yellow cover that plainly said the writer was a woman, Esther Roper. But neither seemed to have noticed that.

ABOUT CONSTANCE GORE-BOOTH

Yeats leaned back, a scone in one hand, and became expansive about Constance Gore-Booth. I dared not deny authorship now. I could only listen and try to eat. He avoided the married name of Markieviez for that once-beautiful daughter of a family that owned big tracts of Sligo, the home of his boyhood.

'Dear, poor Con', he said, flatly, as if saying the clock was five minutes fast. 'Someone told me he met her helping in a soup kitchen some months before she died . . . Soup kitchens in Ireland have a black history'.

I did not know it then, but dear, poor Con, who once reminded him of a gazelle, had given him a chance to get going on a favourite theme of his last years: the Big Famine of ninety years before and the coffin ships that took many of the walking skeletons to America.

'Her Majesty's contribution to the famine fund was five pounds, you know that?'

I did not grasp it at the time, but the truth was I was passing in and out of the life of William Butler Yeats at a moment when a hard, fierce nationalism was replacing the romanticism of half a century before. This was far from Innisfree and the Salley Gardens.

It was all dazzlingly new and astonishing to me, a country boy with a mind hungrier than the Big Famine, when he insisted there could be no boundary to the advance of a nation once its intellectual forces were properly harnessed.

But how, I wondered, could a dream of cultural fusion be achieved other than by governmental power.

'By militants', he said; and he said it so passionately a look of youngness transformed his face. 'By marching men'.

But he did not picture the Irish Republican Army that had gone to earth after losing the civil war ten years earlier, assuming the role of his marching men. He dismissed them as one-dimensional, document-ridden transcendentalists; a combination of aimless lads from the village and shabby-genteel from the town lingering on in an ancient twilight.

The British colonel's daughter, Maud Gonne, who had monopolized the love lyrics in his book *The Rose* when he was twenty-eight, remained a symbol of I.R.A. inspiration as long as she strode the streets of Dublin, gaunt and earnest, in her widow's black. She had been his phoenix—once; but that was over and done with. He referred to her now, almost impersonally, in the casual way one refers to an acquaintance.

'Ah, yes, dear Maud. I seldom see her. Occasionally I have a meal with her, but it becomes difficult sustaining her political viewpoint. I get round this by trying to recollect those things that once amused us'.

George came in then, happy that her husband looked happy, and

reminded him he had promised to call on the poet I
road. He stood up and I helped him on with his wa.
tucked in a woollen scarf.

Yeats had collected his papers when I remembered
autograph *The Winding Stair*. He took the book and cros.
writing table. In spidery writing on the top of the title page
aimless joy is a pure joy—W. B. Yeats'.

I said good-bye to George, then. She stood in the doorway,
autumn light, waving good-bye as her Willie and I crossed the stoi   .dge
over the noisy water.

There was a bus coming and his agility, as he stepped on, surprised me.
He said only two things on the near-crowded bus. Had I the return half of
my train ticket? Oh yes, that was safe in my back-pocket. There was also
the tram fare to Kingsbridge station; had I got that?

That had been salted away, too, but before I could say oh, yes, Yeats
said: 'It's easy to overlook such things', dropped a two-shilling piece into
the pocket of my coat, and then stood up. He stepped off as alertly as he had
stepped on, and waved briefly; and then was gone.

By the time I reached Waterford, that two-shillings was all I had to show
for my call on the great man. I had left the autographed book of poems
behind on the train.

The next time I set eyes on Yeats was that golden August as he walked
down Grafton Street. I had taken to painting shop fronts under Tom
Boylan, and that was achievement because some of the other anthologists
were still minding horses for the farmers around Waterford.

'I'd give anything for a souvenir to remind me of the ould bard', old
Boylan said. 'He's immortal, you know'.

'I haven't got a keepsake to show for that immortal meeting', I said.

'Well, now, you have, indeed', said the old man. 'You have that two-bob
piece'. Then he paused, alarm creeping over his face; 'Oh godalmighty,
you're not going to tell me that, that's gone, too'.

'I am', I said. 'The pair of us have been drinking and smoking it, right
here at the table'.

They didn't go in for credit in a bar like the Bailey, even though you
could say we were kind of on the staff.

NOTES

1. The Bailey is a famous tavern in Dublin which had become an established part of
Dublin life by the middle of the nineteenth century. But it was at the turn of the century that it
began to attract the group of writers, poets and politicians who were to make its name famous.
'The Bailey has the best whiskey and the best food in Dublin,' says Oliver St John Gogarty in
As I Was Going Down Sackville Street. James Joyce refers to the Bailey in *Ulysses* under the name
of Burtons. He used it as the locale for the Lestrygonian episode in the novel. Visitors to The
Bailey will see an unusual relic of Dublin's literary past. This is the door of no. 7 Eccles Street,
Dublin, immortalised by Joyce as the home of Leopold Bloom in his novel. The house itself

..olished in April 1967, and only this door remains, preserved in the vestibule of the
.. ey.
2. Duke Street, off Grafton Street.

De Valera as Play Censor*

(From our Dublin Correspondent.)

An extraordinary situation has developed in connection with the proposed tour of the Abbey Theatre Company in the United States. Negotiations for the tour have been in process almost continuously since May of last year, and in deference to the declared desires of Dublin playgoers no tour was undertaken during the present theatrical season. It was decided, however, to undertake a tour of the principal cities of the United States in the 1934–5 season, and a contract to that effect was duly completed.

Everything was apparently arranged until the time came to inform the Free State Government of the tour, then complications came fast and furious. The necessity for informing the Free State Government, although merely a polite formality on previous occasions, arises from the fact that the Abbey Theatre is in receipt of an annual subsidy from the State. For some years this subsidy amounted to £1,000, but last year Mr. De Valera's Government—'as a measure of economy'—reduced it to £750.

Because of this subsidy there is a Government-nominated member[1] of the Abbey Theatre directorate, and courtesy demanded that the Executive Council be informed of the proposed American tour. On the two last occasions—1931–2 and 1932–3—the players were advertised in the United States as 'By permission of the Government of the Irish Free State,' and if the same advertisements were to be used on the next tour similar permission had to be assured.

When the formal announcement of the 1934–5 tour was made to the Government it was discovered that permission was not to be the formal matter it had previously been: the Government had notions of the plays which should be offered to American audiences as typical of the repertory of Ireland's national theatre. In particular, Mr. De Valera himself held strong views on the plays to be presented, and he caused those views to be brought to the notice of the directors. An interview with the President of the Executive Council was obtained by the directors, and at that interview the intentions of Mr. De Valera were made plain. Neither 'The Playboy of the Western World,' Synge's finest play and most popular with American audiences, nor Sean O'Casey's 'The Plough and the Stars' were to be

* *Manchester Guardian Weekly*, xxx, no. 15 (13 Apr 1934) 296.

included in the repertory. And these two plays had already been advertised as prominent among those to be presented by the Abbey Theatre Players during the tour!

In the course of the interview Mr. De Valera is reported by authoritative persons to have declared that 'he had never set foot in the Abbey Theatre,' and had no knowledge whatever about the plays presented there. He had, however, obtained the views of 'competent representative Irish opinion in the United States,' and it was evidently upon the advice of these people, unnamed and probably unknown, that the Synge and O'Casey plays were to be barred from the repertory. On the first presentation of 'The Playboy of the Western World' in the United States many years ago there were riotous scenes in the theatres, and on one occasion the entire company was placed under arrest on informations placed against it by Irish-American political societies.

At the interview with Mr. De Valera the principal spokesman for the Abbey directorate, Mr. W. B. Yeats, is said to have informed the President that 'he had fought the political societies before, and was prepared to do so again if necessary'; and, furthermore, 'that the Abbey Theatre was not to be regarded as a minor branch of the Civil Service.' It is believed by those closely associated with Mr. Yeats that he would be prepared to lose the annual subsidy to the Abbey Theatre rather than have its liberty to produce whatever plays were deemed worthy of production fettered by the Government.

When spoken to on the telephone at his home at Chalfont St. Giles[2] Mr. Sean O'Casey said he was sorry to learn that matters had come to such a pass, and expressed surprise at the attitude taken by Mr. De Valera in regard to 'The Playboy of the Western World,' which he regarded as one of the most beautiful fantasies ever written. He added that he would prefer to refrain from comment as far as his own play was concerned. Mr. O'Casey's play deals with the 1916 insurrection in Dublin.

NOTES

Eamon de Valera (1882–1975), an Irish political leader; led party of insurgents in Irish nationalist uprising (1916); President of Sinn Fein (1917–26); chosen President of an Irish republican government for which he obtained funds in America (1919); member of Dail Eireann (1919–22) and leader of opposition to Anglo-Irish treaty (December 1921–January 1922) signed by colleagues Arthur Griffith and Michael Collins; resigned presidency; established and presided over Fianna Fail (1924), comprising extreme republicans; took oath of allegiance to King and led Fianna Fail into Free State parliament (1927); President of executive council and Minister of External Affairs (1932–7); Prime Minister (1937–48; 1951–4; 1957–9); President of Ireland (1959), re-elected for seven-year term (1966–73).

On 16 February 1932 Yeats went up to Dublin from Coole to record his vote at the historic election which brought de Valera and the Fianna Fail party into office, with a mandate to abolish the oath of allegiance to the British monarch. Yeats had no objection to the removal of the oath, but he thoroughly disliked the social outlook of de Valera's followers, and his vote was cast for the defeated side. Presently hints reached him that a number of Irish-American societies were putting pressure on the government to exercise a censorship at the Abbey. Whereupon he sought an interview with de Valera, having first stated publicly that he would prefer to forgo the subsidy rather than permit any such interference. Yeats found a charm in his personal contact with de Valera that did not appear in his speeches. On 20 September 1933 he wrote to Mrs Shakespear that de Valera could be compared to Mussolini or Hitler—'all three have exactly the same aim as far as I can judge. . . . The trouble is yet to come I suppose.'

1. George O'Brien, Professor of Economics at University College Dublin.

2. O'Casey at that time was living in a furnished cottage, Hillcrest, Chalfort St Giles, Buckinghamshire, nineteen miles from London.

W. B. Yeats Looks Back; Poet Celebrates his Seventieth Birthday*

In his beautiful home near the Dublin mountains William Butler Yeats, Irish poet of world repute, received yesterday, on his 70th birthday, congratulatory telegrams and messages from the most prominent international figures in art, letters and sciences.

Edith Sitwell,[1] the poet, sent him flowers from Paris, and in a little bound volume came a message from more than a hundred brilliant men and women, including Shaw, Masefield[2] (the British Poet Laureate), Hugh Walpole,[3] Sir John Lavery[4] and Augustus John,[5] saying:—

> We, friends of the arts, wish to offer you on your 70th birthday a token of our admiration. Some of us who have had the privilege of knowing you have felt the encouragement of your sympathy. All of us have known the beauty and strength of your inspiration. We hope that this power which has grown steadily and is still growing may continue for many years to delight mankind.

Dr.[6] Yeats spent the day quietly with his family.

HIS WORK ACCOMPLISHED

Interviewed by an Irish Press representative he said:—

> Looking back on my 70 years I have done all the things that I wanted to do. All my toiling has been with a purpose and it is for others to pass judgment on it. When the movement I am associated with began, Irish literature was held in contempt. No Irish book was reviewed; not even

* *Irish Press* (Dublin) (14 June 1935) p. 7.

Standish O'Grady's fine 'History of Ireland—Political and Philosophi-cal' received a line in any newspaper.

Tracing the early beginnings of this literary Renaissance, Dr. Yeats mentioned the strength it received from the Irish Literary Society[7] in London, with which many great writers and journalists hastened to be associated.

INSPIRED BY GREAT FENIAN

Of his own part he would say little, but I drew from him that his first published piece of writing was a little pastoral play 'The Island of Statues,'[8] after the style of Spenser, published in the short-lived Dublin University Review.

It was the Fenian, John O'Leary, who inspired him to write his 'Wanderings of Ossian [sic].'[9] As a boy of 20 he knew O'Leary in the Young Irish Society in York Street, Dublin, and took part in their many debates.

He says of him: 'A great man who had the capacity to turn my thoughts.'

OLD BITTERNESS GONE

Asked what he thought of Dublin to-day, Dr. Yeats said: 'The great thing that strikes me is the improvement that has taken place in the social life of Dublin.

In my young days Dublin was divided into two classes, Unionist and Nationalist. They never met each other; it was that barrier that destroyed social life in Dublin for me. It was all so vicious that Lady Gregory and I made a resolution not to accept invitations of any kind.

From our own friends on the Unionist side we could only get some kind of hostility, and from the other side there was too much at issue, because we were producing Synge, who was being objected to. For 20 years and more we never accepted invitations and lived just for the Abbey Theatre.

The feud now is not so bitter and will never be as bitter as the old hereditary feud between Unionist and Nationalist. I can get good discussion now on anything and the people do not fly at each other's throats.

I found a new thing in Ireland not so long ago, when ranged around a dinner table were men who had fought against one another in the civil war, discussing affairs with a complete absence of the bitter partisanship that spoiled everything when I was a young man. It is a good sign of the times.

Modern tendencies in literature he found 'too intricate' to talk of with ease, but of Irish writers he claimed that they now held a great position in the world of letters.

FUTURE OF ABBEY THEATRE

'We are getting credit for our own creation,' said Dr. Yeats.

Before the modern movement Irishmen who went to England were looked on as English writers. Even to-day, see how quick the English were to seize on Lawrence of Arabia,[10] who was an Irishman and a member[11] of the Irish Academy of Letters.

The position of the Abbey Theatre, he declared, was as sound to-day as ever in its history.

While, [he said,] all good literature must be national, at the moment intellectual nationalism here has exhausted itself. It seeks new forms, and while the Abbey will continue to produce about four-fifths Irish plays, new formulae of the drama will be shown to our dramatists to study by the production of certain types of Continental play.

Of his own future, Dr. Yeats said simply that he intended to go on writing and was just then engaged in correcting the proofs of his new book.[12]

'And now in my old age,' he concluded, 'they want me to stand as a candidate for the Lord-Rectorship of Edinburgh University. My supporters there have sent me birthday greetings to-day.'

NOTES

In February 1935, after a visit from a lawyer who had come to see him about Lady Gregory's papers, Yeats collapsed and had to be kept in bed for a time. Alarming rumours spread through Dublin, and the secretary of the Pen Club called at Riversdale to enquire. 'Oh, Mrs. Yeats,' he said, 'don't let him slip away before June.' When his birthday came, however, Yeats was fully recovered. John Masefield and his wife crossed to Ireland for the occasion and stayed in Riversdale. To a luncheon party given for the Masefields came Oliver Gogarty, Mrs Llewelyn Davies and Julian Bell, the young English poet. Yeats 'beamed while his Irish playboy Gogarty told one story after another. . . . After luncheon Yeats addressed himself in a very kind manner to Julian Bell and told him to write poetry out of his emotions not out of his opinions. On leaving, Bell said to Mrs. Davies, "At last I have seen a poet who looks like a poet".' (Joseph Hone, *W. B. Yeats 1865–1939*, p. 441). John Masefield and Desmond MacCarthy, who had come to bring English congratulations, spoke at the Pen Club dinner in the evening. Next day the *Irish Times*, the oldest of the Dublin newspapers, published a supplement on Yeats's work.

1. Dame Edith Sitwell (1887–1964), English poet, critic and novelist; author of *The Mother and Other Poems* (1915), *Elegy on Dead Fashion* (1926), *Gold Coast Customs* (1929), *Alexander Pope* (1930), *The English Eccentrics* (1933), *Aspects of Modern Poetry* (1934), *I Live under a Black Sun* (1937) and *Look! The Sun* (1941). The despair of Yeats's friends in the nineties was preparation for a change that came suddenly with certain poets of the twenties, with W. J. Turner, Herbert Read, the Sitwells. 'When I read her *Gold Coast Customs* a year ago,' Yeats wrote to Wyndham Lewis in September 1930, 'I felt . . . that something absent from all literature for a generation was back again, and in a form rare in the literature of all generations, passion ennobled by intensity, by endurance, by wisdom.' In another letter to Dorothy Wellesley dated 6 July 1935 he said: 'In the last few days I have re-read all Edith Sitwell and found her very hard to select from, poem is so dependant upon poem. It is like cutting a piece out of tapestry.'

2. John Masefield (1878–1967) was a close friend of Yeats.

3. Sir Hugh Walpole (1884–1941), English novelist; first novels *The Wooden Horse* (1909) and *Maradick at Forty* (1910); won reputation with *Fortitude* (1913); other novels include *The Dark Forest* (1916), *The Green Mirror* (1918), *The Secret City* (1919) and *The Cathedral* (1922); biographised Anthony Trollope in 'English Men of Letters Series' (1928); wrote a series of chronicles of English social history: *Rogue Herries* (1930), *Judith Paris* (1931), *The Fortress* (1932), *Venessa* (1933), *The Bright Pavilions* (1940) and *Catherine Christian* (pub. 1943); and other novels including *The Duchess of Wrexe* (1914), *Harmer John* (1926), *Captain Nicholas* (1934), *The Youthful Delaneys* (1938), *The Blind Man's House* (1941) and *The Killer and the Slain* (pub. 1942).

4. Sir John Lavery (1856–1941), British portrait and figure painter. Among his best-known canvases are 'Polymnia' (now in National Gallery, Rome), 'A Lady in Black' (National Gallery, Berlin), 'Spring' (Luxenbourg) and 'Game of Tennis' (New Pinakothek, Munich). 'I am pressing upon the Government', Yeats wrote to John Quinn on 29 January 1924, 'the appointment of an Advisory Committee of Artists, and have got Orpen, Shannon and Lavery to promise to act upon that Committee.'

5. Augustus John (1878–1961), British painter. Yeats' first portrait since his hair had turned from brindled grey to white was painted by John.

6. Yeats's first honourary degree from a university was from Belfast in July 1922. In December the degree of Doctor of Letters in Dublin University was conferred upon him. In 1931 he received a similar degree from Oxford University. An honorary degree from Cambridge University was conferred on him the following year.

7. With T. W. Rolleston, Yeats formed at the end of December 1891 the Irish Literary Society of London, and five months later, in May 1892, he founded with John O'Leary's aid the National Literary Society in Dublin.

8. Yeats reached the climax of his youthful verse with his fourth play of 1884, *The Island of Statues*, which he finished in August of that year. He succeeded here in writing a picture play with Spenserian shepherds which, as the subtitle *An Arcadian Fairy Tale* suggests, was completely removed from the world. 'Miss Gonne was here yesterday with introduction from the O'Learys;' disclosed Yeats in a letter to Katharine Tynan dated 31 January 1889, 'she says she cried over "Island of Statues" fragment.'

9. *The Wanderings of Oisin and Other Poems* (London: Kegan Paul, Trench, 1889).

10. Thomas Edward Lawrence (1888–1935). Known as Lawrence of Arabia. British archaeologist, soldier and writer; born in Wales and educated at Oxford; led the Arab revolt against the Turks (1917–18), which he described in *The Seven Pillars of Wisdom* (1926).

11. He was an Associate. The work of 'Associates' was classified as 'less Irish' than that of full members.

12. *A Full Moon in March* (London: Macmillan, 1935).

W. B. Yeats Looks Back; Ireland in the Early Days of Abbey Theatre*

'There may be pure Gaels in the Blasket Islands,[1] but there are none in the Four Courts,[2] in the College of Surgeons, at the Universities, in the Executive Council,[3] or at Mr. Cosgrave's[4] headquarters,' said Dr. W. B. Yeats, in an interview broadcast from Radio Athlone on Saturday night.[5]

You may revive the Gaelic language, but if you do Anglo-Ireland will speak it; you cannot revive the Gaelic race, [he added].

Dr. Yeats recalled the early days of the Abbey Theatre, and said: 'One of the first decisions Lady Gregory and I made was to accept no invitations, but when we came to live in Dublin, to live in the Abbey Theatre as in a ship at sea, Unionist Ireland was a shabby and pretentious England where we would have met nothing but sneers. Nationalist Ireland was torn with every kind of political passion and prejudice, wanting, in so far as it wanted any literature at all, Nationalist propaganda, disguised as literature.

'PLAYS ABOUT LIFE.'

'We wanted plays about life—not about opinions—and with Ireland for their sole theme. A work of art is any piece of life, seen through the eyes or experienced in the soul, completely expounded. We insisted, and the Abbey Theatre to-day still insists, upon every freedom necessary to that exposition.'

To-day it was much harder to get good plays and that was why the Abbey Theatre had changed its policy. A new scenic art had arisen.

They were not going to give up their fine acting, but they wished to add the modern beauty of scene. There the Gate Theatre[6] had been far ahead of them.

The Dublin of to-day, Dr. Yeats said, was incomparably better, gayer, happier, more intelligent and liberal minded.

Dublin was now an Irish capital, with the vigorous thought of a capital city, and was to some extent, a European capital.

* *Irish Press* (Dublin) (14 Oct 1935) p. 9.

NOTES

1. Group of small islands off south-west coast of Ireland, north of entrance to Dingle Bay; in County Kerry.

2. The Four Courts in Dublin houses the Supreme Court, the High Court, a number of registries and other legal offices, as well as the barristers' law library.

3. Of the Irish Free State.

4. William Cosgrave (1880–1965), Irish statesman; identified with Sinn Fein and a member of the Dail Eireann from its beginning (1917); Chairman of the provisional government and President of Dail Eireann (1922); President of the executive council of the Irish Free State (1922–32).

5. I have been unable to obtain a transcript of this interview. A letter from the Controller of Programmes at Radio Telefis Eireann dated 13 June 1973 informs me that their 'script archives would not go back that far'. Senator Michael Yeats, the poet's son, sent me a letter on 24 January 1974 saying that he 'should think it extremely unlikely that anyone made a transcript while the broadcast was in progress. Certainly there does not seem to be anything of the kind in my collection.'

6. The Dublin Gate Theatre was founded in 1928 by Micheál MacLiammóir (1899–) and Hilton Edwards (1903–). Its work was distinct from that of the Abbey; indeed the two theatres were complementary, the Abbey presenting a picture of Irish life in all its phases, while the Gate programmes included drama of every period and every country. See Bulmer Hudson, ed., *The Gate Theatre, Dublin* (Dublin: The Gate Theatre, 1934); *Longford Productions: Dublin Gate Souvenir, 1939* (Dublin: Corrigan and Wilson [1939]); Micheál MacLiammóir, *All for Hecuba* (London: Methuen, 1946); and Hilton Edwards, *The Mantle of Harlequin* (Dublin: Progress House, 1958).

Mr. Yeats Explains Play: Plot of 'Purgatory' is its Meaning; Dramatist's Answer to US Priest's Query*

A definition of the symbolism of his new play, 'Purgatory,'[1] was given to an *Irish Independent* representative by Mr. W. B. Yeats yesterday when interviewed in connection with the question[2] asked by Rev. Terence L. Connolly, Professor of English, Boston College, U.S., at a lecture in connection with the Abbey Theatre Festival.[3]

There is no allegory in 'Purgatory,' nor, so far as I can remember, in anything I have written, said Mr. Yeats. William Blake said that

* *Irish Independent* (Dublin) (13 Aug 1938) p. 9.

allegory is made, not by inspiration, but by the daughters of memory. I agree, and have avoided it.

'Symbolism is another matter. There is symbolism in every work of art. A work of art moves us because it expresses or symbolises something in ourselves or in the general life of men.

'Father Connolly said that my plot is perfectly clear but that he does not understand my meaning. My plot is my meaning. I think the dead suffer remorse and re-create their old lives just as I have described. There are mediaeval Japanese plays about it, and much in the folklore of all countries.

In my play, a spirit suffers because of its share, when alive, in the destruction of an honoured house; that destruction is taking place all over Ireland to-day. Sometimes it is the result of poverty, but more often because a new individualistic generation has lost interest in the ancient sanctities.

'I know of old houses, old pictures, old furniture that have been sold without apparent regret. In some few cases a house has been destroyed by a mesalliance. I have founded my play on this exceptional case, partly because of my interest in certain problems of eugenics, partly because it enables me to depict more vividly than would otherwise be possible the tragedy of the house.

'In Germany there is special legislation to enable old families to go on living where their fathers lived. The problem is not Irish, but European though it is perhaps more acute here than elsewhere.'

NOTES

1. *Purgatory* opened at the Abbey Theatre on Wednesday, 10 August 1938. It is a symbolic one-act play in which an old man and his son pass by a ruined mansion where the old man's high-born mother had lived with her stableboy husband until she died in childbirth. The wastrel squandered her fortune, neglected his son, and finally, in a drunken orgy, burned down the house. The old man relates how he had stabbed his father and had run away while the house flamed. Now, while the spirits of man and wife relive their tragedy, the old man murders his son so that he will not repeat his grandfather's crime. At the fall of the curtain Yeats came forward to say that he had put nothing in the play because it seemed picturesque, but had put there his own convictions about this world and the next. This was Yeats's last public appearance.

2. 'What does *Purgatory* mean?' was the question put by Father Terence L. Connolly during a lecture on W. B. Yeats by F. R. Higgins on Thursday, 11 August 1938 during the Abbey Theatre Festival. Father Connolly said he had read Yeats's play and followed it very carefully when it was produced at the Abbey Theatre the night before. The plot was perfectly clear, but he had to admit frankly that he was still in ignorance as to what it symbolised. Though members of the audience were invited to give their views on the subject, no one volunteered to do so, and the question remained unanswered.

3. Held in Dublin 6–20 August 1938.

An Interview with
W. B. Yeats*

SHOTARO OSHIMA

In the Summer of 1938, after touring Scotland, I visited Northern Ireland
and while staying in Belfast wrote a letter to W. B. Yeats enquiring if it
would be possible for us to meet when I came to Dublin.

Upon my arrival at Phoenix Park Hotel, I found to my immense delight
a letter from Yeats awaiting me. My delight increased when upon opening
the letter I found that it contained an invitation to tea at 4. p.m. on the 5th
of July. For more than twenty years I had kept up correspondence with
him, and his letters to me had always been written in his own hand.[1] This
time, however, the letter had been written by Mrs. Yeats for her husband.
The letter explained at the beginning that he had not been well for a long
time. As I read the letter I had the feeling that he must be very ill.

On the appointed day I walked along the Liffey as far as a bus stop near
O'Connel Bridge. The river was so rich in colour and so pleasing in sound
that later I wrote about it:—

> Smiling at all false dreams of Dublin-town,
> The Liffey flows as it has always flowed;
> Carrying the scraps of joy and sorrow thrown
> On its red ripples, and patient of its load.

I then took a suburban bus, 'Park Gate Tram No. 49' and asked the
conductor where to get off. After getting off the bus I walked down the
village road, on which cows and sheep were mingling with the pedestrians.
The rain was falling so heavily that a streamlet somewhere in the
neighbourhood was grumbling noisily. I was forced to seek shelter in an
alehouse near by.

After a time the rain stopped, and as it was nearly 4 p.m., I felt [sic] the
alehouse and walked along beside a stone wall. When the stone wall ended,
I found myself in front of a gate bearing a bronze plate inscribed with the
letters 'RIVERSDALE.'

Just under the gate a stream, about ten feet wide, was flowing with a
loud noise. Crossing the bridge over the stream, I walked up a slope among

* *W. B. Yeats and Japan* (Tokyo: Hokuseido Press; London: Luzac, 1965) pp. 101–8.

flower-beds beautiful with roses and other flowering shrubs, until I came to a two-storeyed house with a large glazed door and windows. Standing in front of the door with its bronze plate inscribed with the letters 'Yeats,' I looked for a few moments at a beautiful flower-bed on the left. Then just at 4. o'clock I pushed the bell button under the name-plate. Mrs. Yeats answered the door.

Georgie Yeats was brisk in bearing and looked very intelligent and kind. When I introduced myself to her, she greeted me with great warmth and friendliness, as if I had been her intimate friend for many years. After we had exchanged greetings, I was shown into Yeats's study or sitting room through a hall, on the wall of which were hung in a row a series of about twenty *hanga,* Japanese prints, representing *kabuki* performances. They made the hall gay. The room itself looked out over the flower-bed, which, seen through the large window panes, looked very bright.

After a while I heard heavy footsteps coming down-stairs, and Yeats appeared before me. As I shook hands with him, I felt the weight of his poetic achievement in my palm. The old poet had massive shoulders and his grave and shadowy eyes seemed to betray his passionate subjectivity and abundant creative energy. He sat in a chair in front of the fireplace, and to my excitement, I saw a couple of fine Japanese festival dolls, *dairi-bina,** upon the mantelpiece. Although there was the full warmth of a July day, some turf was burning quietly in the fireplace. I thought that the poet, after many years of poetic and political activity, had grown old and needed the additional warmth.

Yeats talked very attractively. But now and then he repeated himself and I could not help feeling the gloomy presence of old age in him. In appearance he was a vigorous man. He was dressed in the same gay coloured clothes as I had seen in his portrait hung above the booking-office at the entrance to the Abbey Theatre. Upon the oak writing-table was laid Sato's[2] sword. It seemed to stand for all spiritual possibilities and human wisdom. It was the very symbol of the poet's inexhaustible imagination.

He talked about Irish literature and I recognized in his words a firm loyalty to the racial tradition. It lent him an inexpressible charm. Then he began to ask me about Japanese literature.

'How are the novels in your country? Are there any poets with racial spirit? Has the younger generation of Japan its own spirit and manner? How is Kan Kikuchi getting along? Are there any playwrights who write dramas marked by national or racial traits?' He asked these questions one after another in rapid succession, so that I could hardly answer them well.

'In big commercial theatres,' I said, 'classical dramas are performed, mainly by the *kabuki* actors. But as for a racial or national revival such as the Irish Renaissance, we have not yet seen any attempt.'

---

* The other day Prof. Kazumi Yano told me that it was he who presented Yeats with the *dairi-bina*.[Oshima].

Yeats was silent for a while. Then he drew a deep breath. The old poet seemed to be in very poor health, but his dignified attitude suggested that he was too proud to admit the fact even to himself. He turned towards the *dairi-bina*, the pair of Japanese dolls in ancient court costume depicting a man and his wife.

'We feel no difficulty in enjoying the beauty your people have created. I would often go for inspiration to the Japanese, who created such great beauty, especially when I was writing plays for dancers. . . . We must have a national literature. Have you seen Synge's *Riders to the Sea* performed at the Abbey Theatre? It is characteristic of our race.'

'Yes,' I answered, 'and I was much impressed at the rhythmical recitation of poetic words in the play. I'm sure there is nothing like that in English literature. We shall have to go to the *noh* theatre to find its equal.'

Yeats nodded seriously and said, 'There was much argument about the performance of the play, and opinion was divided especially on its production. But finally it was decided that the play should be produced in the way that you have seen. There was good reason for coming to that decision. I hope you found in it the ancient, passionate Ireland. A nation or a race should remember its own heroic tradition.'

Yeats seemed rather impatient when I said that some poets of the new generation seemed to pay special attention to politics and social circumstances, and that the central motive of their works seemed to be intellectual anarchism.

'You should not be surprised,' he said, 'to see that the poets of the "New Signatures" are looking for a voice in the new world. They are individualists: they are disgusted and disillusioned with what they see around them.'

At this point I referred to Ezra Pound's *Active Anthology* and said that most of the poems contained in that volume had bewildered us by their novel expression.

Yeats said, 'Even those pieces composed by ellipsis have a triumphant combination of the visual and the imaginative. The usual meanings of words are sometimes distorted in those poems. But even if their poems are sometimes ambiguous, you should admit that young poets are endevouring to discover a new literary technique. Their experiment is the same as that of Verlaine and Mallarmé. They are striving hard to find how they can come near to reality and grasp it firmly.'

It was Douglas Hyde who founded the Gaelic League in 1893, and he was among the first to show the English public the Celtic expression of poetry. He had become the first president of Eire about a fortnight before I visited Yeats. As to Hyde's mission of preserving the Irish heritage, Yeats was affirmative. 'Hyde was quite successful in arousing and displaying national sentiments,' he said. 'Some people are doubtful about the future of Gaelic. But every native language has its own charm. Hyde's Gaelic movement has had a much greater influence than any other movement.

He has done much for the consolidation of national sentiments, thus enabling the Irish people to conceive their own ideals. I'm sure this movement will serve as a model for you Japanese. The Gaelic language has its own peculiar charm to those who speak it as their mother tongue. The revival of this dear tongue will lead to the realization of the Gaelic kingdom. We should also remember Padraic Pearce; he has done much for the Gaelic Revival. The revival of our language owes much to his educational idealism.'

Hyde's *Beside the Fire* has afforded a good example,' I said. 'His manner of copying dialectic expressions faithfully was adopted by Japanese folklorists in recording folk tales.'

'We have also seen the best of Irish literature in the translations of Gaelic poems contained in *Love Songs of Connacht,* and *Religious Songs of Connacht.* They have revived our blighted hopes and the lost life of the Celtic people.'

'Are there any scholars who are endeavouring to revive folk poems?'

'Frank O'Connor and Robin Flower are the best. You will find excellent Gaelic characteristics in Flower's *Poems and Translations.* Besides these two, many other Irish poets are writing poems, adapting freely from the Gaelic legends. The lyrical and narrative poems by Higgins and Clarke belong to this class.'

On the table beside his armchair was the magnificent Kelmscott edition of Chaucer. This book, Mrs. Yeats told me, was given to Yeats by twenty-four of his friends as a present on his fortieth birthday. A golden candlestick standing beside this book glittered in the westering sun which streamed in through the windows.

In those days I was engaged in the work of translating Yeats's poems into Japanese, so I said, 'You remember you gave me permission to publish a translation of your poems in Japan, but I find it very difficult to select poems suitable for translation.'

Mrs. Yeats, serving us tea, answered instead of her husband, 'To be sure, my husband has written so many poems, and he is always rewriting and revising. You may well find it difficult to translate them.'

'If you can afford the time,' said Yeats, 'you had better visit Sligo, Mayo, Galway, Clare and so on; you will find typically Irish scenes in these places.'

'I want to see Lough Gill and, if possible, to see the Isle of Innisfree close at hand.'

'As for the isle I loved metaphysics. I thought there was only one Innisfree, but there seem to be two Innisfrees in Lough Gill. It was no less than fifty years ago and in London that I wrote "The Lake Isle of Innisfree." It didn't matter, however, whether it was a real island or not.'

'The guide book says that the Isle of Innisfree lies beside Church Island and Cottage Island,' I said, and showed him the guide book, pointing to the place where it was written.

Yeats took out a monocle with dark glass from his pocket and gazed at the page for a while and did not say anything more about the matter. Afterwards I visited Sligo and sailed about Lough Gill and saw for myself that Innisfree is not a single island on the lake. There were two islets near by and they were respectively named Church Island and Cottage Island as the guide book indicated.

As I tried to show Yeats the guide book, I happened to come so close to him that I could distinctly hear him breathing hard, perhaps because of his protracted illness. I also noticed, then for the first time in the setting sun shining through the windows, that his hair had turned quite gray with old age. But it seemed to me that his silver hair was glowing like fire with creative energy. With a sense of almost reverent awe for the poet who had been untiringly writing poems in his old age, I asked, 'Are you still writing poems?'

'Yes!' he answered positively with a clear voice.

I was shocked to hear this single word as if struck by a sudden thunder. This curt answer was enough to make me feel ashamed for having asked such a foolish question. His attitude at the moment reminded me of an old *Zen* priest who was asked, 'Are you still pursuing enlightenment?' and answered, 'Away with you! Never ask me a question only to throw dirt at me!'

Indeed, Yeats had never ceased to write poems and his poems had reached us in Japan in golden tones or in passionate silence. It was quite natural that the poet, who was full of great ideas and beautiful images, could not receive my question calmly.

Then Yeats suddenly rose to his feet and, taking up a volume of *New Poems* from the table, handed it to me. I at once recognized that it had been published by his sister Elizabeth Corbet Yeats, since the binding of the book was similar to that of other books of the Cuala Press series. On the flyleaf of the book Yeats had written his signature in advance, which read as follows: 'S. Oshima, from his friend W. B. Yeats, July 5, 1938.'

Pointing to the flying unicorn on the title page, I asked, 'Did Sturge Moore draw this unicorn flying down among stars?'

'Yes, he did,' Yeats answered. 'He isn't in Dublin now. He always stays in London.' And he added in a low voice, 'Now I must take a rest. I feel rather tired. But I have another book to give you; it is the revised edition of *A Vision.*'

I told him that I had a copy of the first edition of the book, that mine was one of the limited edition of 600 copies and that it was numbered 3.

'That's a good number. Thank you for having bought such an expensive edition. But I have revised it since. Please accept this new edition. I will write my signature on it, too.'

Mrs. Yeats joined in our conversation from time to time, and told me about their children in a frank way. 'Our son is going to Trinity College soon, but now he is at St. Columba's School. He is taller than his father, but was once so delicate that we sent him to a school in Switzerland. But now he has become quite healthy. Our daughter is at present in bed with a cold. The weather has been rather bad recently.'

Meantime I asked Yeats for a letter of introduction to Douglas Hyde, for I had been asked by a friend of mine in Japan to get permission from Hyde to translate a book of his. Yeats talked for a few minutes with his wife, and then Mrs. Yeats wrote the letter of introduction on a typewriter. They talked for a long time about how to address the envelope. At last Yeats said to his wife with a smile, 'Mr. Hyde has just become president. The letter must be addressed to his official residence.' And he dictated the address as follows:

> His Excellency
> The President
> Vice Regal Lodge,
> Phoenix Park, Dublin

Then on the top left-hand corner of the envelope he wrote 'Personal' and underlined it.

When I was about to leave, I said to Yeats that I should be much obliged if he would kindly allow me to take his picture and, if Mrs. Yeats didn't mind, together with her. Yeats asked his wife if she had any objections to my request. She smiled but seemed somewhat unwilling.

After I had got out of the house, I stood hesitating for a moment in the front garden, then ventured to ask Mrs. Yeats to allow me to take a snapshot of her husband. 'If you want to take his picture so much', she said, 'why didn't you say so before he went upstairs. He has been very ill of late and has not seen even his brother and sister. It was with a great effort that he saw you. He is very tired.' At the intense tone in which she spoke, I realized how far I had been availing myself of their generosity and made a humble apology. But Mr. and Mrs. Yeats were extremely tolerant of me, for when I was taking snaps of the house and the beautiful flower-bed for remembrance, Yeats appeared at the front door, and sat on a bench just before the ivy which covered the wall. He took out his monocle from his pocket and applied it to his left eye. Rather surprised I hastily took two snaps of him. After a while I said good-bye to Mr. and Mrs. Yeats and left the house still feeling the warmth of the old poet's hand in my palm.

Five months after that, on board the Aquitania on the Atlantic Ocean, I learnt the news of his death. After having sent a telegram of condolence to Mrs. Yeats, I stood alone on deck and gazed on the rolling waves and at the most glorious sunset that I had seen in years. The sight imparted a feeling which seemed as if I had received sad and solemn blow deep in my heart.

NOTES

Shotaro Oshima (1899–   ) is the author of *Ieitsu Kunkyu (W. B. Yeats: A Study)* (Tokyo: Taibunsha, 1927); *W. B. Yeats* (Tokyo: Kenkyusha, 1934); *Studies in Modern Irish Literature*

(Tokyo: Hokuseido, 1956; revised edition, with an additional chapter, 1960); and *W. B. Yeats and Japan* (Tokyo: Hokuseido, 1965). See also his articles 'The Poetry of Symbolic Tradition in the East and the West', *Waseda Daigaku Daigakuin Bungakuku Kiyo (Bulletin of the Graduate Division of Literature of Waseda University)*, no. 10 (1964) 1–29 and 'Yeats and the Japanese Theatre', *Threshold* (Belfast) no. 19 (Autumn 1965) 89–102.

1. There are no letters to Oshima in *The Letters of W. B. Yeats*, ed. Allan Wade (London: Rupert Hart-Davis, 1954).

2. Eisaku Sato (1901–   ), Japanese political leader who was elected President of the Liberal Democratic Party in 1964 and became Prime Minister of Japan.

A Beautiful Friendship*

DOROTHY WELLESLEY

In December 1938 I had taken La Bastide, the villa in the hills above Beaulieu,[1] and W. B. with Mrs. Yeats was staying at a quiet country hotel on Cap Martin. The first evening I went to see him I was astounded at what seemed a miraculous return to health. He looked healthier, and his brain was more active than ever, if such a thing could be possible. He was half sitting up on his bed, much excited. Almost his first words were: 'I want to read you my new play'. And this he did. In spite of the confusion of a much corrected manuscript, he read with great fire. It was *The Death of Cuchulain*.[2] I was much moved, half aware that it was in some sense a premonition of his own death, though I did not know it was to come so soon. After his death Mrs. Yeats gave me the original MS. with a typed version.

Some days later he dined with us to meet Schnabel, the great pianist, and W. J. Turner who was staying at my villa, and who was a friend of both Yeats and Schnabel. Madame Schnabel was there, who knows small English and less Irish. Schnabel could not himself understand much of what Yeats said (which was a great deal) owing to his Irish brogue. They talked about Stefan Georg and Rilke, but the approach of the musician and the poet was so diametrically opposed that points of contact were few and far between. I sat with the Austrian on my right and the Irish Nationalist poet on my left.

On Christmas Day W. B. Yeats and their son Michael, aged seventeen, dined with us. W.B. seemed very gay. He was full of charming stories: the little monkey god who threw down mangoes from the tree; the holy man embedded in the block of ice. He told me afterwards with great pride,

* Extracted from *Far Have I Travelled* (London: James Barrie, 1952) pp. 162–70.

knowing that it had been a good performance, that the stories had been especially for Michael.

*   *   *

We had many delightful evenings with him, Mrs. Yeats, W. J. Turner, and Hilda Matheson. On the last evening, when we all went to see him, we found him as lively and excited as ever. After luncheon at that strangely charming and pagan place, La Turbie, we had motored into the hills behind Mentone, and deep into the gorges beyond the town. Snow on the peaks, brilliant sun, bitter cold. A great exhilaration seemed to be upon us. At about 4.30 we came down from the hills to Yeats's hotel. As I have said, he seemed to us as well as we had ever seen him, full of ideas about his theories of words for songs. I showed him a little song I had made for him—*Golden Helen*—to be printed in the Cuala *Broadsides* 'Yes, yes,' he said, 'It has great poetical profundity.' He was wearing his light brown suit, blue shirt and handkerchief. Under the lamp his hair seemed a pale sapphire blue. I thought while he talked, 'what a beautiful man!' He asked Hilda Matheson to make a tune for *Golden Helen*. She and I went out of the hotel, walking up and down in the rain and darkness trying the tune. When we came back she sang the air. He seemed pleased. His last projective thought seems to me to have been this wish for 'words for melody'. Melody, not music conventionally spoken of: folk ballad, and so on. I from early childhood have craved for this union, words for an air, and this is what we must now carry on.

On this evening also he said, 'The Greek drama alone achieved perfection; it has never been done since; it may be thousands of years before we achieve that perfection again. Shakespeare is only a mass of magnificent fragments.'

*   *   *

On Tuesday he did not come to spend the evening with us as arranged, as he was tired. On Wednesday the Turners left for England and we were busy with arrangements. On Thursday morning I went to see him. He was very ill, in fact I saw he was dying, and I saw he knew it. I stayed only five minutes, fearing to tire him. In the afternoon we went again. Mrs. Yeats had said, 'Come back and light the flame.' I sat on the floor by his bed holding his hand; he struggled to speak: 'Are you writ . . . are you writing?'

'Yes, yes.'

'Good, good.'

He kissed my hand, I his. Soon after he wandered a little in his speech, murmuring poetry. Later that same evening he was able to give Mrs. Yeats corrections for *The Death of Cuchulain* and for the poem *His Convictions*, which he changed to *Under Ben Bulben*. On Friday he was worse, and soon passed into what proved to be his last coma. He had much pain from the heart, but morphia helped him. Next day, January 28th, he was dead. So ended in the material sense this short and beautiful friendship.

NOTES

Lady Gerald (Dorothy Violet) Wellesley, Duchess of Wellington, is the author of *Early Poems* (1913), *Poems* (1920), *Pride, and Other Poems* (1923), *Lost Lane* (1925), *Genesis; An Impression* (1926), *Matrix* (1928), *Deserted House: A Poem-Sequence* (1930), *Jupiter and the Nun* (1932), *Poems of Ten Years, 1924–1934* (1934), *Lost Planet and Other Poems* (1942), *The Poets and Other Poems* (1943), *Desert Wells* (1946) and *Rhymes for Middle Years* (1954). See *W. B. Yeats, Letters on Poetry to Dorothy Wellesley*, ed. Dorothy Wellesley (1940).

    1. South of France.
    2. Yeats had made the prose draft of his last play at Chantry House, and then left for the Riviera with his wife.

Memories of Yeats*

MARY M. COLUM

> Cast a cold eye
> On life, on death,
> Horseman pass by.
>
> *(Yeats's lines for his tombstone from his last poem)*

These are strange lines for the epitaph of a poet who never cast a cold eye on life or death. The last time I saw W. B. Yeats was in June 1938, in his house outside Dublin. He came into the room with his well-remembered, eager step, speaking in his well-remembered, eager voice. But he was changed. Old age that had left him so long untouched was making inroads on his physique. The old energy now came only in flashes. One of his eyes was covered with a black patch; it was blind, and he could use only one eye. 'We are both changed,' he said, examining me with his one eye. 'You were once my ideal of a youthful nihilist.'[1] This was what he used to say to me in my student days when I was so delighted to be Yeats's ideal of anything that I didn't care what the word meant. Nihilism was the romantic form of revolt in Yeats's early days; his friend, Oscar Wilde, had made a first play about Vera, the girl-nihilist.[2] I think, vaguely, in his mind it represented a youthful fighting spirit that went with reading Russian novels, French Symbolist poetry, and Nietzsche. To attribute to anyone a fighting spirit was Yeats's most heartfelt compliment.

    It was wonderful in those student days, after a day's listening to some

* *Saturday Review of Literature* (New York) XIX (25 Feb 1939) 3–4, 14.

minor professor treating literature as if it was sawdust, to go to one of the clubs where Yeats frequently held forth, and hear him talk of art and literature and life and read poetry, especially the poetry of the men he had known. 'I am the last of a doomed generation,' he was fond of saying. That doomed generation included the men of the nineties—in England, Dowson, Oscar Wilde, Lionel Johnson, Earnest Henley, Aubrey Beardsley, John Davidson; in France, it included Verlaine,—not Mallarmé. Contrary to what I have seen in print several times in this country, Yeats never knew Mallarmé, never went to Mallarmé's Tuesday evenings; all the criticism of his poetry built on the notion that he took any part in the celebrated discussions of the Mallarmé group is unrelated to reality. He never knew any language except English, and had no firsthand acquaintance with French literature—symbolist or any other species. But he had met and talked with Verlaine[3] in English and has left a record of the meeting. He knew all the poets who had met a miserable end and he would repeat their poems—Dowson's, Johnson's, Wilde's, or he would repeat Blake or some Elizabethan like Nashe.

Sometimes he would give a formal lecture on poetry or drama. To look back on the situations he was in during those years convinces one that the life of the real artist is always a battle, particularly in the case of a great artist like Yeats, who tried to reform the literary and intellectual life of his country and his period. He was bitterly attacked in Dublin during the heyday of the literary movement; he was so different from other people in his ideas and even in his appearance that they were exasperated by him. Sunk in dreams, he would pass friends or acquaintances in the street with an unseeing eye; he did not consider that many people knew much about poetry, and his assumption of this in his numerous public speeches in the clubs and literary societies of the town got people's backs up. Then there was a number of older literary men who would get up and contradict him at every assembly and tell the audience that literature or poetry could wait—the main cause being the fight for freedom, and the business of literature was to advance the national aspirations.

Until Yeats made himself literary dictator, the subject of discussion at literary gatherings in Ireland was not literature but patriotic ideologies. When he informed us that lines like

> For thy hapless fate, dear Ireland,
> And sorrows of my own

were but conventional sentiment and could not move us deeply, when he became mocking about 'Believe me if all those endearing young charms that I gaze on so fondly to-day' and similar effusions of the national poet, Tom Moore,[4] he reduced over half of his audience to almost speechless rage. Somebody would recover sufficiently to say that Yeats was living in an ivory tower and all the other things men say when they are faced by somebody who takes the discipline of art seriously. At some of the societies and clubs where he spoke he would make an address so stirring intellectually and artistically that the ideas and the words became a lifetime's possession for some of us. But it would be some other speaker, who delivered himself of the humanitarian and political platitudes in fashion, who would be congratulated by the audience.

The newspapers were, nearly all of them, against him and his ideas; even often, such an intelligent journal as Arthur Griffiths's *United Irishman* which later became *Sinn Fein*. Some of the critiques of his most lovely poems both in England and Ireland were ignorant and contemptuous. In Dublin, in the university groups, a few progressive-minded professors supported him; among the students, a group that were considered wild and eccentric were his followers. I was the president of a small Students' Literary Society which followed him around from one hall to another wherever he was to speak, and applauded with hands and feet. The plays in the Abbey Theatre were so sparsely attended that when the members of this Society entered in a body—we were about ten or twelve in number—the audience was appreciably augmented, and Yeats would cast a pleased eye on us. We could be depended on to listen ecstatically to every line of a verse-play; we went, not only to all the plays, but to all the performances of them. Some of our professors a hundred and fifty years after Lessing were still talking about the rules of composition. When, in Synge's 'Riders to the Sea,' the body of the drowned man was brought on the stage, certain professors pronounced this against all the rules of art, and one of the most enlightened of the political weeklies invariably referred to the play as 'a corpse-curtain-raiser.'

The country Yeats faced had had its intellectual life twisted awry with political and defensive preoccupations and its artistic life made anemic through the writers' making themselves mere auxiliaries of political leaders. When writers are too feeble to be able to give artistic statement to great human experiences, they are too likely to swim with the tide and indulge ineffectually in the social and political platitudes that are the fashion. There is nothing for an innovator to do but fight these: Yeats was a wonderful fighter—eager, sardonic, tireless—and he was at his very best when fighting for another man's work. The fight he put up for 'The Playboy of the Western World' was an exhibition of fighting strategy, of immovable courage, of indifference to public hostility such as I have never seen anywhere in anybody else. At the opening night of 'The Playboy' the first act went well, but as the performance went on the uproar began. The man near me who began the hissing was Francis Sheehy-Skeffington,[5] and he was neither narrow-minded nor puritanical. Why did he hiss? Why did the theatre in the end become a swaying mass of angry humanity? I never knew; it was something I could not understand. Yeats was lecturing in England[6] on the opening night; he was telegraphed for, for he alone could handle the trouble and cope with the insistence for the withdrawal of the play. Back he came; he announced that the play would continue for the advertised number of performances; he lined the theater with police and forced a hearing for Synge's play. Synge himself, his face drawn and blenched, would from the front seats from time to time throw a furtive glance at the audience. The demand for withdrawal continued; Yeats announced—these were his words—that neither the house nor the race that bred him had given him a pliant knee, and he was not going to bend before the public. After the play's run had been completed, he told them, he would throw the theater open for discussion of the play.

On the night of the public discussion the streets near the Abbey were crowded with police and there was an excitement as if a revolution had started. A motley mixture of workmen, students, and bourgeoisie in evening dress filled the theater, most of them with denunciatory speeches ready to deliver. Yeats took the platform in full evening dress and faced the crowd. Step by step he interpreted the play, delivering in the process some of his most complex theories of art, one moment cowing the audience, the next shouted down by them. The author of the play, who was no fighter of this kind, stayed at home. When the usual speech about freedom, patriotism came from somebody in the stalls, the audience cheered. But even on the patriotics Yeats was equal to them. 'The author of "Kathleen Ni Holohan" addresses you,' he said. The audience remembering that passionately patriotic play, forgot its antagonism for a few minutes, and Yeats got his cheers. At one moment a student supporter of his took the platform beside Yeats and made a remark which caused nearly all of the few women in the audience to walk out. Myself and another girl-student were the only members of the female sex in sight: we were surrounded by a group of angry males ordering us, if we were virtuous girls, to leave the theater. We stood our ground, and Yeats, who, in spite of his well-publicized dimness of vision, could always see when it suited him, saw our difficulties from the platform and sent a couple of theater attendants to escort us to the stalls among the men in evening dress who, however, did not regard us with a friendly eye, either. I never witnessed a human being fight as Yeats fought that night nor never knew another with so many weapons in his armory. He was then in his forties, but he looked under thirty, a fearless, dominating man in spite of, or perhaps because of, all his dreams and visions and esoteric philosophy.

In the end he won every battle, as men of unbending artistic and intellectual integrity are likely to do. What was he battling for? Perhaps only a few understood, perhaps it never could be completely stated. In one of his poems to the beautiful, stormy woman[7]—as great a fighter as himself—to whom his love-poetry was written, he cries:—

> My darling cannot understand
> What I have done, or what would do
> In this blind, bitter land.[8]

And yet a great poet of his type, an intellectual and artistic reformer, would certainly have more opposition in a larger country, might have found such a place also a 'blind and bitter land.'

But all the fighting he had to do must have altered his personality, for the friends of his twenties would talk of the warmhearted, affectionate, ingenuous boy, while the man we knew was hard, strong, reserved, deliberately living behind a mask, that particular mask which, as he has explained to us, all artists must find for themselves. People who expected to find in him the ordinary simplicities or the ordinary complexities were disappointed and even exasperated. He was very hard to understand; it was hard to correlate the fighting man with the poet, the administrator with the visionary, the 'smiling public man' with the believer in astrology, spiritism, in non-human presences, and in magic. But he was one of those philosophers, adepts, or initiates who believe that all that mankind has ever believed in was true and lasting, existing somewhere, in some realm of knowledge that could be entered.

He had the hard Irish memory for wrongs once done him; I doubt if he ever forgot a friendly deed or forgave a wrong. I think that if he loved or liked any person it was for always. The Greeks, he sometimes said, thought it as great a virtue to hate your enemies as to love your friends; he did both. Like the Greeks, too, he hated old age, and through his later poems runs his resentment that the great energy that was his in his strong manhood was flickering away and could be less and less relied upon to support the tireless efforts of his mind:

> Consume my heart away; sick with desire
> And fastened to a dying animal
> It knows not what it is; and gather me
> Into the artifice of eternity.[9]

Like Swift he has written his epitaph: that last poem which has the epitaph for its conclusion—it appeared in *The Irish Independent*, but has not yet been published here[10]—is full of the old fighting spirit:—

> Know that when all words are said
> And a man is fighting-mad,
> Something drops from eyes long blind,
> He completes his partial mind,
> For an instant stands at ease,
> Laughs aloud, his heart at peace,
> Even the wisest man grows tense
> With some sort of violence
> Before he can accomplish fate,
> Know his work or choose his mate
>
> Irish poets, learn your trade,
> Sing whatever is well made,
> Scorn the sort now growing up

All out of shape from toe to top,
Their unremembering hearts and heads
Base-born products of base beds.

Cast your mind on other days
That we in coming days may be
Still the indomitable Irishry.[11]

This, I think, is his last finished poem, his testament.

NOTES

Mary M. Colum (1885–1957) married Padraic Colum in 1912 and spent much of the remainder of her life in America. Her writings include *From These Roots: The Ideas That Have Made Modern Literature* (1938) and the autobiographical *Life and the Dream: Memories of a Literary Life in Europe and America* (1947). She has also written articles in periodicals on Yeats and reviewed many of his works.

1. 'Nihilism' is total rejection of current beliefs, in religion or morals. In philosophy it means scepticism that denies all existence.

2. *Vera; or The Nihilist* (London: privately printed, 1880).

3. Paul Verlaine (1844–96), French poet at first associated with the Parnassians, and later known as the leader of the Symbolists. Arthur Symons took Yeats in Paris to call on Verlaine, who could speak English. For a record of this visit see V. P. Underwood, *Verlaine et l'Angleterre* (Paris: Librairie Nizet, 1956) pp. 463–4.

4. Thomas Moore (1779–1852), Irish poet who gained reputation as the national lyrist of Ireland by his *Irish Melodies* (irregularly pub. 1807–34) and *National Airs* (1818–27).

5. Francis Sheehy-Skeffington, a nationalist and James Joyce's friend.

6. Yeats was lecturing in Aberdeen, Scotland at that time.

7. Maud Gonne.

8. W. B. Yeats, 'Words', *The Green Helmet and Other Poems* (1910).

9. W. B. Yeats, 'Sailing to Byzantium', *The Tower* (1928).

10. In the United States.

11. W. B. Yeats, 'Under Ben Bulben', *Last Poems and Plays* (1940).

Yeats as I Knew Him*

AODH DE BLACAM

In 1932, when Lady Gregory lay dying at Coole, Yeats wrote[1] to me to tell that she was reading my novel, *The Lady of the Cromlech*, on her death-bed; and he touched on synthesis only to reject it. 'There are two Irelands,' he wrote. His Ireland now, on his own admission, had nothing in common with that of Gaels or of Catholics.

At that time, failing to persuade him that the Gaelic past had value even

* Extracted from 'Yeats As I Knew Him', *Irish Monthly* (Dublin) LXVII (Mar 1939) 204–13. Condensed under the same title in *Irish Digest* (Dublin) III, no. 3 (May 1939) 33–6.

to the pure Anglo-Irishman, I resorted to an oblique argument. I said that
Homer and the Gael belonged to one world; that the House of Penelope
was the true image of many a house that the bards frequented. If Yeats
could not write of High-Kings again, would he not write of Odysseus and
Achilles? I hoped that the poet, though his political change of mind had
turned him against Irish-Ireland, would be true to that *juventus mundi*[2]
which is Homer's, as it is the Gael's. The answer to my plea is in some
poem[3] that Yeats wrote soon after, in which he writes of 'Father Homer' in
a way utterly unsympathetic to the Homeric spirit. The embittered mind
saw no health anywhere.

*   *   *

Away back in 1921 we had hope, for a spell, that Yeats would be
reconciled. He had been living in France, for his health's sake, and had
been reading Péguy's[4] *Mystery of the Charity of Jeanne d'Arc*. He had been
moved by the poetry in which the Saint rejoiced to know that the wheat of
her France and the grapes went to making of the bread and wine which the
Mass changed into the Body and Blood of Christ. With Péguy, he read
Claudel,[5] and, I think, Jammes;[6] and he came home, urging young
Irishmen to familiarise themselves with these new Catholic writers of
France, and to imitate them. In a meditative essay, too, he wrote of his own
advancing years, and wondered whether the time had not come to learn
from holy old women how to compose the soul and make a holy end. It
almost seemed that Yeats, the man we had loved long since, was turning
towards the Catholic Faith. A little later, we thought the same of Bernard
Shaw.

The hope was not fulfilled. Instead, Yeats became more bitter than ever
before, against what we hold sacred. The indecency which marred so
many of his past books now grew more horrid, and the latest book[7] which
he published, less than a year ago, was a repulsive play that we can excuse
only by assuming that the mind which conceived it was unstrung. His
poems, in the last dozen years, were morbid. He wrote of the blood of
Calvary some lines[8] so horrible that I could not quote them; one wonders
how a publisher printed them. He described Bethlehem as the birthplace of
a monster, and lamented the coming of Christianity. How ill this became
the poet who once had charmed us with lines about the child that the Little
People stole,[9] the mice bobbing round the oatmeal chest in a country
house,[10] and the merry playing of the Fiddler of Dooney![11]

*   *   *

When I sat with him and George Russel ('Æ') some years ago, and these
theosophists turned from letters to discuss weird happenings, I was
astonished to hear Yeats say that he had not made up his mind yet whether
there was such a thing as personal survival, individual immortality. Here

was a man in his old age, far-famed as a semi-philosophic author, and his philosophy had not reached yet as far as one of the elementary truths! In truth, he was ill-founded. He wasted genius that ought to have gone to high achievement in groping among issues that a penny catechism would settle for others, whether they were as simple as schoolchildren or as mighty as Aquinas. He knew, he recognised, he proclaimed that art needs prophet, priest and king—that is, faith and authority as well as vision. He had vision, but not faith, and authority he refused. Therefore his poetry went little farther than imaginative emotion; he gave us no Lear, no *Divine Comedy*.

NOTES

Aodh de Blacam was born in London in 1890 and died in Dublin in 1951. He learned Irish in London from Robert Lynd and went to Ireland as a journalist in 1915. Well known under the pseudonym 'Roddy the Rover', he was interned by the Black and Tans for his nationalist writings. His works include *The Story of Colmcille* (1929), *Gaelic Literature Surveyed* (1929), *A First Book of Irish Literature* (1934) and *The Life of Wolfe Tone* (1935). His writings on Yeats include 'Yeats and the Nation. A Surrender to Subjectivity: Why the Abbey Idea Failed', *Irish Times* (Dublin) (13 June 1935) pp. 6–7 (an attack on Yeats and the Abbey Theatre.)

    1. *The Letters of W. B. Yeats*, ed. Allan Wade (London: Rupert Hart-Davis, 1954) does not contain letters to Aodh de Blacam.

    2. Youth of the world.

    3. W. B. Yeats, 'Vacillation', *The Winding Stair and Other Poems* (1933).

    4. Charles Pierre Peguy (1873–1914), French writer who in 1900 founded the journal *Cahiers de la Quinzaine*, in which his chief works appeared. He wrote studies on Joan of Arc, Victor Hugo and Henri Bergson.

    5. Paul Louis Charles Claudel (1868–1955), French diplomat, poet and dramatist who was associated with the Symbolist school.

    6. Frances Jammes (1868–1938), French poet and novelist. For a reference to Peguy, Claudel and Jammes, see W. B. Yeats, *Essays* (London: Macmillan, 1924) p. 537.

    7. W. B. Yeats, *The Herne's Egg* (London: Macmillan, 1938).

    8. W. B. Yeats, 'The Magi', *Responsibilities* (1914).

    9. W. B. Yeats, 'The Stolen Child', *Crossways* (1889).

    10. *Ibid.*

    11. W. B. Yeats, 'The Fiddler of Dooney', *The Wind Among the Reeds* (1899).

Impressions*

WILLIAM ROTHENSTEIN

When I was learning something about drawing and painting in Paris, Grant Richards,[1] then Secretary to Stead,[2] called on me. This would be about 1892. He asked me to stay with him in his London flat, where I met and became friendly with Richard le Gallienne. I went out to see le

* *Arrow* (Dublin) VI (Summer 1939) 16–17.

Gallienne at Hanwell where he was then living, who, on one occasion, produced a photograph: What did I think of that head? I thought it remarkable. Well, it was the head of a young Irish poet, W. B. Yeats. I had not then heard of him, I think to le Gallienne's secret pleasure. But I did not forget the photograph, and a few weeks afterwards York Powell[3] took me to the Yeats's house at Bedford Park,[4] and introduced me to their attractive family circle. When W. B. took rooms on the third floor of a house in Euston buildings,[5] I became one of the intimates there.

Artists and poets, after early promise, often lose control of their gifts. Not so Yeats, who developed a self, eager for spiritual adventure. Anxious to explore the mysteries of life, believing in the holding, and the passing-on of secret wisdom, he was inclined to be over-trustful of those who declared they had experience beyond the human horizon, and sometimes confused spiritualism with spirituality. When Yeats came down, candle in hand, to guide one up the long flight of stairs to his rooms, one never knew what company one would find there. There were ladies who sat on the floor and chanted stories, or crooned poems to the accompaniment of a one-stringed instrument. The masculine company I see more vaguely.

I recollect Yeats coming to meet Stephen Philips [sic][6] at luncheon in my studio at Glebe Place—this would be in 1897—when they talked throughout the afternoon until it was time for supper. For Yeats was rich in theories of the arts, of poetry, painting and the theatre.

'Young man, lift up your russet brow.' I always associate that lovely line with Yeats himself, though his long black hair fell upon a pale forehead under which the dark eyes looked queerly from a white face, and he had the mobile mouth of the imaginatively endowed.

In later years Yeats's resolute gallantry, sustained by ripening experience, became an important force in contemporary life. When Yeats, for instance, was on a lecturing tour in America, Gorki[7] being in the States at the same time, it was discovered that the lady who accompanied Gorki was not his legal wife. No hotel would take them in. Yeats, indignant that no voice was heard in Gorki's defence, himself protested in the American Press, though he knew he was risking a popularity upon which, while in the States, he depended. I have never known Yeats fail in this gallantry. More than anyone I have known he stood for the dignity of the artist, for the integrity of the arts. At a time when men give, often at little or no cost to themselves, ready sympathy for the proletariat, Yeats recognised the claims of those who had a right to power, since they had high courage, superior wisdom and, to Yeats an important aspect, fine breeding.

I recollect telling Yeats, when I was a passionate Balzacian, how Balzac's reward for a writer who had resisted the temptations of social dissipations, to devote himself to entirely his work, was to be the lover of a highly bred and beautiful woman, a countess or even a duchess.

Yeats retained up to the end this sense of the value of fine breeding, since it sets a standard for conduct, as great poetry sets a standard for poets. Indeed, I think of him always as a great aristocrat of letters, aiming ceaselessly to perfect his form and expression, holding in his later work to the phrase of Aristotle which he was fond of quoting: 'To think like a wise man but to express oneself like the common people.'[8]

NOTES

Sir William Rothenstein (1872–1945), English painter who introduced the Indian poet Tagore to Yeats. When the Easter Rising of 1916 broke out, Yeats was staying with the Rothensteins in Gloucestershire.

1. Grant Richards (1872–1948), English publisher and writer; author of *Caviare* (1912), *Bittersweet* (1915), *Double Life* (1920), *Vain Pursuit* (1931), *Memories of a Misspent Youth* (1932) and *Housman: 1859–1936* (1940).

2. William Thomas Stead (1849–1912), English journalist; founded English *Review of Reviews* (1890); introduced so-called American methods, including the interview, illustrations and extras; forced Gladstone government to send Gordon to Khartoum (1884); as a result of his exposure in *The Maiden Tribute of Modern Babylon* of outrages against women and children permitted by law, was imprisoned, but instrumental in obtaining enactment of Criminal Law Amendment Act (1885); devoted himself to advocacy of international peace and friendship with Russia and to psychic research; victim of *Titanic* disaster; author of *If Christ Came to Chicago* (1893) and *The Americanization of the World* (1902).

3. Frederick York Powell (1850–1904), English historian and Icelandic scholar; Professor of Modern History at Oxford (1894–1904); author of *Origines Islandicae* (1905); helped to found *English Historical Review* (1885); author of works on English history and articles in *Encyclopaedia Britannica* and *Dictionary of National Biography*.

4. Yeats's family moved to 8 Woodstock Road, Bedford Park, in 1876. The cessation of rents meant there was less money and Ireland was cheaper to live in, and therefore John Butler Yeats decided he might do better in Dublin as a portrait painter than he was doing in London. In June 1887 they returned to London, where they lived at 58 Eardley Crescent, Earl's Court.

5. In the summer of 1895 Yeats had become independent of his father and moved away from the family and took rooms with Arthur Symons in Fountain Court; then a few months later, when his affair with Diana Vernon began in earnest, moved into rooms of his own at no. 18 Woburn Buildings. The change is apparent in his letters to his father which in 1894 still begin 'My dear Papa', but in 1895 begin 'My dear Father'. The house on the north side of Woburn Buildings still stands, but is now no. 5 Woburn Walk.

6. Stephen Phillips (1868–1915), English poet and playwright; member of Frank R. Benson's theatrical company; won fame with *Poems* (1897); commissioned to write a play, *Paolo and Francesca* (1900); His *Herod* produced by Beerbohm Tree (1900); declined in popularity after *Nero* (1906).

7. Maxim Gorki. Pseudonym of Aleksei Maksimovich Peshkov (1868–1936), Russian writer; wrote first sketch (1892) for a Tiflis newspaper, using name 'Gorki', i.e. 'the bitter one'; author of short stories, novels, plays, several autobiographical and critical works, and biographies of Andreev, Tolstoi and Lenin.

8. Yeats attributes to Lady Gregory the use of this motto: 'When in later years her literary style became in my ears the best written by woman, she had made the people a part of her soul; a phrase of Aristotle had become her motto: "To think like a wise man, but to express oneself like the common people".'—*Autobiographies*, p. 395

Impressions*

W. J. TURNER

I have a capricious memory and it fails me completely when I try to recall how and when I first met W. B. Yeats. Perhaps I should have even forgotton my first meeting with him altogether if there had not been something to remind me, that is, a sonnet I published in 1918 entitled 'Recollecting a visit to W. B. Yeats' which must have been written very shortly after having been taken to see him. As a very shy young man I probably did not speak to him nor do I remember his making any remark to me. This was at his rooms in London, somewhere in the neighbourhood of Southampton Row. The poem is exceedingly and quite unjustifiably gloomy and ends with the lines:

> My God, it is a strange and pitiful sight
> To see the treasury of a poet's room
> And him alone there shrouded in beauty's gloom!

I remember nothing of the others present among whom very likely was Mr. Ezra Pound,[1] with whom Yeats was in close contact at the time.

I did not see him again until many years later, sometime after 1930, when we began to meet at the Savile Club in Brook Street, of which I was a member and where he used to stay on his frequent visits from Dublin. How we met there I cannot recall. Certainly I doubt if he recognised having met me before. This would not have been unusual. One or two members whom he certainly did know complained good-humouredly that he never seemed to see them. He was short-sighted and generally lunched at a small table alone unless he had a guest. But at some time or other he had got into the habit of inviting me to lunch with him. I noticed that he did not seem to have any particular fancies about food or drink and the old club wine-waiter, Frank, was in the habit of assuming that he always took a glass of sherry at his lunch. This invariably appeared without being ordered, and Yeats frequently remarked to me as he drank it that Frank had got it firmly in his head that he drank nothing but sherry.

Yeats had the finest manners and he ate and drank very little for a big man. Later, when through illness he was put on a diet at home he enjoyed escaping from its restrictions in London; but he did not seem to have any very definite tastes in food and would frequently wait to see what I ordered

* *Arrow* (Dublin) VI (Summer 1939) 17–19.

and then have the same. Conversation seemed much more important to him than food; this to me was very strange and very impressive, for I prefer to sit in a dreamy state of bliss when I am eating and not to have to use my mind. Lunching with Yeats, therefore, I felt always as rather a strain, especially as it was not at all easy for me to understand him as he spoke rather indistinctly and often about Irish names and places unknown to me. Everybody knows that Yeats was a most interesting, varied and often very amusing talker, that he had more than a spice of malice and an extremely shrewd and perceptive eye for men's characters and foibles; but his conversation was never casual as most English conversation is, there was always a theme and pertinent matter.

Speaking as an Englishman, I am inclined to be a little astonished at the non-sensuous character of Yeats's imagination. I doubt if he ever, for example, revelled in the flavour of a wine or crushed a grape against his palate with due appreciation. Ideas rather than things excited him. He never ravished with his eye the shapes and contours of things though he probably appreciated colour more than line; but he was most alive to emotional qualities and was drawn to what was noble and passionate, aristocratic, exquisite or mad rather than to what was weighty, slender, massive, delicate, symmetrical or delicious. Whether correctly or not, we English are inclined to look upon this as a typically Irish bias although Yeats' talk was very unlike that of other Irishmen I have known, being much more concrete and thematic. Concreteness was one of the conspicuous virtues of his conversation which abounded in strikingly apt images and phrases. Thus, I remember, when a certain man was praised as having written a very good book, his saying: 'he has written a good book not a very good book, there is no juice in his mind.'

A famous musician once told me that music went on the whole time in his head and never ceased whatever he was doing. I think that in the same way poetry was always present in Yeats's mind. He was constantly turning verses on his tongue, more or less audibly to those near by, certainly audible to himself. I think that this practice of testing aloud his language, as it were, must have been partly responsible for the extreme rightness and directness of his later verse. Few modern poets read their verses aloud, even to themselves; the word has become increasingly unspoken; the writer has begun to appeal predominantly to the eye and the eye overlooks the awkward, vague and redundant more easily than does the ear. It would naturally follow that in such a transformation the music would tend to disappear from poetry. This must be a destructive process, for poetry is a marriage between sound and sense and if the sound is missing it is as if beauty in a marriage were missing and only reason left. This sort of impoverishment of poetry is not as prevalent in Irish as in English writers, because the people in Ireland are more sensitive to the spoken word than they are in England where speech has become much debased and the ear of the middle classes especially dulled.

I should like to mention a quality Yeats had which greatly impressed me and this was the sureness of his instinct and the soundness of his judgment. I should think that he was not an easy man to deceive nor did he attract flattery. His passionate interest in the younger poets and all that they were writing was pure and generous as all true passion is. He had not a spark of envy or jealousy and indeed would linger lovingly and critically on their verses as if they were his own, endeavouring to better them by the same method that he used with his own poetry.

At the time he was selecting the poems for his Oxford Anthology [*sic*]² of Modern Verse he happened to meet me one day at the Savile Club and asked me, after lunch, to consider some suggestion he had to make. He had a copy of a small volume of mine entitled 'Songs and Incantations' and had made new pencilled readings in two of the poems. These he showed me and asked me if I had any objection. It would have been difficult if not impossible for me to give proper consideration to these changes on the spot. I would need time and above all complete solitude even to be able to give my mind to the matter. So I acquiesced and the two poems 'Reflection' and 'The Word made Flesh' were printed in the Anthology with his alterations. I think he totally misunderstood my attitude, for he himself seemed always perfectly at ease and ready to give a considered judgment in the presence of others. It would not, therefore, have occurred to him that I acquiesced merely to rid myself of having to make up my mind before I was prepared to do so. Also, I had swiftly thought to myself 'What does it matter. The poems are already printed.' Anyone who is interested in seeing Yeats's changes can always compare them with the poems when they are finally collected. Personally I very much doubt if one man can improve another man's poems though criticism is sometimes helpful.

Yeats, however, wrote to a friend concerning the alterations in 'The Word made Flesh': 'Turner has given up the vague rhetoric in his poem without a sigh.' In this case any curious reader will be able to compare all three versions: namely the original in 'Songs and Incantations,' the Yeats's version in his Anthology, and my final version in my 'Selected Poems' about to be published by the Oxford University Press. In regard to the other poem 'Reflection' it was only one line which Yeats wanted altered, namely the last line in the last verse which runs:—

7   Undying fires removing far
I   Their unseen presence show
5   Leaving their brightness on dead moons
I   As heavenly suns do.

For some reason Yeats did not like the rhythm of the last line and he altered it to:—

As suns less heavenly do.

We have all heard that Homer can nod and now I know it, for Yeats made nonsense of my line and also in my opinion spoiled the rhythm with his more conventional substitution.

I remember telling an English poet how Yeats had made these alterations in my two poems and he was amazed and said he would never have permitted such a thing.

I cannot share this attitude. Yeats once told me that he and his friends often made suggestions and alterations in each other's work and I cannot see why not. Also, it is interesting to see how the minds of different poets work. Ideally it ought to be impossible to alter a single syllable in a poem or a single note in a musical composition but practically there are many works of great merit where this would not apply.

The extreme sincerity of a man like Yeats would in any case have influenced me since, perhaps, I am not so absolute a lover as he was. Or, it may be that I am more resigned to imperfection and do not mind an apparent blemish or two in my mistress. To every real poet, however, Yeats's wholehearted and all-minded passion for literature could not fail to be invigorating. And he had a similar care and passion for men and women, worshipping what was magnificent, brave and exquisite and disliking the paltry, the vulgar and the mean with a personal integrity that made all his judgments his own.

NOTES

Walter James Turner (1889–1946) was an Australian poet and music critic. He was music critic for the *New Statesman* (from 1916) and dramatic critic for the *London Mercury* (1919–23). Among his books are *The Hunter, and Other Poems* (1916), *Paris and Helen* (1921), *Music and Life* (1921), *Smaragda's Lover* (1924), *Orpheus, or the Music of the Future* (1926), *Music, a Short History* (1932), *Songs and Incantations* (1936) and *The Duchess of Popocatapeth* (1939). In his old age, Yeats was more than ever haunted by the desire to restore the singing side of the poet's art, and he constantly discussed the subject with poets of his acquaintance who had knowledge of music, notably with W. J. Turner and F. R. Higgins. In his Introduction to *The Oxford Book of Modern Verse* (1936), Yeats praised Turner extravagantly; he discovered in him 'the symbol of an incomplete discovery . . . mind recognising its responsibility'. The publication of the anthology was followed by a broadcast from the BBC on modern poetry. Yeats's second programme, 'The Poets' Pub', was on 22 April 1937, with music arranged by Turner, who published a tribute in verse on Yeats's death. See several allusions to Turner in Yeats's *Autobiographies*.

1. Ezra Pound (1885–1973), American poet; one of the leaders of the Imagist Movement; a great experimenter in verse; wrote verse: *Personae* (1909), *Ripostes* (1912), *Quia Pauper Amavi* (1919), *Umbra* (1920) and *Cantos* (1925–40) and outspoken books of criticism, including *The Spirit of Romance* (1910), *Polite Essays* (1937) and *Literary Essays* (1954). Pound made the Irish poet's acquaintance on his first visit to Europe. During the winter of 1912–13 a digestive disorder reduced Yeats to a milk diet for a long period; at other times his head ached and his eyes played the traitor. His life in Woburn Buildings was rendered tolerable only by the assiduous attentions of Pound, who would come to read to him in the evenings and also helped him to health by teaching him to fence. During the winters of 1913–15, Pound acted as Yeats's secretary at a small cottage in Ashdown Forest in Sussex, reading to him, writing from his dictation, and discussing everything with him. Pound's effect upon Yeats's poetry was to make it harsher and more outspoken. It was also Ezra Pound who introduced the *Noh* drama of Japan to Yeats. In 1916 the Cuala Press, owned by Yeats's sister, published Fenollosa's

Japanese plays, translated by Ezra Pound, with a long essay on the drama by Yeats. For Ezra Pound's influence on Yeats see Ernest Boyd, *Portraits: Real and Imaginary* (London: Jonathan Cape, [1924]) p. 238. See also several allusions to him in *The Letters of W. B. Yeats*.

2. *The Oxford Book of Modern Verse, 1892–1935*, chosen by W. B. Yeats (Oxford: Clarendon Press, 1936).

Impressions*

OLIVER ST JOHN GOGARTY

Yeats was the nearest thing to an immortal spirit that I have ever met. I have known holy men, saintly according to their religion who were sanctified, but Yeats was enchanted. You felt something not of this earth earthly when you looked at those eyes, whose gleam it was so hard to catch, swiftly-glancing with all the intensity of Eternity. When I saw that noble aquiline face with the nose so broad between the eyes, I thought of his ancestry from Cornwall where the names Yeats, Gates and Keats are originally one and where there is Phoenician blood with all the magic of the men who brought strange knowledge from the bright strands of the East to the Shadowy Waters of the far West—men who gave Merlin to King Mark and Yeats to humanity.

There was in him a strange and wistful mischievousness as if the King of the Fairies had elected to become a changeling among us. I could never believe that his white hair was anything more than some stage property which he had assumed and which he could lay aside at any moment gaily. He seemed to bear with age voluntarily as one of those whom it could not affect.

He was undemonstrative as he was inflexible in his friendships. He never relinquished a friend.

So richly endowed was he with gallantry in himself that he was prone to attribute it to others. Thus I remember his assertion that Wilde refused to escape in a yacht which was placed at his disposal, 'Because he had in him the old duelling spirit of the Bucks of the Eighteenth Century.' [1]

When you compare him with the greatest poet in England (with the sole exception of the Laureate, who is far more prolific and profound), the late, A. E. Housman, [2] what a more manly and magnificent figure is Yeats! There is no pitiableness or gaol-bird resignation and symbolism about him; he is all nobility and fiery with defiance to the bodily distemper of Death. Admirable and excellent as Housman is in handling the traditional metres, Yeats is a better 'maker'. With the arduous limitations he imposed upon himself he revealed his Mastery.

* *Arrow* (Dublin) VI (Summer 1939) 19–20.

Let us salute the Master whom Death[3] has transformed now as he wished into 'an artifice of Eternity.'

NOTES

Oliver St John Gogarty (1878–1957) was an Irish physician and writer; a Senator in the Irish Free State (1922–36); and the author of *Poems and Plays* (1920), *An Offering of Swans* (1924), *As I Was Going down Sackville Street* (1937) and *Tumbling in the Hay* (1939). There is a poem by him describing an afternoon at 4 Broad Street, Oxford, where Yeats was staying in 1920 until Ballylee was ready. It was Gogarty who removed Yeats's tonsils, 'with exuberant Gaiety' as he wrote to John Quinn, and through whose endeavours Yeats was appointed as a Senator of the recently established Irish Free State. See Yeats's many allusions to Gogarty in *The Letters of W. B. Yeats*.

1. When Oscar Wilde (1854–1900), the Irish dramatist, was charged with homosexual offences his friends urged him to catch the train for Dover while yet there was time. It has been asserted that the authorities held their hands to give him time to make his exit. It is certainly a fact that not until after the last train had left for Dover was the warrant issued for his apprehension. Wilde, however, would not 'run away' and 'hide' and 'let down' his sureties. He had a fortnight's freedom between two criminal trials; and being ordered out of each hotel he tried within a few minutes of his arrival, he went to stay with his mother in Chelsea. Hesketh Pearson in *The Life of Oscar Wilde* (London: Methuen, 1946) p. 306 says that 'W. B. Yeats called at the house in Oakley Street one day with letters of sympathy from people in Ireland.' See also M. Montgomery Hyde, ed., *The Trials of Oscar Wilde* (London: William Hodge, 1948) pp. 77–81.

2. Alfred Edward Housman (1859–1936), English classical scholar and poet; Professor of Latin at University College London (1892–1911) and Cambridge (1911–36); and author of *A Shropshire Lad* (1896), *Last Poems* (1922) and *More Poems* (1936).

3. Yeats died on Thursday, 26 January 1939 and was buried in Roquebrune, France. His body was returned to Ireland in September 1948 and was piped ashore at Galway. His wife, children and brother Jack accompanied the funeral procession to Sligo, where there was a military guard of honour. The government representative was Sean MacBride (Maud Gonne's son), the Minister of External Affairs. The burial took place at Drumcliffe 'under bare Ben Bulben's head', with a stone inscribed as directed in 'Under Ben Bulben'.

As Man of the Theatre*

LENNOX ROBINSON

I have often had to write or speak about Lady Gregory and her work for our Theatre, and I have always said that but for her tireless interest it would have died years ago. Thinking again, I am sure I must modify that statement. It is true that she lived all her life in Ireland and Mr. Yeats had no permanent home here till 1922, and that often very many months passed without his setting foot in the country. But he always loomed in the background, an influence, a critic, and at any moment of crisis a man of

* *Arrow* (Dublin) VI (Summer 1939) 20–1.

swift, forceful action. Lacking his inspiration would Lady Gregory have continued her tireless, very often unappreciated work? I doubt it.

When I joined the Abbey in 1910[1] his days of practical work in that Theatre were over—by practical work I mean the actual production of his plays. After that date the only new plays of his that were produced were *The Player Queen*,[2] certain *Plays for Dancers*,[3] *The Resurrection*,[4] *Purgatory*,[5] *The Words Upon the Window-pane*[6] and the two translations from Sophocles. With the exception of the first play which was produced in his absence, though not actually producing them, he took an active part in their rehearsal. Not, curiously enough; being chiefly concerned with the speaking of the verse, but rather with emotion, movement, scenery, dress and lighting. He would spend half an hour on getting some movement or piece of 'business' to his liking, would cry out in passion—never in temper—at some clumsiness of mine or on the part of the players. To them and to me those rehearsals were a joy and an inspiration for he brought to bear on the play an instinct and an intelligence vastly superior to our own. He was completely lucid in his explanation of what he wanted, but he nearly always demanded something beyond our capacity and he would patiently try in this way and that way to attain his desired result. His plays were too infrequently performed and so he became a little rusty as to what could be done on the stage and what could not—play-producing is like playing on a complicated instrument, an organ, for instance, and the performer needs constant practice. But had his life shaped itself differently, had he devoted all his genius to the stage he might easily have become one of the most distinguished producers in the modern theatre.

But Mr. Seaghan Barlow[7] who has been connected with our Theatre for many more years than I have, recollects that in the early days he was passionately interested in the speaking of his verse and took endless pains with the players over it, demonstrating himself the effect he was seeking for, going over a single line time and time again. He supervised the production of all his own plays and, with Lady Gregory, the production of every play produced in those early days. Mr. Barlow thinks that after some years he despaired of having his verse spoken as he desired, yet he dedicated *The King's Threshold*[8] to Frank Fay in memory of his 'beautiful speaking in the character of Seanchan.'[9] He was slow to realise Sara Allgood's glorious voice and speech and for years looked on her solely as a comedy actress.

Mrs. Martin,[10] for many years a faithful servant of our Theatre, remembers how he and Lady Gregory would curl the wigs, and when an over-officious manager dismissed the whole staff, Mr. Yeats immediately re-instated her. She remembers, curiously, that in those first days he was always called in the Theatre 'Schoolboy Yeats.'

His theories of production can be found in *Plays and Controversies* and elsewhere. I quote this from a note on *The Green Helmet*,[11] it sets down very simply his aims in the production of a poetic play, it illustrates his producer's eye, that eye which must be all-seeing:—

We staged the play with a very pronounced colour-scheme, and I have noticed that the more obviously decorative is the scene and costuming of any play, the more it is lifted out of time and space and the nearer to faery-land we carry it. One gets also more effect out of concerted movements—above all, if there are many players—when all the clothes are the same colour. No breadth of treatment gives monotony when there is movement and change of lighting. It concentrates attention on every new effect and makes every change of outline or of light and shadow surprising and delightful. Because of this, one can use contrasts of colour, between clothes and the background or in the background itself, the complementary colours for instance, which would be too obvious to keep the attention in a painting. One wishes to keep the movement of the action as important as possible, and the simplicity which gives depth of colour does this, just as, for precisely similar reasons, the lack of colour in a statue fixes the attention upon the form.

But he was not only interested in the production of his own plays. After watching a realistic play he would make a dozen criticisms heart-searching to producer and players. I had hung the pictures too high, the farmer's daughters were too clean—('Smear cow-dung on their faces!' I remember him exclaiming,) some actor's wig was atrocious, the scene was too dark. Our supposedly 'good' furniture was undistinguished, therefore he and I must spend a couple of afternoons visiting old furniture shops in Dublin, picking here and there some genuine period-piece and so accumulating a complete set of Georgian furniture. He took pains, as a good producer should, over the smallest prop. He was eager for experiment in the theatre and seized on the idea of the Gordon Craig screens and ours was the first theatre in which Mr. Craig allowed them to be used. He seized on Mr. Granville-Barker's idea of a squared floor-cloth for rehearsal. His was our Peacock Theatre[12] and his our School of Ballet. Had he not been a careful man of business he would have been prodigal in what we spent on the stage, nor did his interest end at it for he would draw my attention to a ricketty seat in the auditorium and carefully inspect the lavatories.

Everything he touched took on a new importance. His presence stiffened a Directors' meeting, he could understand a balance-sheet and cross-examine an auditor. Kind by nature, he could, if necessary, be as pitiless as Lady Gregory. In the years when he visited the Abbey more frequently than lately he remembered almost every part taken by the players and was quick to discern talent in a newcomer and as quick to dismiss another as being without promise, and I seldom or never remember him to have been mistaken. Even in music, of which he had no knowledge and for which he had little liking, he knew what he wanted in the case of his own plays, and had George Antheil's[13] music for *Fighting the Waves*[14] not been the forceful thing it is he would undoubtedly have rejected it.

In short, he was a complete man of the theatre.

NOTES

Lennox Robinson (1886–1958), Irish playwright, novelist and theatre manager. For a study of Robinson see Michael J. O'Neill, *Lennox Robinson* (New York: Twayne Publishers, 1964).

1. Lennox Robinson managed the Abbey Theatre from 1910 to 1914 and from 1919 to 1923. In 1923 the Abbey board of directors appointed him fellow director; he remained a director until the end of his life.

2. *The Player Queen*, a play in two scenes, was first presented at the Abbey Theatre on 9 December 1919. It was produced by Lennox Robinson.

3. *The Dreaming of the Bones*, a play in one act, was first produced at the Abbey Theatre on 6 December 1931.

4. *The Resurrection*, a play in one act, was first performed at the Abbey Theatre on 30 July 1934.

5. *Purgatory*, a play in one act, opened at the Abbey Theatre on 10 August 1938.

6. *The Words upon the Window-Pane*, a play in one act, had its premiere at the Abbey Theatre on 17 November 1930. It was produced by Lennox Robinson.

7. Seaghan Barlow was an actor at the Abbey Theatre, but, as Lennox Robinson relates in *Ireland's Abbey Theatre* (p. 66), 'it is in all other ways that he has shown his genius for the stage. He knows everything in scene-making and prop-making, but, sullen over his cocoa and his Greek, he states he can do nothing. An hour later, everything is done to perfection.' See also Barlow's personal reminiscences, ibid., pp. 69–76.

8. The first performance of *The King's Threshold* was by the Irish National Theatre Society at the Molesworth Hall on 8 October 1903. This production marked a change in Yeats's work, and for many years he turned deliberately to Irish legends, especially to the Cuchulain legend.

9. Frank J. Fay played the part of Seanchan, the Chief Poet of Ireland.

10. Mrs Tessie Martin superintended the cleaning of the Abbey Theatre and was a close friend to Lady Gregory. See her personal reminiscences in Lennox Robinson, *Ireland's Abbey Theatre*, pp. 67–9.

11. *The Green Helmet*, a play in ballad metre by Yeats founded on *The Golden Helmet*, opened at the Abbey Theatre on 10 February 1910.

12. For nine months in the year the little Peacock Theatre, attached to the Abbey Theatre, was used by amateur or semi-amateur societies. Named after its decorations in peacock colours, it opened in November 1925 with a performance of the New Players. It made history when in the autumn of 1928 Hilton Edwards and Micheál MacLiammóir opened their career in Dublin with a performance on this tiny stage of *Peer Gynt*; after a number of productions there they moved to the Gate Theatre.

13. George Antheil (1900–59), American concert pianist and composer.

14. The first performance of *Fighting the Waves*, a ballet play, was at the Abbey Theatre on 13 August 1929. It was produced by Lennox Robinson.

Yeats's Phantasmagoria*

FRANK O'CONNOR

A.E. passed on to me an invitation from Yeats, who was then living in Merrion Square. I found myself alone in a dim, candle-lit room when Yeats entered, tall, elegantly dressed, stern looking with a sideway glance. He always wore a pale, beautifully cut soft suit, full silk shirts, blue during the days of O'Duffy's [1] fascist party, and a huge ring; and when he sat down he washed his hands with a certain consciousness of their beauty. His speech was like his clothes, suave, mannered; he raised his brows and looked down his nose at you; and though he had not yet developed the leaden shuffle of old age, he walked slowly and deliberately, with full and ornamental gestures in the dim candle-light. It was only later when one grew more used to him, that one noticed the expensiveness and beauty of everything about him: the pictures, the masks from his dance plays, the tall bookcases and long orderly table, the silver candlesticks, and that dimness that made rich hollows of shadow everywhere. At first, one was only aware—pleasantly aware—of a touch of dandyism in the lofty, ecclesiasti-cal stare, the ritual motion of the hands, the unction of the voice, and an occasional elaborate mispronunciation like 'weld' for 'world' or 'medder' for 'murder.' And perhaps if one had analyzed those careful sentences of his, one would have found at times the rhythms of oratory rather than the rhythms of good speech—certain cadences linger in my ear.

There was something about him that suggested the bird: the strange inhuman cock of the head; the bird's sloping eyes, which at times seemed to be at the side rather than the front of his face; his long nose, which he tweaked; his laugh, which was abrupt and remote—a caw, Moore called it. Sometimes he laughed without moving his lips, his eyebrows raised, only his eyes smiling, and the laugh dwindled into a sad thoughtfulness as though dying upon the air. Sometimes he laughed excitedly, jerking and moving about, shaking himself within his clothes, stammering slightly; but it was always the eyes that smiled. When he was very happy and forgot himself, animation flowed over him in waves, as I have seen it flow over his sister. He sat forward, arms on his knees, washing his hands over and over, the pose broken sometimes by a loud harsh throaty laugh like a croak and the throwing back of the bird's head, while he sat bolt upright holding on

---

* Extracted from 'Two Friends: Yeats and A. E.', *Yale Review* (New Haven, Connecticut), XXIX, no. 1 (Sep 1939) 60–88.

to the lapels of his coat; sometimes by a tweaking of the nose, most characteristically perhaps by a sudden raising of the index finger for attention. But he was always alert, dramatic, and amazingly brilliant. When he told a funny story, he had a trick of looking suddenly at the ceiling, rolling his eyes with little snorts of laughter, and spreading out his beautiful hands as if he were juggling invisible balls. He was a really lovely man to watch. Every pose was right. The animated fit passing, he threw himself back with his hands before him on the arms of his chair, hanging down, like claws. In a moment of silence, the right hand would be raised as if he were reciting verse to himself and marking the cadence.

Immobile he looked old, stern, a little harassed; in bad humor, the lower lip protruded, and he looked a truly ugly customer. But the moment he grew excited, really excited, there was an astonishing change: he suddenly sat bolt upright in his chair—I must emphasize the rapidity and brilliance of the movement—clutching the edge with his hands or marking every stress furiously with clenched fist, and there was a catch of excitement in the voice—he snorted, sniffed, stammered, glared, the head thrown back and the eyes snapping for an audience while the whole face lit up as from within. I have seen that lighting up only in one other, and in nothing like the same degree. It was astonishing, because, even in extreme old age when he was looking most wretched and discontented, quite suddenly that blaze of excitement would sweep over the face like sunlight over a moor, and from behind the mask, a boy's eager, tense face stammered and glared at you. Trapped, despairing, like a boy's face at a barred window on a summer day, but most exciting to see.

It was my first impression of him. There was no one there but Lady Gregory and myself; I do not even remember what brought it up, but it was all I could speak of for days afterwards. Of the pomposity and arrogance Dublin people never tired of talking of—'the insolence of Yeats' was on everybody's lips—I saw nothing, then or at any other time, unless it were that little touch of dandyism, which I always found very amusing. On the contrary, he had a sort of adolescent eagerness, a passion for abstract conversation, such as I had been used to when O'Faolain and I were boys in Cork, but which did not seem to exist in Dublin, where the eighteenth century lingers and people take pride only in saying witty things, regardless of their truth. Yeats too, when goaded, could say rapier-sharp things, but I think he hated it; never recurred to it, preferred not to talk of fools or bores. We had long wandering debates on Hegelianism, pacifism, communism, during which he frequently worked himself into a fit of excitement, a dog on the trail; leant sideways on one elbow with lowered head and uplifted hand. 'Wait, wait, wait!'—while he thought it out; and sometimes the clash of ideas would release the lightning of a phrase or an anecdote, always perfectly apt.

Being not much more than twenty, I was grateful for his pin-point awareness, so different from A.E.'s dim benevolence. He had a sort of sideway glance round his spectacles—as if he were looking at you round his pose—that was full of knowingness, though I only suspected how much he really saw. That vagueness, that inability to find the cigarettes or remember the names of people he didn't want to remember, was a protective pyschological weakness, probably developed during the timidity of boyhood. He was really diabolically observant, or so I think, and even when I bored him, I was aware that it was I who was boring him, not somebody else, and that he would remember it for me. While it seemed to me that the images on A.E.'s retina were vague, I thought those on Yeats's must have been small, clear, intense, like those of a bird's, watching from a great height the movement of creatures on the earth.

Our relations were always complicated by his feud with A.E. Yeats had discovered Synge and Lady Gregory; A.E. had discovered Colum and Stephens, and Yeats had sneered, 'But was there ever dog that praised his fleas?' That epigram perpetuated the legend that he was pompous and arrogant and ungenerous. The Abbey Theatre suffered and began to perish in a chilly naturalism. One night he asked what I was writing. I told him the theme of 'The Saint and Mary Kate.' He was interested and asked some very acute questions. As I rose to go he said, 'Write it as a play and give it to us for the theatre.' And as I went downstairs I thought how differently A.E. would say that.

There were certain things A.E. gave young writers that no one else could give, or would give, I must add, and his protégés were poor men all. He was as warm and homely as a turf fire. Once when I had been ill, he fussed reproachfully over me like an old hen. 'Why didn't you send for me? I'd have come and cooked you a chop. I can cook a chop very well.' Even now, thought of his goodness brings tears to my eyes.

Yet—here I must fall back into Yeats's phantasmagoria to express what I wish to say, because it is a difficult psychological state of mind—there was too much daylight in A.E. to nourish poetry. I am reminded of that bright glare upon the crude colors of his canvases, and of the masses of shadow among the flickering candles in Yeats's. These two things might almost be taken as symbolical of a contrasted objectivity and subjectivity in the two men, and when I read Synge or Lady Gregory I notice that mass of shadow which they, like Yeats, have in their work. Call it shadow, subjectivity, idealism, humbug, what you will—it is what one needs if one is to live in the garish daylight of a democracy dominated by parish priests.

'You talk about leaving Ireland,' A.E. once wrote to me (I must have been a permanent grumbler). 'But we are born into nations, not because of their harmony with our nature but because their diversity from ourselves excites us to revolt into intellectual self-consciousness. Are not all the Irish writers Pagans or free-thinkers? Is not the nation pious and hidebound? Take care lest in choosing a nation of free-thinkers you do not destroy the diversity between the world without and the world within which makes you a writer.'

As well ask a young man in the provinces not to come to a capital city lest he destroy the diversity between himself and his surroundings! It is an argument one could not imagine Yeats using. He created a phantasmagoria, first of peasant art, then of aristocracy, then an Anglo-Irish myth—all the time balancing that external glare by a corresponding shadow. And I think that we young writers lost in losing that which might have kept us at home and contented with our task.

That fable of light and shadow, of objectivity and subjectivity, is one way of expressing my idea of the old feud between Yeats and A.E., but it was a difference that expressed itself in almost every detail of their lives. Yeats was the small-town boy who had travelled; A.E., the one who had remained at home. I could almost imagine the moment of the first rift, when Yeats, back from London, spoke of some writer who kept a mistress. And A.E., dumbfounded, would repeat, 'A mistress, Willy?' And after that, Yeats would think his old friend narrow-minded, and A.E. would say that Yeats had disimproved since his early days. It is a little tragedy that takes place in every provincial town every day of the week. A.E. was never so dull as with Yeats. All his humor and naturalness seemed to desert him; the chairs were too low for his burly frame, and he almost gave an impression of bleating. And Yeats had a tendency to pose before him. Once A.E. himself told me that he had said, 'All poetry comes of a marriage of the soul and body,' and on another occasion when A.E. praised the verse of—I think—H.D., Yeats replied languidly, 'Merely beautiful ideas in beautiful verse.' I imagine that to A.E.'s sturdy common sense he would retort with a pained, 'That was before the peacock had screamed.' And snubbed, or fobbed off with some image from the phantasmagoria, A.E. would come away in a wild rage, declaring that whenever Yeats talked philosophy he talked nonsense. 'Himself and his peacocks! He hasn't even read Hegel!' And then he would tell how at a séance they had attended as boys, Yeats had bent above a crystal and seen a Great Golden Door, and after a while the Keeper of the Door, until somebody pointed out that all he saw was the reflection of the publichouse at the opposite side of the road and its uniformed attendant. This as we went home together, leaving Yeats muttering among his candles and masks, and A.E. overcome by the heat, sat on the kerb, the most natural of men, hurt because his boyhood's friend had changed so much towards him.

The one was subtle, casuistical, elegant, mannered; a diplomatist who had flattered rich and brilliant women into serving his cause, a man of the world who had been the friend of artists and bohemians; the other, guileless, untravelled, full of universal benevolence but with a nonconformist conscience that occasionally gave out the shrill notes of the 'Old Orange Flute.' A.E.'s guilelessness was really embarrassing. He would take no money for his poems because he thought that simony; and, economic expert though he may have been, he remained a hopelessly impractical man who lived on his little capital and knew nothing of copyright.

'Macmillans are grand publishers,' he said. 'They protect your American copyright as well.'

Yeats was a Catholic, typically a Catholic: there was something about him that reminded you at times of a Roman prelate; fascist and authoritarian, seeing in world crises only the breakup of the 'damned liberalism' he hated; nationalist, lover of tradition and hater of reason and 'mechanical logic.' Russell was a North-of-Ireland Protestant and proud of it. He was a democrat, with leanings towards communism; pacifist, internationalist, despiser of tradition and class, and, in spite of his mysticism, a thoroughgoing rationalist and humanitarian. Injustice or stupidity drove him into a frenzy, and then he seemed to go berserker, with clenched fists raised above his head and incoherent with rage. He would have been delighted if any of us had shown signs of following Heine or Shaw. Once when I had passed some disparaging remark on Shaw's style, he said in a low voice, 'And yet if ever an angel of God walked this earth in the form of a man, his name was Bernard Shaw.'

That disparity continued in their prestige: Yeats a European figure, A.E. little better than a provincial celebrity—a disparity no nature could bear, and I have no doubt A.E. was wounded and bewildered by it. He was just a little bit vain and eager for praise—perhaps because he got so little of it. He was never a man I thought of as happy, as I did of Yeats. Coming to Yeats's door, hearing that rumble of verse being chanted, was like hearing bees on a summer day—a lucky, busy, wicked old man, praising his blessings. Everything came right: fame, theatre, friends, wife, daughter, son—one finds them enumerated again and again in his verse. There was some sense of disappointment over A.E. He showed me the proofs of 'Song and its Fountains.' I noticed particularly the dedication to Yeats 'rival and friend.' Those last revealing words disappeared from the published text.

We saw a lot of one another when the Academy of Letters [2] was being founded. It was Yeats's idea, an institution whose authority might override mob law and fight the absurd censorship of books. A.E. was gloomy. He feared and distrusted those enthusiasms of Yeats and prophesied that the Academy would be asked to award a prize to some of Yeats's protégés.

Yeats's enthusiasms brought out all the boyishness in him. He chased about in taxis, breathless, wiring, intriguing; in private, sinuous and flattering. Once when I questioned the name of some suggested Academician, he said, 'Why worry about literary eminence? You and I will provide that.' But in committee he was very different—masterful and intolerant, sifting words and chopping logic. He was a tyrant who used his position shamelessly to get his own way. Of course, I know but one side of the story, but it seemed to me that Russell, with his North-of-Ireland upbringing, his simple rectitude, was hurt and bewildered by Yeats's devious and incalculable ways. But at the same time he was timid. When he sent his resignation to Yeats, he did not, as he might well have done, complain of Yeats's behaviour. He merely said he would have no more to

do with us 'or a country so given over to the devil' (it was the same cry of
despair with which he afterwards left Ireland, and it seemed to me but the
cry of a sick soul). But Yeats thought that Russell was afraid of a
fight—'For though he is valiant enough when a row starts,' he wrote, 'he
never is in cold blood.' I felt he owed A.E. an apology and told him so.
'Ah,' he said nodding, 'I must smooth him down.' He had been reading a
book by one of A.E.'s young men whose verse he hated, and a few days later
A.E. called to tell me that Yeats had written him, praising the book and
adding, 'As usual you were right and I was wrong.' 'I think that's very
noble of him, don't you?' A.E. asked innocently, and we heard no more of
his resignation. I teased Yeats on his diplomacy. 'Ah, I've known him so
long!' I have told this foolish little story at length because it seems to me
that both men are in it.

*   *   *

Higgins and I were now directors of the Abbey Theatre. I saw Yeats
fairly frequently, in that long room of his, with the French window open on
to the garden, the silver candlesticks, the two marvellous paintings by his
brother, the Indian goddess. His health was failing; he shuffled, panted
heavily, but with his incurable boyishness turned it to sport. He had made
up a sentence the consonants of which helped to control his breathing. He
dieted, and discovered to his joy that his hero, Mussolini,[3] took little but
fruit and milk.

I was always a little shy of him. I feared that I bored him. There was
something about him that was a little outside nature; he seemed to be
aware of you as if from a distance with vision like a bird's. His genius, I
think, had something to do with an extrasensory perception; he saw and
heard things I did not hear, and there are passages in his work, obscure to
me, where I can feel a meaning, a connection, without perceiving it, as in a
bird's movements I can detect purpose without knowing exactly what it is.
I frequently held him up and made him explain himself. He liked that, and
one made a grave mistake in deferring to him or in nodding polite
acquiescence.

Was it this extrasensory perception that made him over-subtle in
business; or that in his boyish, playacting way, he liked to imagine himself a
cunning old diplomatist, weaving spiders' webs of intrigue about us all?
('The Irishman is distinguished,' his father used to say, 'by a love of
mischief for its own sweet sake.') In his relations with Higgins and me I felt
a circuitous and brilliant strategy performing complicated manoeuvres
about nonexistent armies. He did not attend our meetings and pretended
desolately that he could no longer be interested; but once O'Faolain and I
discovered that within five minutes of an Academy meeting he had known
all about it, and I knew he listened to all sorts of greenroom gossip about us.
We were always squabbling about something. Once I snapped, 'I prefer

not to look on my companions as a gang of masked conspirators'; and he replied with a sneer—it was the only time when the mask of impersonality between us was dropped—'You remind me of a character in a story I read once who believed that "no one really intends much harm to anyone else to any considerable extent." ' I suppose he thought me dreadfully simple, and though, within a few weeks of his death, I was compelled to leave the Abbey Theatre Board, I still think those armies mostly nonexistent and his brilliant strategy largely vain. I never could see that he gained anything by it, but perhaps it was the worldliness of the unworldly which helps to keep them sane by making them feel cynical and subtle. He had a trick of doing things out of a generous impulse and then finding mean worldly reasons for them. After I had spoken at A.E.'s graveside and everyone else was wondering what to do, he came over and congratulated me. 'Very fine! Very noble! Have you copies for the press?'

Yet he was always blundering about in that shadow which, in the phantasmagoria by which I explain him to myself, was the thing that protected him against the crudity of life in a priest-ridden democracy and saved him from embitterment and despair. People are already rapidly forgetting what a wretched critic he was. In an early play by Lennox Robinson—'Crossroads' [4]—he saw 'a central idea, a seeming superstition of its creator, a promise of a new attitude towards life, of something beyond logic.' How crazy that sounds to-day! His snobbery—the word is too harsh, but I can think of none better—we all laughed at a little. He felt sure that genius like rank could be hereditary, thinking, I knew, of his son. I suggested that talent might be hereditary, but hardly genius. This made him very cross. Then his face cleared. 'I had an old aunt who used to say, "You can transmit anything you like—so long as you take care not to marry the girl next door." ' One of his last works is an essay on eugenics! [5] The result of some intelligence tests in Scotland had satisfied him that intellect did not improve with the improvement of social conditions; children shifted from slums had shown no improvement over those who remained behind—therefore, with the disappearance of the middle classes, the standard of intellectual life must sink to nothing.

We talked of traditional singing as I had heard it at home and in Venice, which I thought to be the method of singing once practised all over the world. He was very excited and wanted to know if it were like his own singing, which was quite tuneless so far as my ears were to be trusted. He once sang for Higgins a song of his own composition which somebody had said was like one of Moore's Melodies. He told Higgins, too, how he had once gone to Sigerson's, [6] when the old doctor held some old country woman in trance. She passed her fingers over Yeats's face and said 'Poet.' 'Great poet,' she added. 'Musician,' she said at last. 'And then,' added Yeats, 'I knew she was genuine.' But sometimes I think with that queer perception of his he heard things we do not hear; and he had lived so long with the folk mind, the nonreasoning, instinctive mind, that he had an infallible sense of what belonged to it.

That folk sense, that great mass of shadow, of subjectivity if you will at the heart of his work, filling it with depth and luminousness (like the Rembrandt print above my mantelpiece) frequently left me abashed and miserable; for though I am always consciously with the rationalists, liberals, and humanitarians (our first quarrel in the theatre was over a performance of 'Coriolanus'[7] which I thought fascist propaganda), and I write, like any other novelist, out of the logic of circumstance, whenever I see certain plays of his, Lady Gregory's or Synge's, generations of peasant blood in me respond, and I am ashamed of writing, as I seem to do, in a foreign language. He knew that, as I think he knew everything about us, for only once did we talk of folk beliefs. That was at a lunch party when I told him some folk tale I had collected and he turned angrily on me and said: 'Why do you deliberately close your eyes to those things? You know quite well they were once the religion of the whole world!'

It was that religion, philosophy, art of the whole world he tried to approximate to, and he saw in the development of civilization the breaking up into smaller and smaller fragments of what had once been whole. Once, after watching at rehearsal the crippled efforts of some players to be themselves on the stage I said to him, 'Character acting is the end of every great school of acting.' 'The end of everything,' he growled. At another time, after interfering in a rehearsal to stop a young actress sobbing at the great close of Lady Gregory's 'Dervorgilla,'[8] I asked him, 'Is it ever, under any circumstances, permissible for an actor to weep on the stage?' 'Never,' he said, and turned it into a poem—

> Yet they, should the last scene be there,
> The great stage curtain about to drop,
> If worthy their prominent part in the play
> Do not break up their lines to weep.[9]

Another time he walked up and down the foyer with Higgins and myself during a performance by a celebrated English actor with the usual English tendency to pathos. 'When he should have been calling down the thunder he was picking up matches,' Yeats guffawed, stooping and picking up imaginary matches from the ground. 'Picking up matches!'

I have sometimes thought he was a Hegelian only because he could thus believe in the imminent destruction of our world—though the optimistic communist version of it drove him to frenzy. He looked forward to it with fiercer and fiercer gusto, storming or chuckling at all attempts to stabilize. The modern world had got too cluttered up for him. 'All things fall and are built again, and those that build them again are gay.'

He admired Mussolini, Hitler, Stalin, I think, and wrote marching songs for O'Duffy's fascists. He felt himself lost in a world where the poet had no place, and he clung to his boyhood's belief that matter is nothing, that all that has existed still exists and that he could be its servant. In later years he was the born servant—'My mediaeval knees lack health unless they bend'—the Roman prelate, the secretary, the go-between, adept in courtesies and ready to serve any great man because it is in service the moral nature grows. He had done some service for Kevin O'Higgins[10] and would have been glad to serve de Valera. There were times when a likeness to Goethe was overwhelming—and in appearance, too, that became marked in later years—but a Goethe without his Weimar or his Karl August. It is his voice I hear when I read Goethe's words to Falk:

'And if it came to pass with him as with his ancestor, Duke John; if his ruin were certain and irretrievable, let not that dismay us: we will take our staff in our hands and accompany our master in adversity, as old Lucas Kranach did: we will never forsake him. The women and children when they meet us in the villages will cast down their eyes and weep, and say to one another, "That is old Goethe and the former Duke of Weimar, whom the French Emperor drove from his throne because he was so true to his friends in misfortune." '

That is the very accent of the later Yeats—and in his courtesies there was an element of strangeness because he would treat everyone in the same noble way, and even our popular Ministers, as Goethe would have treated some little German monarch. Once we quarrelled before an interview with the Minister of Justice about the banning of Shaw's 'Black Girl.'[11] Yeats had a roll of stiff paper under his arm, and when I asked what it was he showed me—a reproduction of the Sistine Chapel roof! Higgins and I got no chance for our 'mechanical logic,' and the morning was wasted with a dissertation on Michelangelo and the Pope.

I asked him how I should behave as managing director of the Abbey Theatre. 'At one time I deferred to the stagehands,' he said. 'I used to say, "Don't you think this?" or, "Would that be better?" But then I saw I was only embarassing them.' 'When I was managing director,' he added, 'I asked Lady Gregory the same question, and she said, "Give very few orders but see they are obeyed." ' (The advice was admirable.)

He was a great keeper of other people's secrets, and I noticed once or twice how somebody's death released a flood of reminiscence, of a strongly personal kind. He did not understand our casual talk of the business of the theatre, and flew into fury about harmless indiscretions. He never forgave a breach of faith, and was one of the two men of my acquaintance to whom I might have confessed. I never heard him repeat a wounding anecdote of a friend, and even of an enemy (always excepting George Moore) he remembered always what might be praised. He always distinguished between a friend's personality and the character induced by weakness. Once, reporting some shabby trick, he added quickly, 'That, of course, was—the drunken intriguer, not—my friend.' He would endure endless rebuff, deception, and seem as though about to end it—then weaken again—

> . . . but friendship never ends,
> And what if mind seem changed,
> And it seem changed with the mind,
> When thoughts rise up unbid
> On generous things that he did
> And I grow half contented to be blind![12]

It was the quality I most envied and admired him for. Once he came to a meeting to defend an old friend whom I was attacking. He was scarcely able to walk at the time. We had tea together, and when we reached the foot of the steep stairs he begged me to leave him and go on. Going or staying, I didn't know which was worse for a proud man; so I stayed and watched him pause for minutes on each step, gasping, nerving himself for the next, erect, recollected, as though dissociating himself from the body which would no longer obey him. Months later, tweaking his nose, he said with a boyish air of guilt: 'I was wrong, of course. I shouldn't have done that.'

Sometimes I wondered what parts we played in that phantom court whose poet he was. Knowing him, I felt sure he added a touch of the fabulous. 'The theatre was going bankrupt,' he reported himself saying to a London friend. 'I looked round and saw all the successful businesses being run by ex-gunmen. Gunmen! I said, I must have gunmen! And now the theatre is on its feet again.' 'You surely support Mr. Cosgrave's party?' an English aristocrat asked him. 'Oh, I support the gunmen—on both sides.' 'And he turned his back on me and walked away,' Yeats added with a croak of glee.

He was a perfect host, rather like a kind old uncle, forgetful and a little bothered by the tastes of small boys. A lot of nonsense has been talked of his being an astute businessman—again the worldliness of the unworldly being taken for earnest. He was scrupulous beyond measure about money—that was all—and more for himself than others, though never anything but a poor man. He was not ashamed to tell you of his difficulties,[13] for in later years he deliberately talked about things most people do not talk of, and always with such simplicity that there was no embarrassment. When Pat MacCartan[14] and a few other American friends subscribed some money to make his last years happy, Yeats insisted on making the gift public, and at one of our dinners spoke at great length of his difficulties, and of the little pleasures he would now be able to enjoy, 'the things that make an old man's comfort.' It was a speech for an audience of princes, but some of the Dublin wits thought it in very bad taste.

The last time I saw him was to ask permission to dedicate to him the new edition of the two books he had helped with. He blushed like a boy and said gruffly, 'Delighted,' and as if that were not enough, 'honored.' He loved little courtesies, and now I am ashamed because, in a country where Tom is as good as his master, he received so few.

NOTES

'Frank O'Connor' was the pen name of Michael O'Donovan (1903–66), who was an Irish novelist and playwright. Two novels, *The Saint and Mary Kate* (1932) and *Dutch Interior* (1940), are still read and admired, but never created the impact of his short stories. Collections of these include *Bones of Contention* (1936), *Crab Apple Jelly* (1944), *The Common Chord* (1947), *The Stories of Frank O'Connor* (1953), *More Stories by Frank O'Connor* (1954), *Selected Stories* (1956) and *Collection Two* (1964). He was also interested in the theatre and had two plays produced at the Abbey Theatre, *In the Train* (1937) and *Moses' Rock* (1938). From 1936–9 he was a director of the Abbey. Among his non-fictional works are *The Big Fellow* (autobiography; 1937), *Towards an Appreciation of Literature* (1945), *The Art of the Theatre* (1947), *The Road to Stratford* (1948), *The Mirror in the Roadway* (on the novel; 1957), *An Only Child* (1962), *The Lonely Voice* (on the short story; 1963) and *The Backward Look* (on Irish Literature; 1967). When the new Ireland was created by the 'Treaty', the older literary folk, led by George Russell, were mostly advocates of the Treaty, but younger men whose acquaintance Yeats had yet to make—Frank O'Connor, Francis Stuart, Seán O'Faoláin, Liam O'Flaherty—took the side of de Valera and the republicans. In the mid-1930's, as the prefaces to the various plays in *Wheels and Butterflies* show, Yeats's attitude towards the younger generation had greatly altered. He made F. R. Higgins and Walter Starkie directors of the Abbey Theatre and bestowed publicly his benediction on Frank O'Connor and on Seán O'Faoláin, stating to the stupefaction of his listeners at a banquet that 'the future of Irish literature was with the realistic novel.' When he became old, Frank O'Connor, F. R. Higgins and Captain MacManus brought him news of contentions in the town, literary and political.

1. Owen O'Duffy (1892–1944), Irish soldier and member of the Irish Republican Army. He was the Head of the Police in the Irish Free State. In 1933 he founded the Blue Shirts, a fascist semi-military organisation which was split by internal dissensions the following year. He became a Brigadier-General in the Spanish Nationalist Army in the Spanish Civil War. See W. B. Yeats, *Letters*, pp.812–13, 815, 881.

2. It was in Lady Gregory's house that Yeats and George Russell discussed the project of an Academy of Letters which should carry on the tradition of their movement, make known the views of Irish authors on such questions as censorship, and call attention to the respect due to the intellectual and poetic quality in the national life. Bernard Shaw consented to become President of the Academy, and George Russell drew up the rules and the constitution. The formation of the Academy was announced in 1932.

3. Benito Mussolini (1883–1945), Italian dictator who organised Fascism in Italy. Yeats saw in Mussolini's spectacular new regime in Italy personal government at its height and a burst of powerful personality such as he anticipated for the new era in Ireland. He extolled the virtues of government by an elite for Ireland. On 2 August 1924 he spoke at a public banquet of the curtailment of liberty which he foresaw, and referred to Mussolini as 'a great popular leader'.

4. *The Cross Roads*, a play in a prologue and two acts, had its premiere at the Abbey Theatre on 1 April 1909.

5. *Essays 1931–1936* (Dublin: Cuala Press, 1937).

6. George Sigerson (1833–1925), Irish physician and Gaelic scholar. He was President of the Irish Literary Society and one of those promoting the Celtic revival.

7. Shakespeare's play was performed at the Abbey Theatre on 13 January 1936.

8. *Dervorgilla*, a tragedy in one act, was first produced at the Abbey Theatre on 31 October 1907

9. '*lapis Lazuli*', *Last Poems*.

10. Kevin O'Higgins (1892–1927), Irish lawyer and politician who bacame a minister in the Free State government. He was assassinated on his way to Mass. He had been responsible for the Irish Free State's policy of executing anyone found carrying arms during the civil war which followed the signing of the 1922 Treaty.

11. Bernard Shaw's short story, 'The Adventures of the Black Girl in Her Search for God', is a religious allegory, concerned with the Bible, the teaching of Jesus and Islam, and winds up

with the reflection, 'Mere agnosticism leads nowhere.' The story was provocative, and Shaw was viciously attacked, but it became a best-seller.

12. 'All Souls' Night', *The Tower*.

13. 'Yeats didn't have a five pound note until he was over forty,' Sean O'Casey told an interviewer, 'He told me that himself.' (E. H. Mikhail and John O'Riordan, eds, *The Sting and the Twinkle: Conversations with Sean O'Casey* (London: Macmillan, 1974) p. 128)

14. Dr Patrick MacCartan.

No Shore Beyond*

ETHEL MANNIN

Shortly after my return from Moscow I met W. B. Yeats, and began a friendship which Edmund Dulac, and probably other people, considered a little odd, in view of the wide disparity in our ideas, Yeats with his innate mysticism, and I with my then inveterate materialism, but which not only survived but strengthened with the years. But Yeats, full of Burgundy and racy reminiscence was Yeats released from the Celtic Twilight and treading the antic hay with abundant zest. In the latter years of his life because of his health he took only a little white wine and weak whisky and was less racy, but his tremendous Irish wit remained unimpaired.

Once off the materialistic plane of wit and wine, gossip and anecdote, admittedly we did less well. Once Yeats took me to see a Swami[1] in whom he had great faith. The Swami, it seemed, had read my *Confessions and Impressions*,[2] and it was expected we might have an interest for each other. For my part I was willing to try at least once my vibrations on a higher plane. But it was no good. The Swami and I had nothing real to say to each other. And I could not help reflecting that for a man who 'lived by the begging-bowl' the holy man was remarkably well nourished and well groomed of appearance, with creases to the trousers emerging from his robes, well-polished brown shoes, and a gold wrist-watch. When I urged this upon Yeats, he said, Yes, yes, the Swami accepted what was given him. . . .'

An elderly lady with a number of tinkly bracelets came in presently. It seemed she was hostess to the Swami, or some sort of protectress, though later, as it turned out, she quarrelled bitterly both with him and with Yeats. We left the Swami and with the lady adjourned to a restaurant where we met the Dulacs for dinner. Edmund Dulac was probably Yeats' greatest friend. Now Yeats was never good in a crowd; his best audience was one, at most two, and in the buzz of general chatter he began to nod.

* Extracted from *Privileged Spectator; A Sequel to 'Confessions and Impressions'* (London: Jarrolds, 1939) pp. 60–5.

Lower and lower his head nodded, till presently he slept quietly at the head of the table. When such a thing happens it is a nice point for the guests whether to waken their host, or pretend not to notice. On this occasion a waiter mistaking Dulac for the host, and observing that our wine was finished, inquired if we wanted more; which was indeed the case—but you cannot very well prod a sleeping host in the ribs and demand that he attend to his duties and order more wine. It is, moreover, disconcerting when one's host sleeps at table, particularly in a public place, because it is a reflection on the guests. We were in any case a badly mixed party; the combination of Yeats, the Dulacs, and myself, tended, I think, to make us all a bit heavy on the hand.

At about that time I went to a party at the Soviet Embassy; I was to call for Yeats later at the Savile Club as he was to dine with me. At the Embassy I met Ernst Toller,[3] whom I had not met since we had parted in Moscow. We embraced joyfully and drank a number ,of vodkas together in celebration of our reunion and in memory of Moscow. Presently Toller suggested that we should dine together. I told him that I was entertaining Yeats and that he had specially asked that I should not bring people to meet him. At mention of Yeats, Toller exclaimed immediately that that gave him an idea. There was a movement afoot to get Ossietsky,[4] the German writer, in prison in Germany, the Nobel Peace Prize. If he should be awarded this he would most certainly be released from gaol, but to get it he must have a recommendation from some other Nobel prize-winner. Yeats had had the Nobel Prize for Literature—why should he not be the one to recommend Ossietsky for the Peace Prize? Shaw might do it, but Shaw was ill and not to be got at just then, and the matter was urgent. Toller seemed to regard the accessibility of Yeats as a gift from heaven. He was very excited about it. We drank some more vodkas on the strength of the inspiration and finally left in the company of Louis Fischer,[5] who was as darkly, sardonically, disapproving as I had remembered him. It was a pouring wet night and we took a taxi, putting Fischer down somewhere, and Ernst and I going on together to Brook Street. Yeats was ready and waiting in the entrance of the club, wearing the cloak he sometimes affected in the evenings. I explained to him that Toller wanted to discuss something of importance with him; that it was a matter of a few minutes only.

As women are not allowed in the Savile Club it was necessary to find a place for the talk. We came out on to the pavement debating this point and across the road, a little way down the street, the lights of Claridge's glowed through the pelting rain. I forget now which of us suggested we should go there; it was certainly the obvious thing to do from the point of view of convenience, but surely no stranger trio ever crossed that stately threshold. Yeats, tall, silver-haired, be-cloaked, looking so exactly as a distinguished poet might be expected to look and so seldom does, Toller short, dark, 'foreign' looking, wearing a picturesquely broad-brimmed hat, and looking like something out of the pages of *La Vie de Bohéme*, my hatless self, the three of us emerging from the rain and dripping into the brilliance of that most elegant of lounges. But what the flunkeys made of us we did not care, Yeats, because of a natural remoteness which made him at all times to a considerable extent oblivious of externals, Toller and I because we were excited by our plans, and heartened by vodka.

We sat down and ordered drinks and I asked if 'that noise', meaning the orchestra, could be stopped, explaining that we wanted to talk. It was regretted that nevertheless the orchestra must play for its appointed time. Over the drinks—I believe Toller and I continued with vodka—I explained to the non-political Yeats about Ossietsky. Toller followed up eagerly with the importance of Ossietsky securing the Nobel Peace Prize, and how it was necessary to find immediately someone who was already a Nobel prize-winner to support this movement.

I knew before Toller had finished that Yeats would refuse. He was acutely uncomfortable about it, but he refused. He never meddled in political matters, he said; he never had. At the urging of Maud Gonne he had signed the petition on behalf of Roger Casement, [6] but that was all, and the Casement case was after all an Irish affair. He was a poet, and Irish, and had no interest in European political squabbles. His interest was Ireland, and Ireland had nothing to do with Europe politically; it was outside, apart. He was sorry, but this had always been his attitude.

Toller and I looked at each other. Toller's eyes filled with tears. Perhaps, he said, with emotion, perhaps one felt differently about these things if one had been in prison oneself. This, he urged, was not a political matter; it was an affair of life and death, a question of a man's life. He, too, was a poet, but life was bigger than all the poetry ever written.

My own eyes filled with tears. I cannot honestly say whether it was my feeling for Ossietsky, or whether because I was moved by Toller's emotion, or whether it was merely the vodka; it was probably a combination of all three.

But there the embarrassing situation was; Yeats very uncomfortable and Toller and I in tears—and elegant ladies and gentlemen in evening dress all round, and waiters and flunkeys moving about, and the orchestra playing and the chandeliers glittering.

Toller and I pleaded alternately, that Ossietsky was not a political person, merely a liberal writer suffering as so many liberal writers and artists had suffered and were suffering under the Nazi régime; that it might be the saving of Ossietsky's life if he were granted this prize.

Yeats no less stubbornly persisted that he knew nothing about Ossietsky as a writer; that he could not be involved in a matter of this kind; that it was no part of an artist's business to become involved in affairs of this kind. He was sorry. He was very sorry.

His distress was obvious; he was genuinely troubled that there had been made to him this request which he could not fulfil.

Toller and I knew that we were defeated. 'I too am sorry,' Toller said. We blew our noses and called for the bill.

Yeats and I parted with Toller outside in Brook Street and he turned up his coat collar and hurried away through the rain, looking for all the world, with his broad-brimmed hat, and his darkness and his paleness, like the popular conception of an anarchist off on assassination business.

One day, Yeats said, as we drove on, we must talk politics and he would explain himself to me. But he never did. Once in Dublin a few months before his death—and the last time I saw him—we skimmed the surface of the subject, and he was interested in what I told him of Herbert Read's *Poetry and Anarchism* and said that he would like to see the book. In his general dislike of Fascism and Communism and all doctrinaire political creeds and parties he inclined more to the anarchist idea than anything else, and a belief in evolution as opposed to revolution where the social system was concerned, but it was all vague and unformed. Several times he told me that his political philosophy was contained in his 'pamphlet', *On the Boiler,*[7] so entitled, he wrote me, 'in commemoration of a mad ship's carpenter who, in my childhood, used to preach from the top of an old steamboat boiler on the Sligo keys'. (The spelling of quays is his.) Yeats assured me that 'At certain points our political thought is the same.' His 'public philosophy' is contained in *The Vision*—on the fly-leaf of my copy of which he wrote 'I am not so discourteous as to expect my friends to read this difficult book'; his 'private philosophy', as he called it, he did not publish—though *The Vision* is based on it, because, he said, he only half understood it himself. . . .

Yeats was tone-deaf, but even had he not been, his feeling for the music of words as expressed in poetry was such that the idea of setting poetry to music was as much an outrage for him as the wedding of ballet to music is for some musical people. (I once gave an intensely musical person tickets for *Choreatium;* he had never been to a ballet before, and had a passion for Brahms. When I asked him how he had enjoyed it, he replied that by keeping his eyes closed he had been able to enjoy the music.) He had never heard Peter Warlock's[8] setting to his 'Curlew' poems; there had been some dispute and he had never made a penny out of the thing, he said, and even at this stage he still seemed angry about everything in connection with it. I told him that I had a copy of the suite and that I personally thought the music astonishingly 'right' for the poetry; I asked him if he would care to hear the records, and he said that out of interest he would, though he did not approve of poetry being sung. I played the records to him as he sat beside the lily pond in my garden—that is to say I played him one side and half of the other of the first record; he would not hear the suite through; he hooted with laughter—the singer's voice rose when he contended that it should fall, and the whole thing seemed grotesque to him; it was terrible, he said, ridiculous, and proceeded to chant some of the lines in illustration of how they should be rendered to give them the meaning they were intended to convey.

Now when I play the records I feel a little guilty; as though I were doing a mean thing behind his back, for despite Yeats' derision, I still think the music in keeping with the melancholy spirit of the poetry, or, anyhow, what the poetry conveys to my particular ego.

The news of Yeats' death at the end of January 1939 came as a great shock. In his last letter to me, written from Mentone on December 23rd, 1938, he had written that he was in better health than usual and wiring 'Boiler No. 2.' I had written asking his approval on what I had written about him for this book; he replied that I should do as I liked about it; that to ask him to say anything would be to ask him to think of too many things, and he did not want to have to think except when he must. What I had written was 'a pleasant tale and in this atheist age nobody believes anything'. He was not a mystic, he wrote me then, apropos of what I had said of him, 'but on the other hand the author of the last chapter of the half-Russian novel'—*Darkness my Bride*—'is not a materialist'.

His writing was curiously large in this letter; usually it was small and difficult to read; this one had a bold free flow, and the whole letter a sense of lightness, of a careless gaiety. Of the many letters I have from him I have none in the big, free-flowing writing of this last, written a little over a month before his death. Once again I found myself unable to accept the reality of death, the finality of it. And apart from personal feeling, Yeats' death is a most grievous loss to contemporary letters, for as Gogarty wrote me at the time 'we shall not look on his like again'. The national imagination, Gogarty declared, was diminished with the loss of Yeats. But not merely the national imagination; with Yeats the whole poetry of imagination comes to an end; it is the end of the Celtic twilight. The horizon has been reached; there is no shore beyond.

NOTES

Ethel Edith Mannin (1900–   ) is an English novelist and travel writer. Her novels include *Martha* (1922), *Hunger of the Sea* (1924), *Sounding Brass* (1925), *Venetian Blinds* (1933), *The Pure Flame* (1936), *Darkness My Bride* (1939), *Red Rose* (1941), *The Blossoming Bough* (1943), *The Dark Forest* (1946), *Late Have I Loved Thee* (1948), *At Sundown the Tiger*, and *Lover Under Another Name* (1953). Among her travel books are *All Experience* (1932), *Forever Wandering* (1934) *South to Samarkand* (1936), *Jungle Journey* (1950), and *Moroccan Mosaic* (1953). She was married twice—to J. A. Porteous in 1920 and to Reginald Reynolds in 1938. She gave fifty of her Yeats letters to the Yeats Museum in Sligo some years ago, and still has two in her possession.

1. A Swami is a Hindu idol or religious teacher.

2. Ethel Mannin, *Confessions and Impressions* (London: Jarrolds, [1930]; rev. ed. London: Hutchinson, 1936) [autobiography].

3. Ernst Toller (1893–1939), German poet, playwright and political agitator.

4. Carl von Ossietzky (1889–1938), German writer who wrote vigorously in defence of pacifism. He was imprisoned on the charge of revealing military secrets (1931–2) and on the charge of being an enemy of the state (1933–6). While in prison, he was awarded the Nobel

Peace Prize in 1935. The Hitler government considered the award a 'challange and an insult' and prohibited the Germans henceforth from accepting such awards.

5. Louis Fischer (1896–   ), American journalist who was the European correspondent of the *Nation* (New York), serving chiefly in Russia. He is also the author of *Oil Imperialism* (1926), *The Soviet in World Affairs* (1930), *Soviet Journey* (1935), *Why Spain Fights On* (1937) and *Men and Politics* (autobiography; 1941).

6. Sir Roger David Casement (1864–1916), British consular agent and Irish rebel. He joined the Irish Nationalists in opposition to Redmond and to participation of Irishmen in World War I. He went to Germany to ask for armed aid, returned to Ireland in a submarine, was arrested, tried for high treason in London, found guilty and hanged.

7. W. B. Yeats, *On the Boiler* (Dublin: Cuala Press, 1939).

8. Peter Warlock is pseudonym of Philip Arnold Heseltine (1894–1930), English composer and writer of music.

Reminiscences of 'W. B.'*

E. R. W[ALSH]

Sometime in the autumn of 1907 I met Mr. Yeats at an afternoon gathering where I was introduced to him as a young person interested in literature. This was a sure passport to his favour, and he concluded a short conversation by informing me that when in Dublin he was at home to his friends on Sunday evenings and that he hoped I would join them if I liked. From then on, for several years, I spent many memorable evenings at the hotel in South Frederick street[1] where he and Lady Gregory lived.

I was generally the first to arrive, and was greeted with a reassuring courtesy which removed a great deal of the diffidence I felt at first in expressing my opinions. Lady Gregory usually retired early, and until she left the conversation centred round Abbey Theatre affairs, Hugh Lane's[2] modern gallery, current literary matters, or French literature, with which she was deeply acquainted. After she retired talk became less formal, and Yeats took a larger part in it. John Synge, a frequent visitor, spoke least, but there was a reserved power about him which impressed me, and I noticed a shade of deference in Yeats's manner when he asked for Synge's opinion. When he became really interested in a topic Yeats would walk about the room, with head thrown back, and pour forth, in his beautiful powerful voice, imaginative comment or interesting reminiscences. I have heard many other great talkers, but none with his vividness and virtuosity. He loved to talk of the Rhymers' Club; for he knew Beardsley, Dowson and Lionel Johnson well, and the early brilliance and subsequent tragic failure of their lives had touched him deeply. Once, after he had recited Dowson's 'Cynara,' I asked how it was that these men had dissipated their lives away.

* *Irish Times* (Dublin) (10 Feb 1940) p. 13.

He shrugged his shoulders, and suggested the explanation that, having early reached their best where others had touched perfection, they felt there was nothing more in life for them to do!

AN OPINION OF WILDE

Of Wilde he always spoke highly, except once when I mentioned what I thought was Wilde's desire to appear to be a great gentleman, he said: 'Wilde was never quite a gentleman; Wilde was insolent, a gentleman is never insolent.'

He was profoundly conscious of his Irish nationality, and in this respect seemed more truly Irish than many of the fiery patriots whom I have met. Unlike most of the Anglo-Irish he always spoke of the English as a foreign race. Talking to him of a newly arisen English statesman, he commented: 'Yes! they always find the man for a purpose, and put him aside when it is done.' He dwelt on their curious instinctive sagacity, which others regarded as cunning, and he rated them as most formidable antagonists. On this side of his character I think he resembled Parnell, but his interest in politics arose chiefly from a desire to see the Irish question settled, so that our young men of talent might direct their intellect towards the Arts. He dreamed then that Dublin might become a modern Athens.

MYSTICISM

In those days of our acquaintance mysticism and spiritualism formed his religious life. The writings of William Blake and Jacob Boehme deeply influenced him, as did also a friendship with Fionna McLeod [sic] (William Sharp)[3] in Paris. He investigated far into spiritualistic phenomena, and met many of the famous mediums of the time. One important result of these studies was a complete abiding belief in the immortality of the soul. He looked forward to death without fear. 'I know because I have loved life I shall love death also,' he once exclaimed. Like Sparkenbroke in Charles Morgan's novel[4] he regarded death as a desired fulfilment. But philosophy was also claiming him. I well remember the excitement aroused in him by the reading of Goethe's 'Wilhelm Meister,' and I date from that event a desire to follow the great German in his dual activities of poet and philosopher. Plotinus and St. Thomas Aquinas were studied later, and from this period of his life his book 'The Twenty-Eight Phases of the Moon'[5] emerged. The doctrine of this work was founded on reincarnation: every human being returning twenty-eight times to earth and I fear its esoteric nature made it of little interest to Dublin people.

Yeats also strongly believed in astrology, and frequently consulted his horoscope, when about to take any important step. He defended his belief in it by stating that the case for it had never been disproved. Man had merely moved to new interpretations of fate.

GOOD MANNERS

Another book which influenced him in a lighter way was Castiglione's 'Il Cortegiano.'[6] To Yeats perfect graciousness of manner was a part of real culture of the mind, and in Castiglione's description of the Court of Guidobaldo he found the complete picture of this happy union. While he was at no time a snob, this aspiration towards a life of easy, dignified urbanity was inevitably misunderstood by some people. Once he was rebuked for standing up when 'God Save the King' was played at a public dinner, and he wrote a charming reply to his critics, quoting Balzac's dictum: 'In the matter of good manners we are all conservatives.'

Significant, too, in this direction, was an incident which happened to him in London about this time. He had called, carelessly dressed, at Sutherland House, one afternoon to see the Duchess, who had been a constant friend to him. Ushered into her great drawing room he noticed a small group standing apart round a lady. The Duchess came forward to greet him, and immediately said: 'I want to present you to Her Majesty,' and, before he had time to gather his wits together, he found he was talking to Queen Alexandra. He did most of the conversation, however, contrary to the traditions of etiquette, but he learned afterwards that the Queen was very pleased with him.[7]

The ease and lack of all self-consciousness of the party strengthened his desire for a polished society, and the disdain he felt for the bourgeoisie, whose lives were ruled by convention and fear. 'There are only three classes I respect,' he exclaimed, 'the aristocracy, who are above fear; the poor, who are beneath it, and the artists, whom God has made reckless.'

Among the people whom I met at South Frederick street Captain Shaw Taylor came nearest to Yeats' ideal gentleman of the Renaissance. His remarkable personal beauty, and his exquisitely winning way made him irresistible as a conciliator, and Yeats hoped that as he had been the means of bringing about a settlement at the Land Bill Conference, he might also succeed in the larger issue of the Irish question. His early death shattered that hope and robbed Ireland of a promising son.

GEORGE MOORE

George Moore never came to our discussions, for at that time there was little love lost between him and Yeats, who never rated Moore's work highly and did not think it would live. His style was lucid, but undistinguished, and his work governed by logic. For formal logic Yeats had a contempt, maintaining that the work of great writers was guided by intuition and inspiration. Moore must have had some inkling of Yeats' opinion, for he spoke to me with an obviously malicious pity about the failure of 'The Unicorn and [sic] the Stars,' a new play of the poet's which had just been put on at the Abbey.[8]

Yeats married[9] towards the end of the Great War, and thereafter for many years I saw little of him. A few weeks before he left on his last journey to France he came into the Arts Club and chatted to me for about an hour. His conversation was as lively and interesting as ever. His mind showed no signs of aging.

Yeats took his art with intense seriousness. It was a dedication from which neither poverty nor neglect had deflected him in the least. He worked with great industry and believed in no easy path to success in the arts. I once asked him what he thought of a young poet who appeared to show promise. 'He came to me for advice,' was the reply, 'and I lent him a large volume of Chaucer to study. He brought it back to me in a week saying he had read it. Now, it would have taken him several months to master it thoroughly. He will not learn his craft. When the inspiration of youth is exhausted there will be nothing to fall back upon.'

NATIVE SHREWDNESS

In the early days of our acquaintance he knew few people in Dublin, for his strong nationalism excluded him from the ruling Anglo-Irish society. Lady Lyttleton, the wife of the Commander in Chief, a very cultured woman, used to invite him sometimes to dinner. But even she had to be careful about the guests she asked to meet him. He was, therefore, rather a lonely man, for the merely Bohemian company he might have joined had no attraction for him: but I never heard him complain on this account. In character he was wise, kindly and simple, with a good deal of native shrewdness. The latter characteristic came as a surprise to those who regarded him as a mere dreamer, and I remember a Dublin stockbroker relieving his feelings in this respect with the remark, 'Mr. Yeats, if you hadn't become a poet you might have been an ornament to the Dublin Stock Exchange!'

Material success meant little to him, for his ideal was a high, heroic way of life, but when it came he accepted it with a pleasant modesty. He was happiest, I think, in the days when he fought the great battles of the Abbey Theatre when popular clamour against 'The Playboy of the Western World' and, in a lesser degree, against 'The Piper,'[10] threatened to smash the Irish theatre movement. He was vehemently urged by many to take off the 'Playboy,' but he resolutely refused, saying it would be a national calamity to do so. For the great courage he showed then and on other occasions where an artist's right to expression was challenged, he deserved, as the poet Heine wished for himself, that a sword should be laid beside the wreath of laurels on his coffin.

NOTES

1. Until he became a member of the Stephen's Green Club, Yeats stayed when in Dublin at the Nassau Hotel overlooking the College Park. He was at home to his friends on Sunday evenings in this hotel, which Lady Gregory used as a residence, and in which Maud Gonne had also been accustomed to stay when she was in Dublin.

2. Sir Hugh Lane (1875–1915), Lady Gregory's nephew. Yeats first met the young picture

dealer and art collector in 1901, when they were both fellow guests of Lady Gregory. By 1912, Lane's collection of modern French pictures, a part of a modern art gallery founded in Dublin in 1905, had become famous. Lane offered them to Dublin on condition that they should be suitably housed. This created a controversy, in which Yeats took a prominent part. Lane became the unnamed hero of a memorable series of poems entitled *Poems Written in Discouragement* and published in 1913. An event of 1915 which touched Yeats to the quick, both on Ireland's account and Lady Gregory's, was the sinking of the *Lusitania* with Hugh Lane on board.

3. William Sharp (1855–1905), Scottish poet and man of letters who wrote both under his own name and under the pseudonym Fiona Macleod. During the 1880s and the 1890s, the period of *Dr. Jekyll and Mr. Hyde* and *The Picture of Dorian Gray*, masks were very much the wear, and dual personalities the height of fashion. Thus George Russell had to double himself as 'AE'; William Magee distinguished himself as 'John Eglinton'; Mrs Pearl Craigie as 'John Oliver Hobbes'; William Sharp as 'Fiona Macleod'—indeed it long remained uncertain whether William Sharp and Fiona Macleod were two people or one, male or female. See Yeats's account of Sharp's visit to him in Paris in his *Autobiographies*, pp. 339–41. Sharp shared Yeats's occult theories.

4. Charles Morgan, *Sparkenbroke* (London: Macmillan, 1936).

5. Probably Walsh means *A Full Moon in March*, published in 1935.

6. Conte Baldassare Castiglione (1478–1529), Italian diplomat and writer who is known particularly for his celebrated dialogue on ideal courtly life *Il Cortegiano*, which was translated into English as *The Courtier* by Sir Thomas Hoby in 1561.

7. Queen Alexandra knew Yeats's poems, but had not heard of his political manifestos, and had said that she would like to see one of his plays on the stage. See Charles Ricketts, *Self-Portrait* (London: Peter Davies, 1939) p. 112.

8. *The Unicorn from the Stars*, a three-act folk play by Yeats and Lady Gregory, was first produced at the Abbey theatre on 21 November 1907. It was a transformation of an earlier five-act prose tragedy, *Where There Is Nothing*. George Moore, watching the curtain come down on one of the scenes, said to the man next to him, 'Poor Yeats! He's dead!'—Richard Ellmann, *Yeats: The Man and the Masks* (New York: Dutton, 1948) p. 188.

9. In 1917 Yeats proposed to Maud Gonne's daughter Iseult at Coleville; the proposal was rejected. He then married George Hyde-Lees on 20 October.

10. *The Piper*, by 'Norreys Connell' (Conal O'Riordan), was first performed at the Abbey Theatre on 13 February 1908. The play was protested against because it seemed to the members of a certain group to be an unpatriotic revelation of the lack of cohesion among Irish political and patriotic factions.

Castle of the Heroes*

MAUD GONNE

One of our early dreams was a Castle of the Heroes. It was to be in the middle of a lake, a shrine of Irish tradition where only those who had dedicated their lives to Ireland might penetrate; they were to be brought there in a painted boat across the lake and might only stay for short periods

* Extracted from 'Yeats and Ireland', *Scattering Branches*, ed. Stephen Gwynn (London: Macmillan, 1940) pp. 15–34.

of rest and inspiration. It was to be built of Irish stone and decorated only with the Four Jewels of the Tuatha de Danaan,[1] with perhaps a statue of Ireland, if any artist could be found great enough to make one, which we doubted.

The Four Jewels, as Willie explained, are universal symbols appearing in debased form on the Tarot, the divining cards of the Egyptians and even on our own playing cards, and fore-shadowed the Christian symbolism of the Saint Grail, whose legends Willie loved to trace to Ireland.

*   *   *

Our Castle of the Heroes remained a Castle in the Air, but the last time I saw[2] Willie at Riversdale just before he left Ireland for the last time, as we said goodbye, he, sitting in his arm-chair from which he could rise only with great effort, said, 'Maud, we should have gone on with our Castle of the Heroes, we might still do it'. I was so surprised that he remembered, I could not reply. The whirlpool of life had sent the current of our activities wide apart. We had quarrelled seriously when he became a Senator of the Free State which voted Flogging Acts against young republican soldiers still seeking to free Ireland from the contamination of the British Empire, and for several years we had ceased to meet. I stood speechless beside him with the song of Red Hanrahan echoing through my mind, 'Angers that are like noisy clouds have set our hearts abeat'—'Like heavy flooded waters our bodies and our blood', and I realised that Willie and I still 'bent low and low and kissed the quiet feet' and worshipped Her, who is 'purer than a tall candle before the Holy Rood'.

NOTES

Maud Gonne (1866–1953) was an Irish patriot and philanthropist who was engaged in constant political agitation against the British. Yeats proposed to her but was turned down, and in 1903 she married Major John MacBride, who was executed by the British after the Easter Rebellion in 1916. She was the heroine of many of Yeats's lyrics and plays. See Maud Gonne MacBride, *A Servant of the Queen* (London: Gollancz, 1938); 'W. B. Yeats: A Dublin Portrait', *In Excited Reverie*, ed. A. Norman Jeffares and K. G. W. Cross (London: Macmillan, 1965) pp. 1–13 (transcript of the BBC symposium to which Maud Gonne contributed); Curtis B. Bradford, 'Yeats and Maud Gonne', *Texas Studies in Language and Literature*, III, no. 4 (Winter 1962) 452–74; Joseph M. Hone, 'A Scattered Fair', *Wind and the Rain*, III, no. 3 (Autumn 1946), 110 (prints fragments from a diary kept by Elizabeth Yeats: Yeats and Maud Gonne); A. G. Stock, 'The World of Maud Gonne', *Indian Journal of English Studies*, VI (1965) 56–79; Elizabeth Coxhead, 'Maud Gonne', *Daughters of Erin* (London: Secker and Warburg, 1965) pp. 17–77; and Chris Healy, 'Maud Gonne', *Confessions of a Journalist* (London: Chatto and Windus, 1904) pp. 227–36.

1. Tuatha De Danaan = Irish 'Race of the Gods of Dana' or 'Tribes of the Goddess Danu'. They were considered superhuman conquerors of the Firbolgs and Fomorians but were in turn conquered by incoming Milesians who deified, worshipped and enshrined them in fairy-mound underground kingdoms.

2. In the late summer of 1938.

Yeats
as a Painter Saw Him*

WILLIAM ROTHENSTEIN

I remember going one day to see George Moore, who greeted me with, 'I am so glad you have come. I can only think when I am talking!' Yeats could also think in solitude, but ideas, when he was in the mood for talking, seldom failed him. He liked women to be among his audience. A man is at his best talking to women, he said once. So at Woburn Buildings there was usually a circle of green-clad ladies seated on the floor, while he intoned his poems, and Florence Farr plucked at the single string of a rough, primitive instrument, designed by Yeats himself. In those days he was absorbed by spiritualism, and by magic too, affecting to believe in the power of certain words to evoke spirits. He hinted that he had got into communion with dark forces, and told of drawing a circle, from within which he called up spirits, spirits he believed to be on the point of materialising. He told too of an uneducated girl who, going into a trance, spoke literary Chinese. I wondered how Yeats could identify the language!

*   *   *

Yeats happened to be staying with us in Gloucestershire during the Easter of 1916 and I recollect his grave face when he read of the outbreak of the Easter rebellion. He spoke of the leaders as innocent and patriotic theorists, carried away by their belief that they must put their theories into practice. They would fail and pay the penalty for their rashness. He did not then realise how significant the sacrifice was to be for Ireland's future. He obviously felt some discomfort at being safe in England when his friends were risking their lives in Dublin, and fretted somewhat that he had not been consulted, had been left in ignorance of what was afoot.

His heart was in Ireland, yet he had spent the greater part of his life in London. Scornful of certain elements in the English character, he none the less admired the aristocratic quality of English culture; and his relations with English poets, with Dowson, Bridges, Masefield, Binyon, Symons and Sturge Moore, were of the closest. On this account, no doubt, and because he was regarded as the most eminent contemporary poet and man of

---

* Extracted from 'Yeats as a Painter Saw Him', *Scattering Branches*, ed. Stephen Gwynn (London: Macmillan, 1940) pp. 35–54.

letters, he was asked to edit the *Oxford Book of Modern Verse*.[1] While he was in London in connection with this work, I went more than once to see him in his lodgings. On one occasion I found him surrounded with a pile of books, when he asked me, did I know anything of Dorothy Wellesley's verses? He had only lately come upon her poems and was inclined to place her high among contemporary poets.

* * *

In his later years Yeats tended more and more to get away from anything in the nature of aesthetic gesture. Speaking of painting he quoted his brother Jack as saying that he painted to please himself. 'This,' he said, 'is not my attitude to poetry. You must remember your audience; it is always there. You cannot write without it.' He held the reaction against tradition to be tiresome. We have to accept the conditions we find in our own time; within their discipline we can still remain free enough to be ourselves. Not that he had patience with easy acceptance; wherever there is thought there is opposition. He wanted to inspire the youth of Ireland with the national ideals to be found in Berkeley and Swift. A return to clarity, to the poetic expression of what is in the minds of the common people. He aimed to have his poems sung in the streets. Yet there are obscure passages in many of his later poems.

NOTES

For a note on Sir William Rothenstein see p. 250.

1. *The Oxford Book of Modern Verse* (Oxford: Clarendon Press, 1936). The anthology was controversial; in the Introduction Yeats explains his exclusion of the work of Wilfred Owen and of other English war poets on the ground that 'When man has withdrawn into the quicksilver at the back of the mirror no great event becomes luminous to the mind.' See Joseph Cohen, 'In Memory of W. B. Yeats – and Wilfrid Owen', *Journal of English and Germanic Philology*, LVIII, no. 4 (Oct 1959) 637–49; and John Press, 'Anthologies', *Review of English Studies*, I, no. I (Jan 1960) 65–6.

The Man and the Dramatist*

LENNOX ROBINSON

I met him first when I was twenty-two and he was just twice that age. I suppose it was only a young man's impression (I was very inexperienced for my age) but he seemed then to be a middle-aged, if not almost an old man. This is strange, for he kept his appearance of a young man till he was over thirty, perhaps he suddenly put on maturity. At any rate by the time I met him he had an air of great dignity and authority, a poise not a pose. He was often, all through his life, to be accused of being a *poseur*. It was not the case. He had mannerisms of movement and speech as every person of great individuality is bound to have, his pose would have been to try and pass himself off as an ordinary person. He was extraordinarily striking in appearance, tall, slim and his hair still quite black, the beard of earlier years had disappeared. His eyes were strangely placed, one of them was always weak and by the end of his life its sight had gone. This made it forgivable in him to pass a friend in the street without recognition or to fail to identify people in a crowded room. He has talked to me for an hour about the Abbey Theatre, calling me by the name of a previous manager, and then he suddenly stopped, looking at me as if he had only just realised my identity and appearance (yet no two appearances could be in greater contrast than the former manager's, and mine); there followed an apology which did away with any feeling of hurt on my part, for he was always courteous and gentle save when roused to vehemence on some matter of vital importance. In dealing with his inferiors there was no arrogance, no consciousness of superiority, and anyone who ever served him quickly grew to love him.

I have said that when I met him first he was slim; that was not always the case. He could vary, and vary rapidly, from leanness to stoutness. I used to tell him he was like the moon that waxed and waned. He was a very moderate eater and drinker—the most rapid eater I have ever met, and took pains about his figure, doing exercises of some sort to keep himself trim. Up to a few years before his death he could look on occasion extraordinarily young, look like that lovely Sargent[1] drawing done just about the time I met him first, and his appearance at the end of his life can only be described by the one word—noble.

* Extracted from 'The Man and the Dramatist', *Scattering Branches*, ed. Stephen Gwynn (London: Macmillan, 1940) pp. 55–114.

In some obituary notice he was described as unapproachable, and the writer said that no one outside his family ever called him by his Christian name. This is not the case. To his intimate friends he was 'Willie', to his close acquaintances he was 'W.B.' In his early days in the Theatre he was known (but I am sure only behind his back) to players and staff as 'Schoolboy Yeats', perhaps because of his big black tie knotted in a drooping bow which might suggest some schoolboy's uniform. Certainly, in the last years, for me he was always 'Willie' to his face; in speaking of him to ·is friends one generally used his initials.

In his early years he affected the big tie, loosely knotted, the correct wear of a poet of the 'nineties. Then he became more orthodox. He liked clothes and liked them to be correct. He took me aside once in the early days of our association and told me that a gentleman didn't wear a 'made-up' dress-tie. I protested that mine was home-made. He apologised, but a year afterwards he warned me again, and again I protested, but from that time forward was always careful that my tie should be slightly awry. Cats he loved and birds, the wild birds that would be fed at his windows or the canaries in their cages, and he would write quite undisturbed by their flood of song, but it distressed him that they *would* use their bath-water for drinking purposes, and he sought vainly from a bird-fanciers' shop for a cure for this deplorable habit.

He was never a rich man, for most of his life he was a very poor one and he had to be careful of his money. He was a good man of business and advised me as a young man never to waste my time over trivial journalism; if everything was written with care, in a year or two there might be enough to gather into a book of essays. That he had followed this path himself was proved when Mr. Horace Reynolds unearthed contributions to American papers written by him as long ago as 1887, republished forty-seven years later, which make good reading.[2] He loved beautiful things and a beautiful way of living, but he had to deny himself. He was never mean but he was never extravagant, he dared not be; after all, most of his friends were as poor as himself, so it was not very difficult to live simply.

*   *   *

He was the most brilliant conversationalist I have ever known, at once witty and profound. At its lightest his talk was full of anecdote and reminiscence, and if he could fail at times to recognise a friend or a face he had a meticulously accurate memory of facts. His sisters have told me how time and time again, turning up some old letter, they have verified some tiny fact, some insignificant incident which had taken place many years before and which he had written or spoken of with perfect accuracy of date and occurrence. It was dangerous to argue with him on a question of fact, he was certain to be right. You might hear him tell the same story over a number of years, the story never varied, each detail was the same, the very language in which it was narrated unaltered. He could rejoice in telling a Rabelaisian story but, ten to one, if you tried to cap it he grew disgusted. It is maddening that my memory is not like his and that of all the fine talk I have heard from him so little remains. In argument his mind worked very quickly, and having him and George Moore to supper one night in London after the theatre—they were not the best of friends then—it was delightful to sit back and listen to poor Moore fumbling for the retort that was to annihilate; but before the right words could be found Yeats had presented some other facet of the subject, leaving Moore floundering in the background.

*   *   *

During the early days of the Irish Theatre he worked hard at production, producing not only his own plays, but, with Lady Gregory, the other plays in the repertory. Ten years later, when he made me Manager and Producer of the Theatre, his only reason for doing so (I had no technical qualifications) was that I had written a promising play or two, and a dramatist should know his instrument. Consciously or unconsciously he knew that he himself had learned his instrument in those years of producing, and he was now putting a beginner to school. By the time I came to the Theatre, in 1910, the days of his great verse-plays were over, but I made the first production in Ireland of *The Player Queen*, some of the Plays for Dancers, *The Words upon the Window-Pane*, *The King of the Great Clock Tower* and *Resurrection*, and his two translations from Sophocles. With the exception of the first play, which was produced during his absence in England, while not actually producing them, he took an active part in their rehearsal. Strange to say, he had not many, perhaps had not any, theories about the speaking of verse. He hated any affectation of speech; chanting or crooning would drive him frantic, his ideal verse-speaker should have a rich and varied voice and the sense of acting that evokes those qualities. These things come only from constant practice in verse-speaking, practice which makes verse come as naturally from the lips of the player as does prose. If he never got in Dublin the theatre of poetry he had dreamed of, it was not for the want of a few very good verse-speakers—I instance Frank Fay and Sara Allgood—and others who were potentially good; the theatre of his dream failed because the Irish theatre took a different, a realistic path. But that theatre had been founded to be a National Theatre, a mouthpiece for the young writers of Ireland; he had never intended it to be his particular plaything, and when the young writers turned away from poetry, he more and more as the years passed allowed his own work to be put on one side. Lady Gregory might plead, I might plead, it was of little use. He had an artist's pride; he knew he could only rely on an audience which would be polite but indifferent to his work, which would count the moments until the curtain fell on *Deirdre* and rose again on some peasant comedy or some tragedy dealing with an event very close to their own life. Later on, he was to make his own theatre for his peers.

But in rehearsal, if he did not spend much time on the speaking of his verse, he paid great attention to other things—emotion, movement, scenery, dress and lighting. He would spend half an hour getting some movement or piece of 'business' to his liking and would cry out in passion—never in temper—at some clumsiness of mine or on the part of the players. To them and to me those rehearsals were a joy and an inspiration, for he brought to bear on the play an instinct and an intelligence vastly superior to our own. He was completely lucid in his explanation of what he wanted from our players and producer, but nearly always demanded something beyond our capacity; and he would patiently try in this way and that way to get his desired result.

*   *   *

But, while writing of him as man of the theatre, I must not forget that his interest was not only in the production of his own plays. After watching the performance of a realistic play he would make a dozen criticisms, heart-searching to producer and players. I had hung the pictures too high, the farmer's daughters were too clean ('Smear cow-dung on their faces!' I remember him exclaiming); some actor's wig was atrocious, the scene was too darkly lit. Our supposedly 'good' furniture was undistinguished, therefore he and I must spend a couple of afternoons visiting old furniture shops in Dublin, picking here and there some genuine period piece and so accumulating a complete set of Georgian furniture. He took pains, as a good producer should, over the smallest 'prop'. He was eager for experiment in the theatre, and seized on the idea of the Gordon Craig screens; he seized on Mr. Granville-Barker's idea of a squared stage-cloth for use at rehearsal. His was our Peacock Theatre and his our School of Ballet, and had we not been always poor, and he a good man of business, he would have been prodigal in what he spent on the stage.

NOTES

For a note on Lennox Robinson see p. 259.

1. John Sargent (1856–1925), a painter who was born in Florence, Italy, of American parentage. Yeats sat to Sargent, who did full justice to the poet's looks, bringing out the youthful appearance which he retained for so long.

2. In 1933 Yeats gave Horace Reynolds permission to bring out these contributions in a little volume called *Letters to the New Island* (Cambridge, Massachusetts: Harvard University Press, 1934). This book does not testify to early powers of critical expression, but is interesting because it shows Yeats at work on those ideas about Ireland, poetry and philosophy which were to possess his later life.

May Craig Recalls
the Abbey Days*

MAY CRAIG

May Craig is Ireland's senior character actress. Any lesser title would deny
the heritage of half a century's work, most of it on the boards of the Abbey,
which she, together with the other great actresses and actors of her era,
helped to make one of the most famous theatres in the English-speaking
world.

Her actress's life has not been all glamour. There was always the great
sense of participating in something worthwhile, of helping the major Irish
writers to realise their work on the stage, and the attractions of the
footlights and of tours abroad. But life wasn't always easy. When her
husband died she was left with five young children, the oldest barely
twelve. She bought a house and, with this to give her security and her
Abbey salary—which was never very large—she just made ends meet,
week after week.

Now she lives in quiet suburban peace at Booterstown: the sea is at the
end of her road. The comfortable house, with its attractive garden, is
packed with photographs, books and programmes, each of them a link
with some moment in the past.

*   *   *

She got her first audition for the Abbey in 1916, when Molly O'Neill,
who was to have played the part of Raina in 'Arms and the Man,' went
down with flu in London. This is what happened at the audition, she told
me.

'I went down and read the part, and then the producer jumped over the
footlights into the auditorium. I didn't know that Lady Gregory and Yeats
were in the auditorium listening to me, because, when he came back, he
never told me whom he had been speaking to, but simply asked me
whether I would be able to play the part.

'I said that I would, if he could help me do it, and he said "There's one
thing I would suggest: when you use your arms, keep your hands quiet."

* In an interview with John Horgan, *Irish Times* (Dublin) (10 June 1965) W. B. Yeats
Supplement.

'Mr. Yeats, as we found out afterwards, said that he would like to put players in a barrel. Even now, if you notice, the Abbey players don't use their hands much, except for a definite purpose. If we were having a row on the stage, for instance, I could not say GET OUT OF THE HOUSE (here Miss Craig waved her arms about passionately). I was told to get it into my face and my voice . . . *Get out of the house* . . . that's the Abbey tradition.

* * *

'I played with Sarah Allgood, and Molly O'Neill, and Fred Donovan, but I owe the control of my emotions to Sarah Allgood. One day, at a dress rehearsal of St. John Ervine's "Mixed Marriage," after I had tried to show the grief that I felt in one scene on the stage, she caught me by the collar of the blouse and said. "Do you realise what you're doing? You're ruining that act."

' "How," I said.

' "With your sighs and your heaving," she said. "You leave the acting to people who know how to act. You sit still. Have you ever felt grief? When you feel grief, you turn to stone. You have *no* feelings."

'She was wonderful. I loved Sarah Allgood, and I loved Molly O'Neill. They were two completely different people, but both great actresses.

'I can remember another occasion on which we were all together, in Jury's Hotel. Some other directors—like Armstrong of Liverpool Rep—were over. Yeats was there with Lady Gregory—I cannot separate Yeats in my mind from her: they were the foundation stones of the Abbey Theatre—the Abbey players, and possibly one or two other officials. The funniest memory I have of that occasion is one of Yeats playing musical chairs. Nobody would believe it, but he was—and he had a paper hat on.'

* * *

There were other, more direct, encounters with the dramatist as well, Miss Craig remembered. Yeats came down to the theatre regularly. 'He was wonderfully dignified—almost up in the air all the time. He'd come into the room and he'd just bow. He would not talk to anyone except to Lady Gregory or the producer and then go off down to the stalls and watch. If anything was wrong with the acting in one of his plays, he would speak to whoever was producing it—Lennox Robinson, Michael Dolan or Arthur Shields—and *they* would tell us what was wrong. So, of course, we were always on pins and needles when Yeats or Lady Gregory was in front.

'I had a very good part as one of the wives in the Green Helmet and, during rehearsals, it came to stage when, just before the play opened, I went to Lennox Robinson, thrilled with the way I was playing it, and said: "Mr. Robinson, do you think Mr. Yeats is pleased with the way I'm playing the part?"

'Robinson, who was very quiet and gentle, said: "Well, my dear, you'd better go down and ask W.B." He always called Yeats "W.B." It was like asking me to go and speak to the Lord. I went down to the auditorium, where Mr. Yeats was standing. He was very tall, always wore pearl grey suits, his hair was long and white and he wore glasses with a ribbon. He was very majestic, very dignified, and you felt like a crumb on the earth when you were talking to him. You can imagine how I felt when I went to him, and said:

'"Mr. Yeats, are you satisfied with the way I'm playing the part?"

'Now, I'm tall, but he was much taller. He looked at me, from my feet up to my head, and down again to my feet, and walked straight away from me. I didn't know what to think, and then he came back, looked me up and down again, and said:

' "My dear . . . the Abbey directors are lending you the theatre. The author is giving you the words. The electrician is giving you the lights. The scenic artist is giving you the scenery. The stage manager is giving you the furniture. Now, will you tell me, what are you giving?"

'I nearly died! But that, I think, is very essential in young people. It made me realise that I was only saying Yeats's words with no expression or feeling in them. And of course you must put something of yourself into everything you do, but I was giving nothing. Afterwards he told me: "Quite good . . . quite good."

'One of the best moments of my life, particularly in the theatre, was at the final curtain of "The Words Upon The Windowpane" when Yeats came out, just bowed to me, and kissed my hand. Was I thrilled. Oh, I loved Yeats. He was a dreamer. And his words were beautiful.'

Without the Twilight*

EDMUND DULAC

If he was a dreamer his dream was not the self-indulgent illusion of the romancer who pins butterfly wings to lizards' backs to turn them into dragons, tricks out with extravagant tinsel a mirage of ancient or distant lands and is afraid to wake up.

Yeats never indulged in strangeness for the sake of strangeness, that aimless castle-building which takes no account of proportion or relation in the piling up of its material. His imagination was under perfect control. His fantasy is neither sham nor fantastic. It has the quality of unexpected fitness that is inseparable from true invention. The element of surprise in

* Extracted from 'Without the Twilight', *Scattering Branches*, ed. Stephen Gwynn (London: Macmillan, 1940) pp. 135–44.

his imagery comes from discovery, not from wonder. It functions in parallel. The thought is modulated in an unusual key, transmuted into a significant symbol; an unforseen richness is disclosed behind familiar things, as is disclosed the delicate tracery of gold and colours on those Javanese puppets of cut-out leather that had only shown as black shadows on a white cloth.

His method of work had nothing about it of the unreal or the spectacular. He hardly knew the ecstasy of the picture-poet who rattles off his lines in a frenzy of inspiration. A word, a phrase would find an echo somewhere in his thoughts. He would sit beating his knee with one hand, or walk about the room, his words measured to his pace, muttering them over and over again in a sort of incantation. And if the magic worked, if the word, the phrase awakened a particularly exciting train of fitting associations, he would set all this out in simple, ordinary prose. Elaboration in poem form came afterwards.

*   *   *

Read again the poems written in the last ten years. How much of the conventional dreamer is there left? How much of the romantic aloofness? Yeats was certainly more detached than most, but his ivory tower had many doors and many windows all wide open on to life. Nothing was neglected or despised. Only he made a choice among the people and the things that went by. And the tower was never lost in the clouds. He never blundered in his dress or in his gestures, he never missed a train, he never fell into a pond, he never lost a precious thing. In fact he was often more precise in his actions—through, perhaps, some well developed subconscious power of attention—than many less romantic people. I have seen him return from a long walk at night, in the country when the sky was pitch black and the roads a network of mud-pools, with his shoes spotlessly clean. I was bespattered to the knees.

NOTE

Edmund Dulac (1882–1953), British (naturalised) artist, illustrator and stage designer. He designed the masks and costumes for Yeats's *At the Hawk's* Well. In January 1918 Yeats asked him to cut a medieval-looking woodcut of Giraldus Cambrensis, which would really be a portrait of Yeats, and later used this as a frontispiece for *A Vision*.

Yeats as Irish Poet*

F. R. HIGGINS

I remember him telling me some years back that most of his poems were composed to some vague tune, some lilt. Indeed, when we were together, he sang in his own uncertain, shy way, some of these poems. Whenever these poems were again repeated, at later dates, he always sang them to the same halting lilt. All poetry, Yeats frequently said, was song; and his *Oxford Book of Modern Verse* was largely compiled by him on that principle. In song-writing, Yeats took more than a literary interest. He wanted the songs of Irish poets sung among Irish people. In writing his own songs, we worked together welding his occasionally meandering words to Gaelic tunes. That exercise was latterly his constant delight—an enthusiasm afterwards fructifying in our jointly edited volume of Broadsides[1] made from Irish traditional songs, the songs of our friends, and our own songs. Convival meetings of Irish poets should be the occasion for song production. It was a frequent idea; for him the social gatherings of the Irish Academy of Letters should take place in the upper room of some Dublin public-house, where the poets present would sing their own work. Such gatherings did take place, songs were sung, including Yeats's—but not in an actual public-house. Poetry must be brought to the people by song.[2]

*   *   *

From his wise, anecdotal memory, his sustained interest in Irish mythology and life—from these every quaint experience, passionate phrase or queer thought became grist to his creative mill; while his own brooding on character gave an almost passionate importance to the commonplace. Yet Yeats stood abreast of his age—writing out of our realities and what to him was reality—most modern among moderns, without being modernist. And through all his works appears one clear image—the image of himself, up to the end eager, youthful, impression-able, in his fierceness or foible. I shall never know an Irishman greater than W. B. Yeats. For fifteen years I was acquainted with him; for half of that time I knew him intimately as a close and constant friend: most generous, most frank, full of zest and humour, a magnetic personality, always

* Extracted from 'Yeats as Irish Poet', *Scattering Branches*, ed. Stephen Gwynn (London: Macmillan, 1940) pp. 145–55.

arrogantly the Irish poet. The night before he left Ireland on his last journey we were together in his room, talking poetry as usual. The new poem *Under Ben Bulben*,[3] on which he still worked, he again read for me. I was elated, yet curiously sad. After midnight we parted on the drive from his house. The head of the retiring figure, erect and challenging, gleamed through the darkness, as I looked back; while on the road before me, my thoughts were still ringing with the slow powerful accents of his chanting:

> Irish poets, learn your trade,
> Sing whatever is well made,
> Scorn the sort now growing up
> All out of shape from toe to top,
> Their unremembering hearts and heads
> Base-born products of base beds.
> Sing the peasantry, and then
> Hard-riding country gentlemen,
> The holiness of monks, and after
> Porter-drinkers' randy laughter;
> Sing the lords and ladies gay
> That were beaten into the clay
> Through seven heroic centuries;
> Cast your mind on other days
> That we in coming days may be
> Still the indomitable Irishry.[4]

NOTES

Frederick Robert Higgins (1896–1941) was an Irish poet who, in 1935, was co-editor with Yeats of *Broadsides*, a poetry magazine. He was also a founding member of the Irish Academy of Letters and Managing Director of the Abbey Theatre, for which he wrote *A Deuce of Jacks* (1935). His main literary reputation rests on his poetry, *Salt Air* (1924), *Island Blood* (1925), *The Dark Breed* (1927), *Arable Holdings* (1933) and *The Gap of Brightness* (1940). Higgins was Yeats's chief protege among the poets of the younger generation in Ireland. Higgins's writings on Yeats include 'Yeats and Poetic Drama in Ireland', *The Irish Theatre*, ed. Lennox Robinson (London: Macmillan, 1939) pp. 65–88; 'The Poet of a Dream: Where "Beauty Is Taut, Passion Precise"', *Irish Times* (Dublin) (13 June 1935) pp. 6–7; and 'As Irish Poet', *Arrow* (Dublin), W. B. Yeats Commemoration Number (Summer 1939) 6–8. On Higgins see Patrick J. Byrne, 'Manager of the Abbey: The Late F. R. Higgins', *Accent*, II (Winter 1942) 92–4; and W. R. Rodgers, ed., 'F. R. Higgins', *Irish Literary Portraits* (London: British Broadcasting Corporation, 1972) pp. 169–84.

1. *Broadsides*, issued monthly by Cuala Press, Dublin, started in June 1908 and folded in May 1915; there were eighty-four issues in all.

2. In his old age Yeats was more than ever haunted by the desire to restore the singing side of the poet's art, and he constantly discussed the subject with poets of his acquaintance who had knowledge of music; notably with F. R. Higgins and W. J. Turner.

3. In *Last Poems*.

4. Ibid.

Meetings with Yeats*

HUGH KINGSMILL

A few months before the war, walking through Cork one morning, I saw a poster with these words on it: 'Hitler mentions Eire twice.' I had just been thinking of the effect England must have had on the Irish consciousness from Henry II down to Lloyd George, a brutal, powerful land just beyond the horizon always about to disgorge ships and troops upon its weak, poor neighbour. The poster showed me the other side of the Irish situation, how galling it was to Ireland to be ignored when it was not being laid waste, and what pleasure the nearest modern equivalent to Cromwell could give by casting a casual glance in the direction of Drogheda.

This Cork poster came back to me a few days ago when I was reading the letters exchanged between Yeats and Lady Gerald Wellesley.[1] Anglo-Irish writers have always drawn even more attention to themselves than to their books. With Swift one thinks first not of *Gulliver's Travels* but of the tortured soul no longer lacerated by savage indignation, and so with the others, Goldsmith the wise zany, Sheridan witty even in the gutter, Wilde witty even in the dock, Shaw on a tub in Hyde Park, George Moore and shaded lamps, Yeats and Celtic Twilight. With Yeats, however, this urge towards self-dramatisation was more embarrassed than with the others, both because he was more of a poet and because he had a less clear idea of the self he wished to dramatise. His effect on those who met him began by being mysterious but ended by being only mystifying.

The first time I met him was in the autumn of 1912, when I was supposed to be helping Frank Harris to edit a ladies' paper called *Hearth and Home*. As Harris took no interest in anything but the salary he drew and the expenses he managed to extract from his unfortunate fellow-directors, I was free to write what I liked, and hearing that Yeats was living behind St. Pancras Church, hardly a hundred yards from where I was, it seemed to me that I could fill a page of *Hearth and Home* with very little trouble if Yeats would give me an interview. At this time he was in his later forties, and apart from his convenient situation I was anxious to see one of the most famous writers of the day. Getting no reply to my letter, I went round one morning after breakfast, rang the bell and waited in some nervousness for the door to open. The house was one of a row in a thoroughfare for pedestrians but not for traffic, an isthmus connecting two streets, a faded unpushful backwater

* *New Statesman and Nation* (London) (4 Jan 1941) pp. 10–11.

with two or three small shops, and perhaps a shoemaker who subsisted on resoling shoes and a tailor who did not aspire beyond turning old suits. Presently the door opened, and there unmistakably was Yeats, in a dressing gown, a narrow dark passage behind him. Some moments having passed, during which I had a feeling as if his body were being slowly reanimated by its soul, returned for that purpose from some far region, Tibet perhaps, I explained who I was. Yeats, pushing his straggling hair back from his forehead, murmured: 'Yes, yes, I remember. . . . Will you come upstairs?'

Seating himself in an upright armchair between the fire and a table on which a large volume rested, he said, in answer to a question put by me from the far side of the table: 'I do not read my contemporaries. I cannot see their faults, for I share them, and so I read only in men who have been dead two or three hundred years. In them I am able to distinguish what is of permanent value from what is trivial, what is temporal.' He opened the volume on the table. 'This morning I have been reading in Donne, though indeed Donne has no faults.' He smiled in a wan, abstracted way, as though the faultlessness of Donne were a mystery he had lost all hope of communicating with others. A little later, having mentioned Baudelaire, he paused to spell the name. I told him I knew it, and he explained that a journalist in New York had made him speak of 'Bandolier'. Taking advantage of a slight relaxation in his attitude, I asked if he thought Oscar Wilde a snob, a crudely framed question, but I had just been reading Harris's *Life of Wilde*, a work devoid of nuances. 'Wilde was not a snob,' Yeats answered. 'He was an Irishman; and England to an Irishman is a far strange land. To Wilde the aristocrats of England were as the nobles of Baghdad.' Frank Harris, I said, held that it was a nervous collapse not courage which prevented Wilde from fleeing the country before his trial. Did he agree with that view? 'Wilde', Yeats replied, 'was an Irish gentleman. It was with him a point of honour to face the trial. It could not have occurred to him to act otherwise.'

My next meeting with Yeats was in the summer of 1924, at Maloja, in the Engadine.[2] He was sitting outside the Palace Hotel with Lennox Robinson whose lively friendliness was in strong contrast with Yeats's gloom. Introducing myself, I mentioned the interview of twelve years earlier, and he said he remembered it, and that it was the best interview he had had, his sombre expression leaving me to infer what the other interviews were like.

He was spending two or three days at Maloja as the guest of my father, the head of a tourist firm, and Yeats's part in the arrangement was to deliver a lecture to the visitors at the Palace Hotel. Shortly before his lecture the headmistress of a fashionable girls' school came up to me and said: 'I saw you this morning sitting on a sofa with Mr. Lennox Robinson. You were talking with him for half an hour. Didn't you feel proud?' This amiable lady was not below the general level of Yeats's audience, which, when Yeats recited 'Innisfree' with an air of suppressed loathing, beamed ardently at him, as though ready at a word to fall in behind him and surge towards the bee-loud glade.

Yeats had changed a good deal since 1912. He was stouter, and carefully as well as picturesquely dressed. An aristocrat had been superimposed on the poet, and his small black eyes, hard as marbles, looked out upon the world with a mixture of contempt and mistrust. One evening when I was sitting with him and Lennox Robinson we were joined by H. A. L. Fisher,[3] whose very proper eagerness to hear what Yeats thought of various famous writers brought out no responsive geniality in Yeats, his tired disdainful air quickening only at the name of Balzac, whose romanticisation of any and every form of power seemed to move him deeply. 'All Nietzsche is in Balzac,' he intoned, and on my expressing some surprise at this opinion, in view of Nietzsche's contempt for Balzac as a vulgarian obsessed with money, Yeats gave me an angry look and withdrew into himself for a minute or two. Mr. Fisher, who was my tutor at Oxford, where I failed in my Finals, clearly being no more anxious than Yeats to hear further from me, I did not intervene again.

On another occasion a story I told brought out a certain humour which I had not suspected Yeats of possessing. 'That is bizarre,' he said. 'I like what is bizarre in life. A short while ago I was asked by John Harris to give a lecture in Cambridge. The father of John Harris is a surgeon in Harley Street, and when I went into a barber's shop the barber was speaking of the father of John Harris, who, he said, was in reality the only surgeon in London, the others being merely his agents. A patient, the barber said, would call upon one of these men, who would be reputed to be skilful in some branches of surgery, and an operation would be arranged. But when that patient was under chloroform, the father of John Harris would come up through a trap door, perform the operation, and vanish before the patient was again conscious.' Yeats laughed, there was a cunning gleam in his eye, and he looked very Irish.

Lady Gerald Wellesley compares Yeats with Coleridge. Each was a teacher as well as a poet, and neither achieved anything approaching what was expected of him. But whereas the genius of Coleridge is like a sunken treasure ship, and Coleridge a diver too timid and lazy to bring its riches to the surface, the genius of Yeats is like a rare plant, and Yeats a skilful, pertinacious gardener wrestling vainly with the weeds and sterile soil of Protestant Ireland.

NOTES

Hugh Kingsmill (1889–1949) was a British novelist and biographer, whose works include *The Return of William Shakespeare* (1929), *Samuel Johnson* (1933) and *D. H. Lawrence* (1938).

1. *Letters from W. B. Yeats to Dorothy Wellesley*, ed. D. Wellesley (London: Oxford University Press, 1940). Dorothy Wellesley was Lady Gerald Wellesley, Duchess of Wellington.

2. Engadine is the name of the narrow valley of the Inn River in eastern Switzerland.

3. Herbert Albert Laurens Fisher (1865–1940), English historian.

W. B. Yeats*

JAMES STEPHENS

I've had quite a number of meetings with Yeats in Dublin, in Paris, in London, and in Kentucky. Of course, I had met him many times with other people, and of course, those kind-of meetings don't count anyway. In his latter years whenever he came to London he formed a habit of ringing me up and asking me to go and see him. I always took a ring from another poet as a kind of royal command. And I always remembered that telephoning was one of the many things which Yeats didn't do very well.

Apropos of that, I was with him once in Dublin, but of that visit I only remember my departure. Yeats was seeing me out. We were walking down the stairs, when up the stairs came a maid carrying in her arms Yeats' son,[1] then aged about three years. The huge-headed infant gazed very sternly at his father, and Yeats, thinking he ought to say something to his own baby, murmured a couple of lines from John Donne, in whom he was then greatly interested. He said to the baby:

> The Chapel wants an ear, Council a tongue;
> Story, a theme, and Music lacks a song:

The infant looked at him with no reverence, and roared in a titanic voice: 'Go away, Man!' Yeats and I went abashed away.

In the hall the telephone bell rang. Yeats answered it. He listened very carefully, and then he said, 'Yes, O yes, yes, yes,' and he hung up. As he let me out he said sadly, 'That was a message from the Government. I never,' he went on, 'can understand anything that the beastly machine says. I'll go round with you to the office and ask them what that message was about.'

I asked him did he always take a taxi to a house that rung him up to find out what it was all about, but he answered that he usually did nothing about it, he just hung up, and left the sequel to be dealt with by Fate, Time, Chance, and Circumstances.

So when he rung me up I felt for him and listened diligently, for I also find some trouble in understanding telephone language, which often says nothing except, 'Hello, are you there, don't ring off, hello, are you there. . . .'

---

* Extracted from 'W. B. Yeats (1942)', *James, Seumas & Jacques: Unpublished Writings of James Stephens*, chosen and ed. with an introduction by Lloyd Frankenberg (London: Macmillan, 1964) pp. 67–72.

On these occasions when I went to his hotel, or his club, we were always alone, and we always talked poetry. I should qualify that statement—Yeats' intention was that we should talk about his poetry, or, more closely still, that he would talk about his poetry, and that I should listen heartily, and interrupt as little as was possible.

But it never turned out that way, for I was as unstoppable a sayer of my own verse as he was of his, and quite unconsciously, the instant a man says a poem to me I say two quick ones back at him, and as I nearly always shut my eyes when I am saying a poem I never know whether my companion is asleep, or only yawning. No one, not even Yeats, can do anything to a man who has his eyes shut and is away in full flood upon no earthly sea.

Yeats and I, however, were very well-mannered with each other. There is always a point of distrust between two men who have any manners at all in private. Still, I'm inclined to believe that Yeats and I were the only poets with good manners that ever lived. When he had finished a poem I always asked him to say it again and when I had finished one he as scrupulously invited me to repeat *the last verse*.

Yeats was really only interested in his own poetry. He complained to me once that people kept writing to him about the work of new poets, pointing out that as he was 'interested in poetry' he must read, praise, and help the new-comers. But, he said, almost angrily, 'I'm not interested in poetry. I'm only interested in what I'm trying to do myself, and there aren't enough hours in days and nights for me to get through what I'm at. Besides,' he went on, 'out of any ten poets who are pushed on you by literary ladies, nine are no good, and the tenth isn't much good.'

One day—this was in Paris—I asked him what he did about books that were sent to him for signature. He became quite thoughtful about this, and then he became very happy. And then he told me this story:

He was dining once with Thomas Hardy, and as they were finishing their coffee he asked Hardy the very same question: 'What do you do, Hardy, about books that are sent to you for signature?'

'Yeats,' said Hardy, 'come with me, there is something upstairs I want to show you.' At the top of the house Hardy opened a door, and the two poets entered a larger room. This room was covered from the floor to the ceiling with books. Hardy waved his hand at the odd-thousand volumes that filled the room—'Yeats,' said he, 'these are the books that were sent to me for signature.'

About a year before his death I went to his hotel, and was shown up to his bedroom. The great poet was in bed, with a dressing-gown about him and a writing-pad on his knee. We talked for a little, and then he said thoughtfully: 'All my life I've been bothered as to how writers get on with their work in winter. If,' he went on, 'if you sit at a table you get stiff hands and frozen feet, and then the stuff you write can only be warmed by sticking it into the fire.'

I agreed that, barring being boiled alive, being frozen to death was the worst torment of a literary life. 'But,' said Yeats triumphantly, 'I've found out how to conquer cold feet. My feet are never cold now. Come over to the bed, Stephens,' he said, 'and I'll show you.'

He threw the coverlets off. He was fully dressed under the bed-clothes, and had a dressing-gown on over his ordinary clothes. But it was his legs that delighted me. 'There,' he said, 'you can't get cold feet if you wear these.' He had on a pair of huge rubber fisherman's boots that reached to his thighs. 'Inside these,' said he cunningly, 'I have on a pair of woolly slippers, and I'm as warm as toast.'

He was anxious to know how I worked. I told him that I didn't work much at verse. Almost any of my books have been written in about a month: the verse comes in a rush, three or four pieces a day, and when it's finished I don't write any more for perhaps a couple of years, and I don't even try to, because I don't want to.

Yeats was astonished at this, especially at the not wanting to. 'I,' he said, 'work at it all day and every day. I hunt poems the way a hound hunts rabbits. I prowl about poetry the way a hungry wolf prowls about a hen-run. . . . What is your best poem?' said he.

'I don't know,' I replied, 'I've a different best one every few days. . . . At the moment,' I went on, 'I'm in love with two of yours: "Byzantium" and a little scrap that you seem to have written at a teashop table.'

'I love that table-top poem myself,' he said, 'but I don't think it has the strangeness, the syntax, that makes a great poem.' I chided him there—''Tis the highest movement you ever reached in your life, or that any man has reached in a century!' And thereupon I said ten lines of his own poem, 'Vacillation,' to him.

NOTE

James Stephens (1882–1950), Irish poet and novelist. When he received the Polignac award for imaginative literature in 1913, Yeats went to London to make a speech on his compatriot's work at the Academic Committee.

1. Michael Butler (now Senator) Yeats (1921–   ).

W. B. Yeats*

MICHÉAL MACLIAMMÓIR

Many of Tessie's[1] prophecies came true, and we were playing Paul Raynal's tragedy, the *Unknown Warrior*, when Yeats saw us for the first time, and I knew that it was because he was there that I gave the only

* *All for Hecuba; An Irish Theatrical History* (London: Methuen, 1946) pp. 72–5.

performance that came within miles of what I had dreamed. The Peacock[2] is so small that I could see him plainly as he sat there by Lady Gregory's side and knew that his attention was held. We three, Coralie,[3] Hilton,[4] and I, were the only characters in the play and, comparing notes between the acts, we decided that there is no such stimulus in the world for the actor as to know that there is in the audience some one whose mere presence calls forth the best that he can give. I think we all acted better that night than we had ever done before, and we tumbled into our dressing-rooms when all was over in an ecstasy of exhaustion.

The next day an invitation arrived for me from Lady Gregory to lunch with her at her hotel and meet the poet. I was a little late from a prolonged rehearsal, and when I was shown into the familiar room, he rose to his feet, tall and slow and stately, as grey as time, as vague and as vivid as a dream, and advancing with a curiously hesitating step, his right hand raised as if in benediction, he said, 'You told Lady Gregory you had wanted to meet me for fourteen years: you are exactly fourteen minutes late.'

I said it had seemed like forty, to which I naturally expected he would ask, 'years or minutes?', to which in turn I would have said, like Lady Bracknell,[5] 'Both, if necessary, I presume', but he wouldn't play up so early in the day and, sinking into his chair, he murmured:

'*You are a magnificent actor.*'

For this I was genuinely and totally unprepared, and felt uncomfortably on the verge of tears, but there was nothing to do but simper. This was all very bad, and I became suddenly shy, shyer than I had felt since my first rehearsal on the stage of His Majesty's when I was ten.[6] I murmured something quite unintelligible to myself but which I felt horribly would be not only understood by him but ignominiously seen through, and took refuge in Lady Gregory, who had the air of watching a sacred snake to whom she was high priestess, and a mouse in whom she had placed a certain gentle faith.

This, then, I thought was Yeats, not alone the poet I had dreamed of all my days, not alone the seer, the visionary, the father of a whole nation's reawakening, but a most formidable man as well, an acrobat whose range was limitless, who threw you neatly to the ground before you were well within reach, and who, as you lay shocked and stunned, stood over you and paid you dazzling compliments; and remembering certain plays of his, I thought, 'It's more than the Noh drama you've learned from Japan.' The next move came then, and it was as unexpected as the last, for after a little dreaming into his waistcoat—he was in purest grey from top to toe—he looked up with that rare and lovely sidling dark smile of his and almost shouted, 'How do you do?'

So I was helped to my feet again, and the comedy would recommence. And although I knew it was incorrect to answer this strangely inquisitive English form of salutation, which for no reason is put as a question, I said I was very well, thank you, and how was he? He reassured me about his health, and then said something really kind and amusing about rehearsals being beyond time as Portia was beyond reproach; and presently we all sat down to lunch, and it was beautiful to see how meekly he took Lady Gregory's advice as to what he should eat, choosing roast mutton rather than curry, as the lesser, he observed, of two evils. He compared Raynal's tragedy to Racine and Corneille and suddenly, as though a flame had fallen upon his mind by some mention I had made of Verlaine, he began to tell stories, not of Sligo as I had half-hoped he would, but of the London of his early years, of Wilde and Dowson, of Aubrey Beardsley and Lionel Johnson, and two hours rolled away in a sort of fabulous enchantment.

The people who dismiss him as a man by saying that outside his work he was a poseur whose rudeness and arrogance were unbearable, are those who cannot have known him. Of course he could pose, of course he could be both rude and arrogant. He could indeed be anything he chose, and the ability to assume all these qualities at will is a bare necessity of life for him who would spend his time in Dublin, whose passionate and almost quixotic worship of mediocrity is coupled with an instinctive mistrust of the first rate, a permanent sense of discomfort in its presence, and a malicious determination to drown it in a storm of envy and belittlement.

> *What have I earned for all that work, I said.*
> *The daily spite of this unmannerly town. . . .*[7]

Not that Yeats showed bitterness for the city for which he had laboured with such titanic energy. He had never turned his back on those wavering points of fire he tried so valiantly to blow to flame, though he no more than Shaw could have been 'enamoured of failure, of poverty, of obscurity, and of the ostracism and contempt which these imply.' Yeats held on to the end, and who shall blame a delicate man, labouring through the hateful storm, if he wraps a cloak about his head?

No, his pose, if he did pose, was to me a wholly delightful and half-humorous one that concerned itself chiefly with a strange and erratic timing of effects. His tempo in conversation was as skilful and as full of variety as a fine actor's and had about it something of bewilderment and of bizarre surprise. 'The popular theatre', he said unexpectedly that day, breaking abruptly from a description of Beardsley and booming out his words as though he were speaking from a great distance, 'had corrupted the audience of my youth', and a sudden stillness fell as he crumbled his bread while I waited for an utterance and Lady Gregory passed me the butter. But the slow smile, as George Moore had said, 'trickled back into his countenance' and he began a superb story of a man who sat in the gallery at the first London performance of the *Doll's House*. The man had not enjoyed his Ibsen at all, and after the slamming of the door when Helmer cries 'She has gone!', he had called out 'Yus, and so' as my bloody shilling!'

He asked me for stories about Tree[8] and about the legends of ghosts in

Galway, where I was still spending much of my time, and I begged him to tell me of Fiona Macleod, 'that miraculous liar', and of Florence Farr and the Avenue Theatre; and when I got up to go he invited me to his house, and his manner as he stood by Lady Gregory's side, making a sort of Rodin[9] group in the silver afternoon light, was friendly and simple.

NOTES

Micheál MacLiammóir (1899–   ) is an Irish actor, director and dramatist noted for his work both in English and Gaelic. In 1928 he became Director of the Galway Theatre (Taibhudhearc na Gaillimhe) and, with Hilton Edwards, founded the Dublin Gate Theatre. Both theatres often played his dramas, the best known of which are *Diarmuid and Grainne*, given both in English and Gaelic, *Ill Met by Moonlight* and *Where Stars Walk*. He has also written *Theatre in Ireland* (1950). His writings on Yeats include 'Problem Plays', *The Irish Theatre*, ed. Lennox Robinson (London: Macmillan, 1939); 'Yeats, Lady Gregory, and Denis Johnston', *Bell* (Dublin) IV (Apr 1943), 33–6; and, with Eavan Boland, *W. B. Yeats and His World* (1971).

1. Mrs Tessie Martin, who superintended the cleaning of the Abbey Theatre and was a close friend to Lady Gregory.
2. Micheál MacLiammóir and Hilton Edwards were first playing at the Peacock Theatre, attached to the Abbey Theatre, before they moved to their permanent building in 1929. See Micheál MacLiammóir, 'Peacock Theatre', *All for Hecuba* (London: Methuen, 1946) pp. 67–8.
3. Coralie Carey, the actress.
4. Hilton Edwards, the actor and co-founder of the Dublin Gate Theatre.
5. In Oscar Wilde's *The Importance of Being Earnest*.
6. Micheál MacLiammóir made his debut in 1910 as Alfred Willmore in *The Goldfish*.
7. W. B. Yeats, 'The People', *The Wild Swans at Coole* (1919).
8. Herbert Beerbohm Tree (1853–1917), English actor –manager and half-brother of Max Beerbohm.
9. François Auguste René Rodin (1840–1917), French sculptor.

The Yeats I Knew *

MARY M. COLUM

As he walked along the street or appeared in the Abbey Theater or at any one of the innumerable literary and dramatic societies, he stood out from the indifferently dressed men around him as carefully garbed, with a studied bohemian elegance, an elegance influenced, no doubt, by the aesthetics of the nineties and by Oscar Wilde.[1] Sometimes he would be in dead black, with a flowing tie, sometimes in a strange shade of brown; in

* Extracted from *Life and the Dream: Memories of a Literary Life in Europe and America* (London: Macmillan; New York: Doubleday, 1947; Dublin: Dolmen Press, 1964) pp. 127–45.

the evenings he wore a black or brown velvet jacket. This dressing set off his personality, as did his rhythmic speech and his gestures. I suppose there was a great deal that was studied about his appearance in those days, and the charge of posing that was often leveled at him had a certain foundation—that is, if one had not enough insight to take the whole personality into consideration. A good deal of his posing was due to the fact that he really was not very much at home with ordinary people, did not know much about life as lived by the rest of us and had not a great variety of friends. Then, human energy and human interest even in the most powerful personalities are limited, and unless people can put on some mask, the outstanding ones can be drained of energy by the demands upon them of people and of the world. Yeats, then, played the role of the artist, the man who devoted his life to the practice of art and the furthering of art. It was often said of him in Dublin that Lady Gregory's influence had made him snobbish; I really do not think he needed any external influence to make him snobbish; at this period he was afflicted with a variety of snobbishnesses that were a sight to behold and an experience to encounter. First of all, his genius, the nature of his intellectual interests, placed him to some extent apart from the bulk of humanity; then, in addition to the common Irish notion of high descent, he had, like Villiers de l'Isle-Adam, the ideas of the romantic poets of a noble and chivalrous ancestry, an ancestry devoted to high causes. If he had had his choice he would have liked to be at the court of a Renaissance prince or duchess, or even with Goethe's Duke in Weimar.[2] Added to this romantic snobbery, he had a curious bourgeois snobbery mocked at by George Moore, and it was very hard for Yeats to mock back at Moore. Yeats might be able, as he certainly was at times, to adopt the grand air of a Renaissance prince, but he often failed in ordinary good manners, and he certainly was no match for the easy courtesy of an estated gentleman like George Moore or the considerate Lord Chesterfield manners of James Joyce. Yeats often gave an odd impression of being not only ill-mannered but insensitive; James Stephens once told me that he had cultivated this mask of insensitivity as a protection against the world and against the slings and arrows that were so often launched against him.

II

Nevertheless, there was an unaccountably coarse streak in him such as I have never encountered in any other outstanding artist. But he seemed to have none of the vanity that so many writers have, and, absorbed and absent-minded as he was, he gave no impression of self-centeredness. His enthusiasms were for causes—the cause of art, the cause of Irish nationality, the cause of love and friendship. His very snobbery was in the cause of the superior human being devoted to the higher disciplines and to beauty. He made a cult of discipline which in later life made him take a romantic view of the fascist movements in Europe. Yet in a strange way he did not equate discipline and self-control. 'Art gives everything', I have heard him say, 'to self-surrender, never anything to self-control.' It was his devotion to art, to his country, that made him work so hard in Dublin to make people understand poetry and literature. He worked so hard that I think much of his mysterious illness in later years which the doctors diagnosed by such queer names was due to the fact that these labors of his in his prime had so exhausted him. I have seen him put such immense emotional and intellectual energy into a talk to an audience of about twenty or thirty, some of them inimical, as would have projected a major scene in one of his verse dramas, and neither for this nor for his work in the theater did he get any financial return; he did not even at the time get much of any other sort of return, either—little gratitude, and that only from a few. In one of his poems to the beautiful, stormy woman who inspired so much of his love poetry, he wrote:

> My darling cannot understand
> What I have done or what would do
> In this blind, bitter land. [3]

And yet a great poet of his type, an intellectual and artistic reformer, would certainly have found more opposition in a larger country where the practical man of affairs dominated; for him an industrial country might also have been a 'blind, bitter land'. But he never wavered; no matter how strong the opposition he encountered he went steadily toward the goal he had visualized, the creation of a national theater and a national literature. 'The dogs bark,' says an Arab proverb, 'but the caravan goes on.' There was plenty of barking and snarling in Dublin, but day by day the caravan went on.

In his own esoteric way he took note of our student exchequer. I was deputed by the little college society of which I was president to approach the Abbey box office and explain that the cheapest ticket, one shilling, was a little above our student budget, as we went not only to each play but to every performance of it, which meant every night for a week. The Abbey secretary, Fred Ryan, a young man whose life was also devoted to causes, interviewed me with some perplexity.

'I don't think our license permits us to change the price,' he said. 'You will have to see the head director, Mr. Yeats. He is now at rehearsal. I will find out if you can see him.'

He came back in a minute from his investigation. 'Mr. Yeats will see you in about ten minutes.'

I waited in the foyer of the Abbey Theater in an ecstasy of nervous fright and delight. In a little while W.B. came out from rehearsal, exhausted and remote from the world, his lips still murmuring lines. Fred Ryan held a low colloquy with him and then presented me.

'This is the president of the Twilight Literary Society. The society is asking for reduction in the price of tickets.'

W.B.'s eyes were dimmed. His gaze went beyond me. But he woke up.

'I remember,' he said. 'You wrote the box office a letter about this, didn't you?'

This was matter for surprise: it had never struck me he would read the letter himself.

'Would eightpence be all right?' I interjected nervously.

'Eightpence!' he repeated dreamily, raising his arm in the familiar gesture. 'Eightpence!' he repeated. He nodded to Fred Ryan and walked out the door. Ryan and myself were left a little uncertain of the result. 'I think it's all right,' he said in a soothing voice. 'Mr. Yeats wants you in the audience. We will give you twelve tickets for eight shillings.' The society, I should mention, numbered twelve.

NOTES

For a note on Mary M. Colum see p. 246.

1. It is largely due to Gilbert and Sullivan's *Patience* that many people believe Wilde to have been the founder, or at any rate the chief exponent, of what is known as the Aesthetic Movement. The aesthetes were not a group of men banded together to pursue a common object, which is the natal meaning of the word 'movement'. There was a number of people who, each in his own way, had brought about a certain result. The so-called Movement was in the air, never in committee. The poet, the painter, the architect, the sculptor, the dress designer, the house decorator, the furniture maker, the printer: these had reacted against the stereotyped art and craft of the period, and their general tendency was called aesthetic; the work of each being in some way related to the rest, though the relationship was never clearly defined and few of the artists would have claimed kinship with others working along the same lines. Such divers characters as Ruskin, Morris, Pater, Swinburne, Whistler, Woolner, Rossetti, Burne-Jones, Henry Irving and even those satirists of the 'Movement' Gilbert and Sullivan, were part of the tendency; but it may be doubted if any of them would have cared to be called aesthetes, and the last two would have rejected the appellation with scorn.

2. In 1775, at the invitation of Charles Augustus, heir apparent to the Duchy of Saxe-Weimar, Goethe settled in Weimar, then the literary and intellectual centre of Germany.

3. W. B. Yeats, 'Words', *The Green Helmet and Other Poems* (1910).

Reminiscences of Yeats*

OLIVER ST JOHN GOGARTY

In a room in the old-fashioned Nassau Hotel, which looked northward into College Park, Dublin, a group of authors and actors had banded together in the early 1900's to read new plays and to settle by vote which plays

* *Mourning Became Mrs. Spendlove and Other Portraits, Grave and Gay* (New York: Creative Age Press, 1948) pp. 211–24.

should be produced, and where and when. The idea of thus introducing democracy into art was George Russell's. Though it gave the actors, who were all amateurs, an opportunity to meet the playwrights, it also provided the stimulus for arguments that lasted, in some instances, for months. For their productions the group hired cheap halls, such as St. Theresa's Hall in Clarendon Street and a kind of clubhouse in Camden Street, and between rehearsals they held lectures on art and on the drama. So began the literary movement that was later to become the world-famous Abbey Theatre and the Irish National Theatre.

Yeats, Russell (AE), Colum, Synge, Lady Gregory, perhaps Maude Gonne (I say 'perhaps' for there was little love lost between the ladies), and the two brothers Fay, Frank and William, were present on one of the rare occasions when I attended a meeting of the Literary Theatre, as the group then called itself. Synge's *Riders to the Sea* had just been read, and was received with grave silence. At last Yeats exclaimed, 'Aeschylus!' and inclined his head. Everyone agreed, including the man beside me, who asked in an awe-struck whisper, 'Who is Aeschylus?' Ever ready to impart information, even when the readiness outruns accuracy, I replied, 'A man who is like Synge.'

This is my earliest recollection of meeting Yeats. I often try to remember who it was who introduced us. The probability is that it was the democracy of the occasion that brought us together. No one formally introduced us. We just met.

I had first heard of Yeats from J. E. Healy, an editor of the *Evening Mail*, a somewhat conservative Dublin paper. Healy was a scholar of Trinity College, and his admiration for Yeats's prose impressed me very much. I began to suspect that I was missing something by my devotion to out-door sports. As a matter of fact, I was missing the beginning of what turned out to be the Irish Renaissance. I was missing the poetry of the period and the most important poet of his time. When I at last met Yeats, who looked every inch (and there were seventy-three inches of him) a poet, I wondered why Healy had referred to his prose.

In those days of 1902, Yeats looked exactly like the charcoal drawing John Sargent had made of him. The sketch shows a gaunt, upright young man, with a shock of dark hair falling over the left brow. Sargent had caught a gesture of Yeats's body-making itself. The jaw is clear-cut and firm. The mouth is beautifully modelled. The nose is aquiline, with great breadth between the eyes, one of which—the right—is noticeably lower than the other. Around his long throat is a soft collar and flowing silk tie. Since the drawing is in black and white, it conveys no idea of the complexion of the poet. His cheeks were russet brown, his cheek-bones touched with color. His mouth was remarkable for the translucent lips that were soft and red like the berry of the yew. He had a charming voice with mellow tones that quickened with his thoughts. He was tall and dark and looked mysterious in a mitigated light. There was about him a strange aloofness—a remoteness—and he had a way of withdrawing into himself, the effect of which was as though someone had suddenly turned off a light. His aloofness, however, was probably prompted by shyness, which he threw off only when aroused.

The writers and actors who unknowingly were infusing a soul into Ireland dedicated their time—in some instances, all their time—and their energy to the work of an Irish National Theatre. They were earnest, intense, and devoted men, following the artistic leadership of Yeats and Lady Gregory, who, incidentally, demanded servility of all her acquaintances. Neither Joyce nor I had pliant knees, and so we kept each other company.

It was Lady Gregory who decided that Yeats's friends were to present him on his fortieth birthday with a copy of the rare Kelmscott Chaucer, which had been printed at Kelmscott by that fount of energy, William Morris, a friend of both Yeats and his father. At the time, I had not seen Yeats for three years—through no neglect of mine, but due rather to his residing in London. I used to see him when he stayed at the Cavendish Hotel, which was within half a dozen doors of my home in Rutland Square. I recall that Joyce and I were passing the place in a tram one evening, and I pointed it out to him, mentioning the Chaucer birthday presentation. Without a word, Joyce left the tram. In those days you were not obliged to wait at a tram or bus stop. I saw him hurry to the hotel and disappear inside. Afterwards, Joyce told me that Yeats himself had opened the door of his apartment, and that without prefacing his remark he had bluntly asked Yeats how old he was.

'What did he say?' I asked.

'He told me that he was forty.'

Silence. . . . You had to prod Joyce for information, for he rarely volunteered anything.

'And what did you say?' I persisted.

'I said, "I am sorry. You are too old for me to help. Good-by." '

Jealousy or resentment of the Lady Gregory 'outfit' may have prompted Joyce's behavior, although he was defying nearly everything at the time. It was strange, however, how Yeats could be impressed by such brazen rudeness. Perhaps audacity attracted him. In any event, he had an astonishing faculty for being able to disassociate a person from his actions. Yeats never allowed his critical judgment to be swayed by his personal likes or dislikes. For instance, many years after the birthday misadventure, Yeats told me that since he had read Joyce's *Ulysses*, every other kind of writing seemed insipid.

Joyce and I were walking down Sackville Street past Byrne's, the stationer's, when he told me of the foregoing incident. He announced it with an air of challenge, but I made no comment. Inwardly I was shocked. I have respect for gifted men, and I could not see how Joyce could help Yeats. Without warning, Joyce turned abruptly into the shop, which sold a few cheap books in addition to newspapers and stationery. As I glanced in the window my eye caught a little paper-bound book, *Lays of the Moy* by Gerald Griffin, a young namesake of the better-known poet. The little volume had caught Joyce's eye, too, for when asked why he had rushed into the shop, he answered with almost a sigh of relief, 'I was seeing if they were better poems than mine!' Perhaps jealousy was the explanation for Joyce's rudeness to Yeats. It was never directly manifested except on rare and trivial occasions such as this, but I suspect that it was there all the time.

Apart from the farcical situations which arose from time to time, it has always been my impression that Yeats's association with the occult retarded the acceptance of the dramatic movement in Ireland. His dabbling in astrology, magic, seances, mysticism, and the occult in general, however, was secondary to the devotion of his life—Poetry. In other words, Yeats dealt in mysticism merely to enrich the subconscious, from which all inspiration flows. With AE it was otherwise. Russell preferred philosophy to poetry, even though for him philosophy was largely theosophy. An acquaintance of mine, whose parents were Irish and Spanish, complained that all Irish poetry was 'anent'; that is, it referred to something other than it said. This was particularly true of AE's poetry. 'Anentness' made the populace suspicious, and especially so since they felt that the Abbey Theatre had little use for Roman Catholics. It remained for Yeats to overcome this unpopularity, but it took twenty years to make the grudging admit that his patriotism was pure, selfless, and ideal.

On the other hand, I have never looked lightly upon Yeats's tampering with the spirit world—not since the time he entered a room in my house in Ely Place, Dublin, stood in the doorway, and said, 'There is a presence here, I smell incense.' Yeats had had no way of knowing that my wife and I had just been talking about a friend—a priest—lately dead. Yeats used to say that to talk about a dead person is to bring their ghost about you. Since then I have never scoffed at ghosts.

Yeats loved to detect in simple people simple beliefs. He once told me of an incident that took place when he was traveling by train to Galway. Yeats had just been elected Senator of the Irish Free State. A countryman, finding a door in the corridor locked, turned to him and said as though all things were possible to a man in an exalted position, 'Will you open it, Senator?' There was a hint of amiable malice like that of a leprechaun in Yeats's appreciation of humorous adventures of this sort, and from them he derived an enjoyment out of proportion to their significance. For instance, Yeats once remarked to Lady Gregory, 'I hear that the Sister Superior of the school where Gogarty's daughter is said to her: "There are five bad men who are destroying Dublin: Russell, Yeats, Liam O'Flaherty, Lennox Robinson, and—" she stopped.' Evidently, the fifth man was Gogarty, and the idea amused Yeats no end.

Yeats hated hatred. This probably explains why one so word-compelling had few terms of invective or of scorn. His nature was too deep for hatred. His only retaliation against George Moore's attacks on him was to attempt to pillory Moore in the dialogue of some play. Moore had at one time likened Yeats to 'an umbrella forgotten at a picnic.' Yeats retorted that Moore looked like 'a face carved out of a turnip.'

On one occasion, however, repartee failed Yeats altogether. He had applied for permission to read in the great library of Trinity College. Every applicant must take an oath in Latin swearing not to damage books. Yeats must have applied to Mahaffy,[1] because it was Mahaffy who sent him a copy of the oath, with the quantities marked for pronunciation by Mahaffy himself, and the message, 'For I have a sensitive ear.' I offered to write a sardonic reply to Mahaffy, but Yeats would have none of it. For all I know, he took Mahaffy's insolence lying down.

And yet Yeats had wit enough to defend himself. On one of his three visits to the United States, which he grew to like the more he knew of the country and its people, he was reading his poetry to an audience in Pittsburgh when a woman who turned out to be a teacher of elocution challenged his method.

'Will you kindly tell me, Mr. Yeats, why you read your poetry in that manner?'

'I read my poetry as all the great poets from Homer down have read their poetry.'

But she was not satisfied.

'Will Mr. Yeats give me his authority for saying that Homer read his poetry in that manner?'

Unhesitatingly he answered, 'The only authority I can give is the authority a Scotchman gave when he claimed Shakespeare for his own country, "The ability of the man justifies the assumption." '

Yeats always regarded England as a foreign country though he resided there frequently and had many friends there. As an Irish poet, in him all the traditions and sentiments of Ireland met. He was impatient of England, a country so largely composed of bourgeois. To him the bourgeois mind was a 'middle-class' mind. His cry was for a return to the simple folk, to the heroic folk. When Yeats heard that in Russia Lenin had declared religion to be the 'opium of the masses,' Yeats remarked, 'In England H. G. Wells is the opium of the middle classes.'

Yeats was susceptible to beauty to the end of his days. Some shrewd journalist in San Francisco was the first to notice that interviews by male reporters only bored Yeats. From this he deduced Yeats's preference for female society. This is far too dogmatic. That Yeats admired American women for their *chic* and for their intelligence was undoubted. He had compared them to English women, to the disadvantage of the latter. And this remark, made somewhere in New York, was very badly received in London. But Yeats could take his place among men and was often the most forceful of them all when it came to dispute. J. M. Hone, in his life of Yeats (Macmillan, 1943), states, and is not out of place here:

He had the powerful lower lip which reveals the born orator and the born pugilist; a certain disdain, a certain pugnacity is necessary both to the pugilist and to the orator. In addressing large audiences he was sometimes uneasy at the start, and would then stride up and down the platform in a rather surprising manner before he attained his natural distinction of bearing, his gravity of utterance, and his rhythm. His voice was musical, touched with melancholy, the tones rising and falling in a continuous flow of sound. He lingered on certain words as if to avoid a hiatus, as it were, but the pauses when they occurred were timed and still full of sound, like the musical pauses in the execution of a master. This cadenced utterance was most characteristic. . . .

Being as he was the most rhythmical of verse-makers, naturally he loved the sound of words. I recall an incident which may seem to be somewhat facetious, but it is such a good illustration of what I mean, and it is so characteristic of Yeats that I may be forgiven for repeating it.

In his old age, he was accustomed to go abroad to sunnier climes to escape the Dublin winters (to say nothing of Dublin summers). One year, when he was wintering at Majorca, he was attended by a Spanish doctor who had written a letter to Yeats's Irish doctor. Wishing an interpretation in the words of a layman, Yeats showed me the letter. I read a quaint sentence to this effect:

'We have here an antique cardio-sclerotic of advanced years.' Not wishing to impart the gravity of such a message, I said that it was doctor's Greek to me, and that it would be all Greek to him. He insisted, however, and so I read rather slurringly, for the letter boded little health. 'Read it slowly and distinctly,' he ordered. There was no escape, and so I read it slowly and distinctly. He inclined his head. 'Read that again.' He followed the cadence with his finger. At last as the sound died away, he exclaimed, utterly ignoring the meaning:

'Do you know that I would rather be called "Cardio-Sclerotic" than "Lord of Lower Egypt"?'

How, it may be asked, can a poet have a musical ear and yet be, as Yeats was, completely tone deaf? Many tales are told of Yeats's tone deafness. In spite of his early experiments with a psaltry to wed words to music and of the co-operation of Dolmnetsch the musical instrument-maker and of the actress, Florence Farr, Yeats was bored by music, which he did not trouble to understand, and he was bored worse by the extenuation of words for the sake of the music. Compton Mackenzie, the Scotch novelist and patriot, told me that when he had attended a concert in Dublin with Yeats (it was on some official occasion, the Tailteann Games, I think), they had entered the box just as John McCormack was singing Yeats's 'Down by the Salley Gardens.' Mackenzie drew Yeats's attention to the song. Yeats listened for a moment and then when he had at last caught a word or two, remarked, 'Oh, the deadly audibility of the fellow.' And Lady Gregory records that when the pianist Rummell gave a recital at the Abbey auditorium for the actors, who for reasons of safety could not leave the theatre between matinee and evening, Yeats fell asleep during the playing of Beethoven's 'Moonlight Sonata,' and upon awakening said that he had dreamed that there was a storm going on.

In his middle age Yeats's health improved. He could swim with me in the half-frozen deep water of Dublin Bay at Sandycove. At this time, he affected to have a bad memory. Indeed, he added this to his fund of 'withdrawals' to avoid bores or to escape tedious conversation.

One day I had occasion to remark in his hearing that Aeschylus called Memory the 'Mother of the Muses.' From that day on Yeats never forgot a thing.

Yeats could be simple as a child and childlike when some new thought struck him. To those who did not understand him, or who were jealous of him, his unconscious attitudinizing appeared to be a deliberate pose. Sir William Watson was one who made this great mistake. Here is what he wrote, and I know he meant Yeats, for I knew Watson well:

> I met a poet lately, one of those
> To whom his life was one continual pose.
> A wise man this, for, take the pose away,
> What else were left 'twould pose the gods to say.

I never told Yeats of Watson's lines. Perhaps if I had, he would have given us an epigram such as the one he gave AE when AE asked him to praise a poet whom Yeats regarded as an imitator:

> You say, as I have often given tongue
> In praise of what another's said or sung,
> 'Twere politic to do the like by these;
> But was there ever dog that praised his fleas? [2]

I have written so much about Yeats's foibles that it is time I tried to describe him in the vein that has made him the chief poet of our time.

Yeats composed with what appeared to be great mental agony. With his hands behind his back, his head down, or suddenly looking up, he would pace the floor, humming and murmuring to himself until the poem arose from the rich darkness within him. I observed him at work at my house when he was composing 'What Finger First Began,' one of the songs in a late play of his. It was suggested by a Chinese legend that those who hear aerial music are listening to the music of a lost kingdom.

It took him several minutes of humming to get the second line.

> What finger first began
> Music of a lost Kingdom? [3]

As the rhythm-wedded words came, he wrote them in pencil on odd pieces of paper. I found many such pieces of paper in my study when he had finished his poem.

When Yeats read poetry, it mattered not whose it was, he always got the pitch of the verse, as it were, by murmuring to himself with an intensity of interest that he always exhibited for poetry. He was most generous, always interested in other people's work, and did not appear to realize what a favor he was conferring by altering or correcting entire lines. When I wrote *A Serious Thing*, during the Black and Tan atrocities, for the Abbey Theatre, Yeats told me that if I left out the psychoanalysis of Pilate's wife who 'had a dream,' it would be one of the most powerful political plays ever written, for I had compared the resurrection of Lazarus in answer to a divine call to the *risorgimento*[4] of Ireland. The Black and Tans in the audience were too stupid to see the irony—they applauded the piece. I could not leave out the analysis of Pilate's wife, however, because I believed that this new sophistry would wreak havoc upon untrained minds, and I wanted to kill it by ridicule in its cradle. I did not succeed, and spoiled instead what could have been pruned into a good play had I listened to the Master.

When he was reading my book of verse before recommending it to his sisters' press, the Cuala, Yeats would offer suggestions that I invariably accepted gratefully. 'Intensity' of phrase was one of his aims, the pouncing and surprising word. I have a list somewhere of the alterations that Yeats made in pencil and which I adopted in my book. It is not of sufficient interest to recall them now, but I remember that almost an entire stanza of 'Palinode' was written by Yeats. He was generous in all things but in this especially.

There are few things in this life which give as much satisfaction as the friendship of good and famous men. To have known someone as strange as Yeats is, like Poetry, 'its own exceeding great reward.' There was an aura about the man that was almost palpable. You could feel his presence in the dark even if you had not met him for a year. It was as though he had more spirit than his body could contain, and it stood about him like the aura round the moon. There was inspiration in his presence. From Augustus John's lips I borrow a sentence that he applied to Lady Gregory's nephew. It is more appropriate to Yeats, 'He was one of those rare ones who, single-handed, is able to enrich and dignify an entire nation.' I would add, 'And to redeem it.'

NOTES

For a note on Oliver St John Gogarty see p. 256.
1. John Pentland Mahaffy (1839–1919) Provost of Trinity College Dublin.
2. W. B. Yeats, 'To a Poet, Who Would Have Me Praise Certain Bad Poets, Imitators of His and Mine', *The Green Helmet and Other Poems* (1910).
3. W. B. Yeats, 'At the Grey Round of the Hill'.
4. A resurgence of (nationalistic) feeling.

Yeats, as I Knew Him*

EDMUND DULAC

Many people who otherwise admire him as a poet look upon him as a dreamer, playing with Occultism and symbols in order to impress his public, and in some ways as a poseur, even as a bit of a snob. He was, in fact, none of these things.

When I first met him round about 1912 he naturally appeared to me as the Great Poet with all his characteristic mannerisms: the slow, deliberate gait, the hand raised in a gesture between a salute and an episcopal blessing, the intoning delivery that seemed to some people to be pure affectation. But I felt that with a man who could write as he did, who could talk as he did, who, in conversation, displayed such subtle culture and had otherwise such naturally gentle manners, all that could not be mere posturing, and the first superficial impression soon gave way to a feeling of sympathy which, by good fortune, I found to be mutual. We had in common many intellectual and aesthetic interests so that, presently, we became close friends, and our friendship, which grew more and more intimate as time went on, lasted till the end of his life, that is more than twenty-five years. And it is because, throughout those years, I had occasion to see him from many different angles that I feel I can give what I believe to be the true interpretation of his so-called pose and affectation.

This world being a stage, we all need, in order to act our part, a background and an audience, especially if we are artists, poets or public figures.

But there is a great difference between acting a part for the benefit of the gallery and *living it for the sake of one's soul.*

What I particularly want to emphasize is that *Yeats did not act a part for the benefit of the gallery.* It was more the gallery and the background that played a part, and an important one, in the whole of his make-up. They were the necessary condition of his intellectual and poetic life. He did not act to please a certain audience or to intrigue and impress by the use of symbols and other occult practices. He did not frequent aristocratic circles out of snobbery. His work, as well as his life, were characterized by a very marked sense of design. I don't know much about poetry but I don't think I am far wrong in saying that Yeats' poetry is, in the main, based on images and patterns. If he took an interest in occultism, in symbols and in astrology, if

* Extracted from *Irish writing* (Dublin) no. 8 (July 1949) 77–87.

he had a love of ritual, if he liked aristocratic culture, it was because he was always looking for a design into which he could fit the world, his life, his emotions and in consequence, his work.

As far as the aristocratic circles he frequented are concerned, they were, as I have said, also essential to his background. It was clearly not out of snobbery that he cultivated such connections. They had to fulfill very definite conditions of good manners, culture and behaviour, in fact they had to contribute to the ritualistic part of the picture, although he did not mind sometimes exaggerating their virtues to himself in order that they should fit better. If he had any snobbery in another sense, it was about the peasant—the Irish peasant especially—or the man of the people. In the ideal world that he was constantly trying to construct round him there would have been a Court entirely composed of clever, refined and brilliant people, where artists would have occupied a prominent position. The artists would have been in a sense initiates, following ancient traditions. They would have been helped in their work by the peasant or the man of the people, who would have been the craftsmen, the players or the musicians. He found however, in practice, that he could only realise a very thin substitute for a Court, but he never lost the hope of creating a body of craftsmen to weave beautiful fabrics or decorative tapestries, and of forming companies recruited from the farms and the shops of the village. And he succeeded in this to a great extent when he founded the Abbey Theatre. All his life he dreamt of musicians who could be trained to chant verse in some kind of primitive style. For he hated the ordinary professional singer with such passion that it led to the one and only quarrel—a brief one—we had in the course of our long friendship.

All this was the inevitable condition of the part he liked to play to himself in relation to a background that was as necessary to him as formulas, test-tubes and retorts are to a scientist. One cannot in any way call that a pose. A pose is something that is put on for the occasion. A poseur is an entirely artificial person. The true poseur either never drops his pose before his friends—for fear of being thought a humbug—or if he drops his pose the whole of what he is supposed to be disappears with it.

But with Yeats the whole of what he was, and the whole of what I have called his background, his interest in mysteries, his ideals, remained precisely the same whether he was among intimates or before one of his audiences. Before his public he was, as I suggested, acting the part of the poet at Court and went through the ritualistic gestures, intonations and pronouncements that were in keeping with the part. But this kind of ritualism was not necessary with his intimate friends. His friends were not part of his audience, they were with him behind the stage, associated, not only by a community of interests, but also by bonds of human sympathy.

And I may say that I seldom found sympathy so sincere, so real and so simply and kindly expressed. There were, naturally, many occasions when I had to ask him to spend an evening with people who were eager to meet him. Not only he never refused but he went out of his way to be entertaining without pontificating, and to make my friends feel quite at home with him, especially when the friends were people of no particular importance. It happened sometimes that I would arrange these meetings in order to dispel the impression that he was the self-absorbed, aloof person they thought he was. I only needed to hint at what I expected of him and he would make it a point to take a personal interest in the people concerned and to keep them amused with a series of his priceless anecdotes just as if he were himself an ordinary man. It also happened that some people were shy or too excited in the presence of the Great Man, and there were moments when things became not a little embarrassing. But Yeats was never embarrassed or annoyed and showed always, on such occasions, the most extraordinary patience. One night I had arranged for an American who wrote poetry of sorts and his wife to dine with Yeats at a favourite restaurant. The American was one of his passionate admirers and it had been the dream of his life to meet him. That man and his poetry could never have interested Yeats in the least. Nevertheless, he talked as he could talk when he was in good form, and as the dinner went on the American became more and more excited; at last he could hold out no longer; he put out his hands, half closed his eyes and very solemnly said: 'Now Mr. Yeats. Won't you give me a message from your heart?' Yeats was rather taken aback, and in the silence that followed, the American gentleman's wife, who had taken only a distant interest in the poet, was heard to remark to my wife: 'You see. The trouble with all that rich Continental food is that it makes one apt to suffer from congestion of the lower intestine.' 'What's that?' said Yeats. But he did not turn a hair, and went on talking. Whether what he said could be considered as the message expected I dont know, but when the dinner was over and we had said goodnight, Yeats turned to me and whispered: 'Was that all right? Did I do it well?' Some time after, he remarked in a letter, speaking of the dinner: 'That American saint or Yogi of yours sounded too friendly and beautiful . . .'

Another time the guest was a very dear man I was very fond of, who was intelligent, cultured and a good poet. But he was also abnormally shy, and in order to brace himself for the meeting with the Great Poet he had worshipped all his life, he had taken a little stimulant, and the cocktails served before dinner were unfortunately just too much for him. However, we sat down, and Yeats pretended not to notice that there was anything wrong. Before the coffee, thinking that poetry might have a beneficial effect on the condition of our friend, might so to speak, wake him out of his trance, I asked Yeats to recite the last poem he had written and had read to us a day or so before. It was 'The Curse of Cromwell.'[1] He did not have the lines with him, but said he would do his best to remember. So he started:
    'You ask what I have found and far and wide I go.
    Nothing but Cromwell's house and Cromwell's murderous crew.
    The——'

'Atchoo!' went our friend.

Yeats was cut short. 'I forget what comes next,' he said.

'Wait a moment.' He paused and then went on:

'The lovers and the dancers are beaten into the clay——'

'Atchoo!' went our friend.

The line was lost again. Yeats brushed his hair back once or twice. After another pause he found it:

'And there is an old beggar wandering in his pride——'

'Atchoo!' went our friend.

After the next sneeze Yeats had completely lost the hang of the poem. He shut his eyes for a moment and said: 'I'll start all over again,' and to the accompaniment of no less than seventeen sneezes, he managed to get through. Anyone else would have not only given up in despair, but been extremely offended. We are all, naturally, rather embarrassed, except our friend who was too far gone and could only mumble: 'Mr. Yeats. I have now realized one of my greatest desires,' and collapsed. Yeats patted him on the shoulder and smiled as if nothing had happened.

NOTE

For a note on Edmund Dulac see p. 291.

1. W. B. Yeats, 'The Curse of Cromwell', *Last Poems*.

W. B. Yeats*

W. R. RODGERS (*editor*)

FRANK O'CONNOR:[1] There was a peculiar sort of innocence about the man—an extraordinary innocence.

SEAN O'FAOLAIN:[2] I confess I never warmed to him because I felt there was an absence of *bonhomie*[3] and simplicity about his nature, at any rate as he presented it when one met him. Whether that was part of a pose or of a mask that he put on I don't know, but it kept one at a certain distance. I respect that. Certainly there was no reason why he shouldn't go masked if he wanted to, but you would sometimes wish that he'd drop it and say 'Hello', or talk in a natural way, as we talk among ourselves.

* Extracted from 'W. B. Yeats', first broadcast on BBC in June 1949. Reprinted in *Irish Literary Portraits; W. R. Rodgers's Broadcast Conversations with Those Who Knew Them* (London: British Broadcasting Corporation, 1972) pp. 1–21.

O'CONNOR: But I think he did. I never felt any of that difficulty that you seem to have felt with him at all. Yeats only posed when he was shy or embarrassed. I kept on telling people, 'Now for God's sake don't call him sir, because if you call him sir he'll start posing.'

W. K. MAGEE:[4] It would be very hard to say whether he was simple or not, but I don't think he was a poseur—certainly not consciously.

O'FAOLAIN: I remember once Edward Garnett[5] told me how, when he was very young and they were both poor (in the days when W.B. used to have to black his heels so as to cover up the holes in his stockings), they'd walk from his digs to Edward's digs and back again, and back again, all night long, absolutely forgetting everything in the most natural way. And once Edward invited him down for a week-end to his country cottage, and he arrived with nothing but a toothbrush and a bit of soap. Edward said he was absolutely innocent. That was quite evident, there was no pretence about it, although he had seen the same man in the box at—I forget what theatre—when a play of his was on, standing up as he used to do in the Abbey Theatre at the head of the stairs, looking around. On view. Clearly an actor.

AUSTIN CLARKE:[6] He'd also something else we couldn't copy, that was a marvellous black lock of hair; when he spoke and chanted and waved his arms, the lock of hair would fall over his brow, and with a gesture he would fling it back, and then it would fall down again. Well, we didn't know how he had trained it.

O'CONNOR: I remember when I was first in Dublin, going to a party and being very shy. Mrs Yeats signalled to me to come and sit beside her. She said, 'I knew you were shy, because you did exactly as Willie does when he's shy, you ran your hand through your hair.' And after that I just looked to see what he did with his hands and I saw that the man was frequently shy.

O'FAOLAIN: Let's try and get an example of this alleged pose which I say he had. Was it a habit or was it conscious? The way he had of not recognising people, who themselves felt that he must really know them perfectly well. A way of saying 'Hello Tierney' when it was really Binchy, or of saying when he meets Mary Colum in the street—she told me herself—intoning 'I hear a voice from across the seas. It is a girl's voice but I do not know whose it is'.

O'CONNOR: Yes, he would say that, if he knew the person concerned. When he went into a room it was always a toss-up whether he would behave as a shy man and go up to Tierney, as you say, and say 'Hello Binchy', trying to pretend that he knew him, or whether, as he more often did, with me at any rate, he would just hold out his hand and say, 'Who have I?' That was the admission that he was blind, which he didn't like to make normally.

DOSSY WRIGHT:[7] That is quite right because he has passed me time out of number in the street. If I didn't want to speak to him I didn't bother, but if I had to speak to him I went up to him, and he knew me at once, but otherwise his head would be in the air and he'd pass anyone. His thoughts were miles away.

BRINSLEY MACNAMARA:[8] I remember one such meeting with him myself. He brought me walking round Stephens Green. And as we went around he told me lots of things about plays, and he finished up by saying something which may have some bearing upon what we're trying to work out now about whether it was a pose or not with him. He said, 'A man, an author, should always try to keep the company of his superiors, never of his inferiors.'

O'CONNOR: A very wise remark. Very wise.

DR RICHARD BEST:[9] Well, he was always very dignified, and he wasn't without a sense of humour, but when he said something humorous, because he saw the humorous side of things, he bent his head and clasped his hands together as if he were washing them in invisible soap and laughed slightly, but always in a most dignified way. Yeats, so far as I can remember him, was always in full dress, as it were; he never let himself down. I used to think that, if he had been called upon to play the part of Pontifex Maximus, he would do it most naturally, without ever having to act. He was always like that. But to tell you the truth, I never felt quite at my ease with Yeats, as I did with George Moore, let us say, and other people, because Yeats was always on a plane, as it were, above me; he always lifted the conversation into a higher plane.

MACNAMARA: The only thing he never really got used to was the fact that poets and writers might be found sometimes in the public houses of the town, and he never ventured into one of them. There's a story that Yeats once approached Fred Higgins[10] and he said, 'Higgins, do you know I have never been in a pub in my life and I'd like to go into a pub.' So Higgins came to me and he asked me what was the most likely pub now to which we might bring Yeats without horrifying him too much by what he'd see there in the shape of literature and other things. And we decided on one pub, and Higgins went along with him there, and they called for some mild drink and Yeats looked around and he said, 'Higgins, I don't like it. Lead me out again.'

O'FAOLAIN: There's no trouble about meeting O'Casey or O'Flaherty in a pub, and talking to them and chatting as man to man, which you never could do with Yeats. It seemed to me he did put a barrier between himself and his fellow men by the technique that he employed.

O'CONNOR: You see, the real problem is that Sean [O'Faolain] is assuming all through that it's necessary and desirable that poets should sit in pubs and call one another, as we do, Sean etc. I don't think that's proved.

O'FAOLAIN: I don't think it's necessary, I think it occasionally happens—I personally very rarely go into pubs, but I'm capable of doing it on occasions, and I think if it *never* happens then a poet is liable to be thrown into an extraordinary kind of isolation, and may develop what I can only call a sort of fake Brahminism. And it seems to me that that poet's technique of protecting poetry may result in a fake Brahminism that must infect his own work.

O'CONNOR: Well, I maintain that infect is the wrong word, and that poetry *is* Brahminism—it's the soul of a man alone with himself.

O'FAOLAIN: That is a nineteenth-century romantic conception of poetry.

O'CONNOR: Very well, it *is* a romantic conception of poetry, but it is none the less a conception of poetry.

O'FAOLAIN: That takes Yeats back to William Morris, and Ernest Dowson, and Francis Thompson, and Pater, and Dobson, Lionel Johnson, and to Beardsley . . .

O'CONNOR: And to Dante?

O'FAOLAIN: To all that Yeats grew up with as a young man during fifteen of the most influential years of his life in London towards the end of the century, years during which he wrote some of his most mannered and artificial poetry. His great triumph was to shake off that influence. It took years and years.

MACNAMARA: But didn't the bulk of Yeats's poetry come out of that romantic conception of poetry, or out of the period when that was the conception of poetry that it maintains?

O'FAOLAIN: That's true, and I have no doubt that probably Yeats sitting at his desk and writing his poetry was, as it were, perfectly natural and innocent with himself so long as he didn't let that thing infect him. The outward signs were in his manner of dress: the cane, the lovely grey suit, the carefully chosen colours, the long hair, the flowing tie. All that theatrical pose must have come between him and his own natural self.

O'CONNOR: Bless my soul—that a man's taste in shirts stands between him and his own natural self—where is art getting to?

O'FAOLAIN: Down the drain of *fin-de-siècle* romanticism.

O'CONNOR: Well, the other thing is just getting down the drain of sloppy democratic feeling—I mean, you just be dirty because everybody else is dirty.

o'faolain: Oh come, come! There's no need to go to that extreme. T. S. Eliot wrote his poetry absolutely personally, absolutely originally, in a rolled umbrella and a bowler hat coming out of a bank.

o'connor: Well, don't you feel that *that* poetry had been infected, in your own word, by the umbrella?

o'faolain: No, I do *not*. I think it was necessary for Eliot to live like a Londoner in order that he should get down to the reality of his time, place and self.

clarke: Well, I think that it is a great pity that the poet, like the soldier, the clergyman and many others, hasn't some specific dress, or at least part of a dress to distinguish him, say, from the businessman. As a young poet I wore an enormous bow-tie—it was of shimmering gold and green—and I was very proud of it. The reason I wore that bow-tie was because in Dublin all the poets wore a bow-tie. Yeats, appearing frequently at the Abbey Theatre, had a magnificent black tie, which we could copy in other colours. But when I came to London for the first time I found that poets no longer wore any specific sign or symbol of their art. They were all dressed in hard stiff white collars, like businessmen. It was the time of the Georgian school, and I think it would have been better for the Georgian poets if they had worn flowing ties. It might have saved them from the terrible rush and pressure of the modern world. It might have protected their art. Look what happened to the Georgian school. I attribute that solely to the fact that they did not wear flowing ties, like the Irish poets!

o'faolain: Do you never get the feeling that Yeats is an old-fashioned poet belonging to an old-fashioned period?

macnamara: But yet he was able to go on and adapt himself to the new realistic time and the new conception of poetry. You consider Yeats's later work—it's altogether in contrast to the earlier, and to that romantic conception of poetry.

o'faolain: The gods were good to him. They let him live long into his maturity. But he is a nineteenth-century poet. Our last romantic.

macnamara: I think he was always pretty near to the realistic quality of his own country. Even when he was living in the days of pose, in the big tie and a velvet coat in London, he could write very realistically about the death of Parnell, and the effect it was going to have upon his country.

o'faolain: You mentioned the name of Parnell.[11] Probably Parnell and old John O'Leary[12] the Fenian were his two great heroes, men who, like himself, had gone down into the gutter. But you remember in his autobiography he says, 'You must *not* go down into the gutter if you want to have authority over people. You must keep yourselves from them.' He did live a remote and isolated life, and the result of it was that he *could* speak with the voice of authority. AE didn't, and he did not speak with the voice of authority. Nobody today has the same authority that he had.

o'connor: That was really what motivated his kind of Fascism; it wasn't Fascism, it was a worship of dictatorships, of authority.

mrs iseult stuart:[13] One day he presented me to an extremely vulgar lady with a title, whom I, being very young, snubbed, not out of snobbishness but out of extreme shyness. He was extremely indignant about that. He thought that to snub a person with a title—no matter how obtained—was a horrid thing and not at all correct. Nevertheless, although he had this love of titles, although he thought it was a great thing to be a senator, he did love real nobility.

o'connor: He used to jeer at my Socialism. 'Damned Utopianism,' he'd say.

lennox robinson:[14] Well, Frank, my impression of Yeats, of course, is about twenty years or more earlier than yours, when I came up from the wilds of County Cork, not knowing anything, only having written a couple of plays and meeting Mr Yeats at the Nassau Hotel with Lady Gregory. I'd never met either of them before. It was afternoon and Mr Yeats was late; he came in not in the magnificent way that you're talking of, but remember this is twenty years earlier . . .

o'connor: Twenty years humbler. You must remember that when I met Yeats first, he was an old, very authoritative, rather Olympian figure: very tall, very dignified, all his gestures were sweeping, his voice had a soft, oratorical cadence which comes back into my ears even now. There must have been another and very different Yeats when he was younger, because I remember AE describing him with a sort of longing in his voice, the boy with a beard, as AE used to say, who used to come into his bedroom at two o'clock in the morning to recite some new poem which he'd written.

magee: I was at school with Yeats. He was a much older boy than I—he seemed to me quite a young man, he had a beard. I got to know him quite well and we were friends. We used to sit together in class and I even used to cog from him in examinations. He was a little uncertain, I think, with the headmaster, Mr Wilkins. He wanted to start a naturalist club in the high school, and I remember sitting opposite the two of them when they were talking and noticing the smile on Wilkins's face while Yeats was talking. He didn't take him seriously. And he used to call him 'the flighty poet'. He came in quite casually and went off whenever he wanted. He would announce that he wouldn't be there tomorrow and so on, in a way that excited my envy. I remember being greatly struck by his making friends with a very unpopular boy, walking up and down with him, and I was wondering what they were talking about. And I think it was simply a sort of interest in the soul of this boy that made him talk to him.

o'connor: 'Soul claps its hands and sing and louder sing
        For every tatter in its mortal dress.'[15]

best: I remember hearing Yeats give a lecture—it may have been an Irish
Literary Society lecture—I think it was the late Dr Sigerson[16] who was in
the chair, and I was tremendously impressed by Yeats's final remarks,
where he quoted something of an Italian poet who described the way he
was being tossed in a storm and he saw amid the waves a flame, and he
recognised that that flame was his own soul, and if the waves overwhelmed
it then he was lost for ever, but gradually the storm subsided and the flame
burned bright, and Yeats said, 'That is Ireland,' and he wound up his
address in this most impressive way. That was Yeats at his very best, I
remember. Old John O'Leary came in . . .

> Beautiful lofty things: O'Leary's noble head;
> . . . Maud Gonne at Howth station waiting a train,
> Pallas Athene in that straight back and arrogant head:
> All the Olympians; a thing never known again.[17]

MAUD GONNE McBRIDE:[18] I was twenty, and William was twenty-one
when we first met, and it was through John O'Leary. Willie's father was
painting his picture and I never saw a more beautiful head than John
O'Leary had. Willie and I had the deepest admiration for him. As I said,
Willie was then twenty-one and I was twenty, and he was extremely proud
of that one year's seniority. He looked much younger than I did, because
he was rather a dishevelled art student—for he intended to be a painter like
his father. John O'Leary used to say, 'Your vocation is to be a poet. You
have that in you,' and then he would make him read some of his early
poems.

> Had I the heavens' embroidered cloths,
> Enwrought with golden and silver light,
> The blue and the dim and the dark cloths
> Of night and light and the half-light,
> I would spread the cloths under your feet:
> But I, being poor, have only my dreams;
> I have spread my dreams under your feet;
> Tread softly because you tread on my dreams.[19]

MADAME McBRIDE: 'Don't you understand in the spiritual world, in the
faery world here,' he would say, 'everything is the reverse. Therefore your
poems are children, and I'm the father and you're the mother.'
    Willie and I fought very hard; he went on all those committees really to
help me more than anything else; but he was wonderful at a committee
meeting and used to be able to carry things very often.

> O but we dreamed to mend
> Whatever mischief seemed

To afflict mankind, but now
The winds of winter blow
Learn that we were crack-pated when we dreamed.[20]

MRS STUART: I have known him to be wonderfully on the spot when he absolutely had to be, when there was nobody, no grown-up, extrovert grown-up, to take the burden, but when there were tiresome things like, when travelling together, seeing to the luggage, or getting a cab or anything like that, then Willy would fall into a great abstraction, from which I learnt a great lesson myself, not to be there on these occasions.

ROBINSON: Look at his connection with the BBC. He gave certainly three recitals for the BBC, every time they loved him more and more, and they gave him more and more money, and in the end they wanted to give him the best battery, the best whatever they could do to his home in Rathfarnham, and they said, 'Have you got electric light in the home?' He had to wire back to his wife to find whether they had electric light in the home—he hadn't.

ANNE YEATS:[21] We acquired a wireless. For a long time he wouldn't have one, he didn't like them, then when we acquired one, the first evening it was turned on, he was listening to it, and he couldn't hear very well, so he put his hand to his ear, and said, I beg your pardon?'

O'CONNOR: Yes, I can well believe he was impractical.

ROBINSON: He wasn't impractical! He could do a balance sheet better than anybody I know.

WRIGHT: But he was an extraordinary man in that way meeting with the company. He would be talking of the Greek gods or something, and then he'd suddenly say, 'Well, we've heard all these figures, but what I want to know is what we have lost and what we have gained in pure simple words.'

BERTIE SMYLLIE:[22] I think I was the first person, certainly the first person in this country, to know that Yeats had won the Nobel Prize. I was on duty at the *Irish Times* office that night, when the message came over the Creed machine to say that for the first time an Irish poet had won the prize, which amounted to quite a considerable sum, I think between seven and eight thousand pounds. I was rather friendly with Yeats at the time, and it was fairly late in the evening, getting on to eleven o'clock I suppose, and I rang him up at his house, hoping that he didn't know the news. He came to the phone himself—he *didn't* know the news. I said, 'Mr Yeats, I've got very good news for you, a very great honour has been conferred upon you,' and I was rather enthusiastic and gushing at the time, and I said, 'This is a great honour not only for you but for the country,' and I could tell that he was getting slightly impatient to know what it was all about, so I said, 'You've been awarded the Nobel Prize, a very great honour to you and a very great honour to Ireland,' and to my amazement the only question he asked was, 'How much, Smyllie, how much is it?'

ROBINSON: Well, I say he was tough. I say that from the moment I met him he was tough, and he was tougher and tougher as his years went on; and when he was a senator and when he had this position and when he defended divorce and when he defended censorship he said, 'Nobody can touch me, because I'm so important.' And on this question of censorship he said, 'I want to read all the dirty English Sunday papers because I will read the last words of every murderer. Whereas, if I buy the *Observer*, I will read the last words—alas! not the *last* words—of St John Ervine on the theatre.'

MRS STUART: I remember Yeats telling me that the greatest prose line that was ever written which had its own particular prose rhythm—which was as great as verse rhythm—was in Emerson: 'The stars, the stars everlasting are fugitives also.'

ARTHUR HANNAH:[23] I can remember Yeats well, he came into our shop quite a lot. As a matter of fact, all he bought from us were detective novels. On one occasion he came into me, reprimanded me, said I had sold him a detective novel in which there was far too much detection. Well, then I sold him an Edgar Wallace and he went out very happy.

ANNE YEATS: Detective stories and Wild West might not seem to come under the category of what I call guided reading, but father read a great many of them, though mother always had to vet them to make quite sure that they had happy endings. But about the Wild Wests, too; when he was ailing in Majorca, he was very ill at the time, and delirious, I remember he was telling mother, 'George, George, call the sheriff!'

MACNAMARA: He began to be altogether more natural, and towards the end of the period when he was a senator here, he spoke and acted rather like any ordinary man. He played golf and went around.

SMYLLIE: Well, of course, the idea of WB taking up golf was rather amusing to us who knew him, and he came to me and suggested that possibly I might help him, so I did. I was a member of a Club called Camikmines, and of course the Great Man left everything in my hands; there was another young man called Duncan, and we had to provide all the clubs, we had to do everything. I'd a small car, a little MG, and the first day we were going up, I handed WB his bag, and he said, 'Smyllie, this is my quiver'—he always insisted on calling his golf bag his quiver. However, we started off, we played several times, and he'd make a wild swipe at the ball, let the club fall on the ground, and walk off with his hands behind his back in the characteristic Yeatsian fashion, leaving myself and Duncan to pick up the quiver and the club and to look for the ball, which was very important—for the ball was very rarely to be found. He used to drive the ball into a clump of furze bushes or into a ditch or anywhere, about, say, ten yards from the tee, and we lost several balls this way. But a rather characteristic thing about this was that the next game we went out to play, WB noticed we had been losing all these balls and we had been providing him with new ones—not new ones, actually, we knew too much about it for that—but old ones. The next day he came out, and every time he hit the ball and lost it, he used to produce a half-crown from his pocket, and hand the half-crown either to myself or to Duncan in compensation for the ball that had been lost.

ANNE YEATS: We used to play croquet quite a lot in Rathfarnham. He was a very good croquet player and he used to hit a ball at the far end, seemed to concentrate a lot on it, and I don't think he played to win, but I think he liked winning the game like anybody else. I remember somebody came to tea and cheated to let him win, and he never played with her again.

NORAH McGUINNESS:[24] That was a singular honour, because very few people I think were asked to play croquet with him. I believe he took the game very seriously indeed and really enjoyed winning a game, so I feel that I did what I was supposed to that day, because he won the game, but then I'd never played croquet before.

MISS MACNIE:[25] He was very anxious to play it, and one time they took a house out in the country and there was a croquet lawn there, and he was very anxious to come up against some competitor. So he asked a friend of mine if she could produce some person to play a game with him. She produced a young daughter of hers who had never played a game in her life before. However, she played the game with WB and it was impossible not to win because WB's shots were not the best in the world. At the end of the game he looked very disconsolate and, as my friend put it, if it had been announced to the world that he was the worst poet in the world he couldn't have looked more dejected. And he walked across to my friend and he said to her: 'You must have had her trained.'

MRS STUART: Willy walked on land rather like a swan or a pelican without too much certitude but was very different in the water. He was a wonderful swimmer and could swim for ages under water and reappear after a great distance. When we were bathing together, I was always struck by the extraordinary agility and ease he had in the water and athletic power. He was also very fond of kites. We had bought one which he said was inadequate, and he himself altered this thing, and used to run along the shore on a windy day, and the kite flew at a great height and that was a great pastime.

SEAN McBRIDE:[26] He used to come and spend some time with us in the summer at a house at the seaside in Normandy—a place called Colville, not very far from Bayeux. He used to be very keen on flying kites, and we used to spend hours together on a long strand flying them. He was able to get kites to a marvellous height. He'd apparently always been keen on it, because I remember he told me that his father in Sligo made some kites which he flew. After that, my next vivid recollection of Yeats was when my mother was in prison in England in 1918. I went to stay with Yeats and Mrs Yeats in Galway, outside Gort, near Coole, near Lady Gregory's house.

O'CONNOR: Oh, Lady Gregory was a terrifying old lady, and I was once telling Mrs Yeats how terrified I used to be of her, and she said, 'Oh well, Willie was the same. After we got married we went to stay at Coole, and Willie felt it was really time to assert himself. I suppose he was getting on for fifty at the time, he was a famous man, a most distinguished man, and a married man, and he felt he simply must break the rules of Coole House. Now one of the rules was that you could not have animals in the house, and WB, being famous and married and middle-aged, decided that he must defy the laws of Coole House and bring Pangur. So Pangur was duly brought on the train, and loaded on to the side-car to take them to Coole House. But half-way up the drive to Coole, the famous public man suddenly got cold feet at the thought of the frosty visage of that old lady in the big house, and he tapped the driver on the shoulder and said, 'Drive to the stables,' and Pangur was put into the stables and late that night, when the old lady was fast asleep, WB went down in his slippers and rescued Pangur and brought him up to his bedroom, so that he never really succeeded in asserting himself against the old lady up to the day of her death.

Now, Anne, tell us something about what it's like to be the child of a famous man.

ANNE YEATS: I think chiefly, almost the first thing I remember—at least, I don't remember, I was told it—was calling him Willie when I was still in my pram, and a voice coming out of the window, firmly saying, 'You are not to call your father Willie!' and then I replied, 'Willie Dada, Willie Dada,' which I take it didn't go down very well, either.

MAGEE: I don't wonder because everyone in Dublin called him 'Willy' and I think it rather irritated him. The name that he said was the finest name was Michael, I think. I was rather interested when he called his son by that name.

MISS MACNIE: Even people who knew him a great deal better than I did have never mentioned that he was a perfectly splendid father, and that Mrs Yeats was an equally splendid mother and wife. But to me, meeting him as I sometimes did at teatime, when he came in, he was perfectly delightful with his children. And it really was a very amusing thing to watch WB coming in with his head well up as he always held it, and with his hands clasped behind his back followed by Michael who, by the way, never spoke until he was about four years of age, and who at that time was about two feet high; he used to walk in after his father in the most sedate manner possible, with his hands clasped behind his back and keeping pace with his father, exactly like his father, just a miniature image of him. It always used to make me laugh every time he did it. Anne was very amusing too. She was wiser than Michael, and when her father would come in after he had played bears or elephants with Michael, he used to lie down flat on a sofa between the two windows and this was part of a game apparently, because Anne would always run across the room, open the door, go outside, shut it, then bang it open and rush across the room and jump flat on her father's prostrate body on the sofa.

MISS MACNIE: Oh yes. Anne and I discussed a point about that at one time. I said to Anne, 'Were you afraid of your father?' And she said, 'I was terrified of him.' And I said, 'Well, what an extraordinary thing, so was I.' He was the only person in the world I ever was frightened of, and I was, I was afraid of her father. I said, 'Why was it?' 'I don't know,' said Anne, 'there's no explanation so far as I'm concerned, because he never laid a finger on us, he didn't believe in corporal punishment, and he never touched either Michael or me—never punished us in any way—and yet I was afraid of him.'

ANNE YEATS: We had to be frightfully quiet really about the house generally; I remember once Mike and I were fighting, rather more than usual, and mother couldn't cope with us, so she sent father in. He just sat down in the chair, and intoned in full voice, 'Let dogs delight to bark and bite' and then got up and went out of the room. He was rather awe-inspiring, I think, on the whole. You always had to stay rather quiet, and then he was writing quite a lot.

MRS YEATS: [27] Yes. He had to be absolutely alone, so completely alone that even when an infant was in the room and silent, he had still to be alone, because no personality must be there at all. It wasn't a matter of merely being spoken to or interrupted or anything else, but he had to be in absolute isolation in a room wherever he was writing.

O'CONNOR: He was one of the hardest workers that I have ever come across. I know George Moore jeers at this business about his writing four lines in a day and his reaching his record of seven lines. But if you'd seen exactly how much labour those four or seven lines had cost him, you wouldn't think it was anything like a bad day's work; because he would recite a single line hundreds and hundreds of times in succession. Even in the middle of a conversation with you—he would be talking about politics perhaps, and quite suddenly he would lift the right hand and would begin to beat time and you would hear him recite a line a couple of times and then the hand would drop again and he'd go on with the conversation, just as though nothing had happened. [28]

MRS STUART: For most poets it seems to me that concealment and secrecy is necessary before their work can come to anything, whereas with Yeats, it was quite different. He had to exteriorise everything he wrote before he wrote it in talk and discussions, and even ask for advice, and then he would begin to write the first draft and talk it over more, and the second and so on.

> Everything he wrote was read,
> After certain years he won
> Sufficient money for his need,
> Friends that have been friends indeed;
> 'What then?' sang Plato's ghost. 'What then?'[29]

ROBINSON: He was an awfully human person, because he loved his children, he loved birds.

> All his happier dreams came true—
> A small old house, wife, daughter, son,
> Grounds where plum and cabbage grew,
> Poets and Wits about him drew;
> 'What then?' sang Plato's ghost. 'What then?'
>
> 'The work is done', grown old he thought,
> 'According to my boyish plan;
> Let the fools rage, I swerved in naught,
> Something to perfection brought';
> But louder sang that ghost, 'What then?'
>
> What shall I do with this absurdity—
> O heart, O troubled heart—this caricature,
> Decrepit age that has been tied to me
> As to a dog's tail?
> 　　　　　Never had I more
> Excited, passionate, fantastical
> Imagination, nor an ear and eye
> That more expected the impossible—
> No, not in boyhood when with rod and fly,
>
> Or the humbler worm, I climbed Ben Bulben's back
> And had the livelong summer day to spend.
> It seems that I must bid the Muse go pack,
> Choose Plato and Plotinus for a friend
> Until imagination, ear and eye,
> Can be content with argument and deal
> In abstract things.[30]

SMYLLIE: You know, I never believed that WB knew anything much about philosophy, though he talked a great deal about it, but he invented a philosophy of his own, which was rather amusing. One very interesting and amusing thing occurred, when he was expounding this highly esoteric theory of his one night up in the Arts Club. And among those present was a little man called Cruise O'Brien, [31] a very brilliant journalist, and one of the very few people who could be rude with impunity to WB. WB gave him, as he very often gave me, a fool's pardon. This night, at any rate, he was expounding this philosophy of his which was connected in some queer way with the phases of the moon; he was telling us all about the twenty-eight phases of the moon and he had equated every phase against some historical figure. He said, 'Number one—the highest phase—is perfect beauty.' With a respectful silence for a few seconds we all listened, and then he said, 'Number two was Helen of Troy—the nearest approximation to perfect beauty.' And he went right round the twenty-eight, or rather twenty-seven, phases and finally he came to the last, and then he said that the lowest form of all is Thomas Carlyle and all Scotsmen. This shook us all a little bit and Cruise O'Brien spoke up at once, 'WB,' he said—he'd a very mincing voice, Cruise—'have you ever read a word of Carlyle? You say Carlyle is the lowest form. Oh come! Have you ever read a word of Carlyle?' 'Carlyle, Cruise, was a dolt,' said WB. 'But I insist, WB, did you ever read one single word of Carlyle?' 'Carlyle, I tell you, was a dolt.' 'Yes, but you haven't read him.' 'No, I have not read him, my wife, George, has read him and she tells me he's a dolt.' That was the end of the philosophical treatise for the night.

MRS STUART: I think the main idea was that the human cycle was similar to lunar months but divided into twenty-eight periods of successive reincarnations. But I really think I'm not quite the person to talk about the phases of the moon, because Yeats gave me such a very flattering position in it, placing me phase fourteen, which is one of as near complete beauty on earth as can be attained, and as near complete subjectivity also, because at phase fifteen you do not incarnate on earth. Similar in beauty but beginning to work towards objectivity is phase sixteen at which he placed my mother, but there the first impulse is towards action again. I had a cat, a black Persian, in Normandy at the time when the thought of the phases of the moon was beginning to take shape in his mind and this cat used to dance wonderfully in the moonlight, take huge leaps. And in a queer way, I think that gave the kind of poetic urge to the idea which otherwise would have been a little bit too coldly philosophical.

NORAH MCGUINNESS: His book, *A Vision*, had just been published, and he started talking about it over dinner. I think it was even at the first course he started talking about it. So I said to him that unfortunately I hadn't read his book, I'd only heard it discussed. I don't know what sort of kink Mr Yeats had, but he got it into his head that I'd read his book. I even hesitate now when I think of that dinner, because there were about five courses to be got through and Mr Yeats started asking me my opinion on various aspects of the book, about various passages, and I tried to assure him again, 'No, I haven't read it, Mr Yeats.' He seemed to ignore that, but fortunately for me when he asked me a question he didn't seem to expect an answer. So I struggled through the fish and the entrée and fruit, whatever it was—and I felt at the end I had come through fairly well, because I hadn't given away the fact that I hadn't read the book, seeing that he'd made up his mind that I had.

Well, it was one of his famous Monday evenings, which as everyone knows were very sacred evenings, inasmuch as women were never admitted to these evenings. I thought that perhaps I'd be released when I left the dining-room, but not at all. Mr Yeats said, 'Come up to the study.' So I thought, 'Oh well, it's only for a few minutes and I'll be asked to go.' So I went up to the study and there were several young men whom I was introduced to. I don't remember who the young men were, except one who was Sean O'Faolain, and years afterwards he told me it was also his first visit to Yeats, and he was really more in awe of me than Mr Yeats, because he thought I was the blue-stocking of all the world at that time.

MISS MACNIE: There was a young man who came across here from England, a rather objectionable and pushing young man, who came uninvited to one of WB's evenings. He was announced by the maid and found himself in the room with WB and George Russell standing at the mantelpiece talking busily to one another. WB saw him, I think, but he took no notice whatever. He was an uninvited guest and as such WB didn't acknowledge him. The young man walked across the room, stood beside WB and George Russell for a moment or two and then went across and sat down in a chair beside a friend in the corner. WB paused for a moment or two, looked across at the corner and then very slowly and very, very erect walked forward to the corner and said very politely to him, 'Sir, you have not been invited. You are not welcome. Will you please go.' And he walked across the room and opened the door and closed it after this young man.

CLARKE: So far as the younger generation of poets are concerned, here in Ireland, Yeats was rather like an enormous oak-tree which, of course, kept us in the shade, and did exclude a great number of the rays of, say, the friendly sun; and of course we always hoped that in the end we would reach the sun, but the shadow of that great oak-tree is still there.

O'CONNOR: He lived a deep interior life and all the outside things counted practically for nothing—unless he concentrated on remembering them. I remember his once quoting to me a lovely poem of Eleanor Wylie's and he quoted it with an intensity of passion that I never heard him give any other poem. 'Live with a velvet more: go burrow underground.' And he burrowed underground quite a lot. I got the impression that right up to the end he remained a very shy, gentle creature.

MRS YEATS: Yes, a great many people thought this. I often felt it was very sad that there were so many people that he himself would have liked to meet. I will just give you one example only, and that was Arnold Toynbee.

He only met him in the last year of his life, and he was introduced to him one lunch by Miss Hilda Matheson. He'd longed to meet him for, I may almost say, years, because he thought that his thought was part of his own scheme. And you see, that meant a great deal to him, that meeting. But he would never have written to Toynbee to ask him of he might go and see him. That was a curious kind of shyness on his part that he wouldn't approach the great man.

CLARKE: Well now, that is rather curious. I'd gone down to the Seven Woods at Coole as a very young enthusiast in a romantic way, and I crossed a wall into the domain, and came into a dark wood which was surely the Wicked Wood of the poem, in which there was a witch, and then I saw another bright wood ahead, and I moved towards that. Suddenly through the leaves I saw a glimpse of blue, and for a moment, being very young, I almost felt here was an elemental spirit; and then I said no, if this is the great domain, it's a peacock. I crept forward, I looked through the leaves, and there, crossing the grass towards a Georgian house, I saw a tall figure in a marvellous sky-blue watered silk raincoat holding fishing-rods and lines and all that fierce tackle of the country gentleman, and I said to myself, I'm in the wrong domain, this cannot be the Seven Woods. Then I looked again, and I recognised dimly from those frontispieces of the books that it was the poet himself, disguised as a great country gentleman and sportsman; as a young romantic poet of the Irish movement, I was shocked and disappointed.

> Between land and water he grew,
> Between low and high,
> To both the man ran true,
> Arrogant, shy.
> Enough that out of the two
> (And their commotion)
> The salt root rose and grew
> Into a green reed, a wavering blade
> That between land's night and sky's light
> Saw red, ran wild, and tongued the imperturbable ocean.

Malachi Stilt-Jack am I, whatever I learned has run wild,
From collar to collar, from stilt to stilt, from father to child.
All metaphor, Malachi, stilts and all. A barnacle goose
Far up in the stretches of night; night splits and the dawn
      breaks loose;
I, through the terrible novelty of light, stalk on, stalk on;
Those great sea-horses bare their teeth and laugh at the
      dawn.[32]

NOTES

William Robert Rodgers (1909–69) was born in Belfast; became Presbyterian minister in Armagh (1934–46); BBC producer and script-writer (1946–52); elected to the Irish Academy of Letters as a distinguished Irish and Ulster poet (1951). His books include *Awake* (1941), *Europa and the Bull* (1952) and *Ireland in Colour* (1956). See Darcy O'Brien, *W. R. Rodgers (1909–1969)*, Irish Writers Series (Lewisburg: Bucknell University Press, 1970)

   1. For a note on Frank O'Connor see p. 270.

   2. Seán O'Faoláin (1900–   ) was educated at University College Cork and Harvard. He lectured in the United States for some time then returned to Ireland, where he was recognised as another of the new voices in Irish writing with his first short story collection *Midsummer Night's Madness* (1932), which earned critical praise and clerical disapproval. Other collections include *A Purse of Coppers, I Remember! I Remember!* and *The Stories of Sean O'Foolain.* He has also written novels, *A Nest of Simple Folk* (1933), *Bird Alone* (1936) and *Come Back to Erin* (1940); a play, *She Had to Do Something*, performed at the Abbey in 1937; as well as historical biography and other non-fiction, including several articles on Yeats.

   3. Simplicity; good nature; heartiness.

   4. 'John Eglinton' (William Kirkpatrick Magee) (1868–1961), Irish essayist and poet who was a school friend of Yeats.

   5. Edward Garnett (1868–1937), English writer and father of David Garnett, also a writer.

   6. Austin Clarke (1896–1974), Irish poet.

   7. Adolphus Wright, actor and director.

   8. Brinsley MacNamara (1890–1963), Irish dramatist.

   9. Dr Richard Best was a distinguished Gaelic scholar and linguist. He was long associated with the National Library of Ireland. A well-known Dublin character and friend of James Joyce and Oliver St John Gogarty, he appears under his own name in *Ulysses* (the National Library episode).

   10. For a note on F. R. Higgins see p. 293.

   11. Charles Stuart Parnell (1846–1891), Irish Nationalist leader.

   12. John O'Leary (1830–1907), Irish Nationalist leader.

   13. Iseult Stuart, the daughter of Maud Gonne. She frequented artistic and literary circles in Dublin and London and married novelist and playwright Francis Stuart.

   14. For a note on Lennox Robinson see p. 259.

   15. W. B. Yeats, 'Sailing to Byzantium', *The Tower* (1928).

   16. For a note on Dr George Sigerson see p. 270.

   17. W. B. Yeats, 'Beautiful Lofty Things', *Last Poems.*

   18. For a note on Maud Gonne see p. 281.

   19. W. B. Yeats, 'He Wishes for the Clothes of Heaven', *The Wind Among the Reeds* (1899).

   20. W. B. Yeats, 'Nineteen Hundred and Nineteen', *The Tower* (1928).

   21. For a note on Anne Yeats see p. 205.

   22. Bertie Smyllie (1919–   ), Editor of the *Irish Times* for a lengthy period. He is best known for his encouragement of young writers, many now established as leading authors, whose work he first published in his newspaper.

   23. Arthur Hannah, the proprietor of Hanna's Book Shop in Nassau Street, and friend of Yeats.

   24. Norah McGuinness, a distinguished Ulster-born artist. A close friend of the Yeats family, she lives in Dublin.

   25. Miss Macnie, a Dublin caricaturist. Some of the first examples of her work are to be found in the Dublin Arts Club, of which she was a founder member.

   26. Sean MacBride, son of Maud Gonne MacBride and a prominent senior counsel at the Dublin bar. One-time Minister of External Affairs, he then became Secretary of the

International Commission of Jurists in Geneva. He is also a founder member of Amnesty International. A Nobel Peace Prize winner in early December 1974, he is presently Commissioner for MAMIBIA

27. Mrs Yeats was the wife of W. B. Yeats; born Georgie Hyde-Lees. She influenced his poetry through her interest in spiritualism. See W. B. Yeats, *A Vision*.

28. 'My poetry costs me endless labour,' said Yeats. 'Other people write fine poetry with no trouble at all to themselves.'

29. W. B. Yeats, 'What Then?', *Last Poems*.

30. Ibid.

31. Conor Cruise O'Brien (1917–   ), Irish writer and diplomat.

32. W. B. Yeats, 'High Talk', *Last Poems*.

Reminiscences of Yeats*

FRANK O'CONNOR

For the rest of my life I nourished something like an inferiority complex about the old lady[1] until long after Yeats' death. Mrs. Yeats revealed to me that he was as terrified of her as I was. She had always treated him as a talented but naughty child. When at last he married and took his young wife to Coole, he felt the time had come for him to assert his manhood. No animals were permitted in Coole—which, considering what most Irish country houses are like, seems to me to be kindness to Christians—and Yeats was fond of his cat. Now that he was a married man, a mature man, a famous man, he was surely entitled to his cat. So Pangur was duly bundled up and brought to Gort. But as the outside car drove up the avenue of Coole the married, mature, famous man grew panic-stricken at the thought of the old lady's forbidding countenance. He bade the jarvey drive him first to the stables. There Pangur was deposited until, everyone having gone to bed, Yeats crept out in his slippers and brought him up to the bedroom. Yet till the day she died he secretly nursed the hope of being able to treat her as an equal. Nobody who had not been squelched by her could realise the relief with which I heard this.

*   *   *

* Extracted from *Leinster, Munster and Connaught* (London: Robert Hale, 1950) pp. 237–43, 250–1, 256–61.

'Everybody in Dublin is worried to death about what George is saying of them in his new book,'[2] Martyn said one day to Yeats. 'I'm the only one who never worries.'

'Ah, Martyn,' replied Yeats, 'that's only because you don't know what he is saying about you.'

'What is he saying?' growled Martyn.

'That you started the pro-cathedral choir, not because you liked choirs, but because you liked choirboys.'

'The scoundrel!' shouted Martyn, turning purple. 'I'll have the law on him.'

But a few days later Yeats met him again, his old smug, philosophic self.

'Oh, Yeats,' he said, 'about that thing that George wrote——'

'Yes?'

'He's not printing that part, he tells me. It's only a chapter he reads to his friends on Saturday nights.'

*   *   *

The truth is that of all the men I have known there was none who cast a more eager eye on both life and death. He was a blazing enthusiast who, into his seventies, retained all the spontaneity and astonishment of a boy of seventeen. I remember well the first night I went to his house—the occasion that was damped by the presence of the old lady—and Yeats entered the dim, candle-lit drawing-room, tall, elegantly dressed, stern-looking—a figure to terrify a young man more forthcoming than myself. And then the extraordinary change which came over him when he grew excited; the way he sat bolt upright in his chair, snorted, sniffed, stammered, glared, the head thrown back, while the whole face blazed from within. It was astonishing, because even in extreme old age, when he was looking most wretched and discontented, quite suddenly that blaze of excitement would suddenly sweep over his face like a glory, like a blast of sunlight over a moor, and from behind the mask of age a boy's eager, intense, appealing face stammered and glared at you, trapped and despairing, like a boy's face behind a window on a summer day.

When we weren't quarrelling, which was often enough, we usually got on well, because his adolescent eagerness, his passion for abstract conversation, was the sort of thing I had been used to when Sean O'Faolain and I were boys in Cork and made ourselves intellectually drunk over 'objectivity' and 'subjectivity,' Keats and Shelly. We had long, excited and very muddled arguments about Hegelianism, Fascism, Communism, pacifism; and sometimes the clash of ideas would release the lightning of phrase or anecdote, always perfectly apt. Once when I quoted the remark of an Irish politician that 'the great difference between England and Ireland is that in England you can say what you like so long as you do the right thing, in Ireland you can do what you like so long as you say the right thing,' he capped it with 'My father used to say that the great difference between England and Ireland is that every Englishman has rich relations and every Irishman poor ones.'

He published two volumes of my translations from the Irish, and did it with such enthusiasm[3] that he practically rewrote the lot. I met Gogarty about that time, and he said: 'Yeats is writing a couple of little lyrics for me, so I'd better drop in and see how he's getting on.' I made one small effort at interfering in the writing of my own poems, but it was not welcomed. It was in the line 'Has made me travel to seek you, Valentine Brown.' 'That's a bad line,' I said. 'You can say, "Has made me travel to you," or, "Has made me seek you," but you can't say, "Travel to seek you." Why not "Has made me a beggar before you, Valentine Brown"?' 'No beggars! No beggars!' he roared.

His first enthusiasm after I got to know him was the establishment of an Academy of Letters, and he had a lovely time chasing about in taxis, giving lunch-parties, sending wires and pulling wires. He was an outrageous old flatterer. At that time I hadn't even published a book and was being accepted into the Academy on trust, but when I asked whether Mr. Somebody or Other was important enough to be a member Yeats replied: 'Why worry about literary eminence? You and I will provide that.'

Then he became a Fascist and started parading Dublin in a bright blue shirt. In his early revolutionary days he wanted the secret society he belonged to to steal the Coronation Stone from Westminster Abbey. In his Fascist phase he wanted the Blueshirts to rebuild Tara and transfer the capital there. He had neighbours who, he decided, were Blueshirts too, and these had a dog. Mrs. Yeats, who was democratic in sympathies, kept hens, and the Blueshirt dog worried the democratic hens. Naturally, Yeats supported the dog. One day Mrs. Yeats' favourite hen disappeared, and she wrote to the neighbours to complain of the dog. By return the neighbours replied that the dog had been destroyed. Mrs. Yeats, who was very fond of animals, was conscience-stricken, but Yeats was delighted at what he regarded as a true Blueshirt respect for law and order. One evening he called at my flat in a state of high glee. The democratic hen had returned safe and sound and Mrs. Yeats was overwhelmed with remorse. Another victory over the democracies!

Then I became a director[4] of the Abbey Theatre, and our rows went on almost uninterruptedly until his death. He wanted 'Coriolanus'[5] produced in coloured shirts, in hopes of starting anti-Fascist riots as in Paris, but I dug in my heels about that. In time I almost became one of his enthusiasms myself, which was flattering but rather embarrassing, as he had fathered more bad art and literature than any great writer of his time. 'Within five years,' he told me once, 'So-and-So will be a European figure.' 'Russell,' he said to A.E., who was refusing to enthuse over another of his protégés, 'I wish you and I had the same chance of immortality as that young man.' But one liked the boyish eagerness which prompted it, the questioning way he read you some God-awful poem and tried to persuade you it was 'profound,' 'Shakespearean,' 'the greatest thing produced in our time.'

In his later years he got into a perfect fever over eugenics.[6] It began by his asking me one night if I thought genius could be passed on from one generation to the next. I said I thought not; talent, perhaps, but not genius, and he got very cross, and only then did I realise that he was thinking of his son Michael. Then his face lit up, and he said: 'I had an old aunt who used to say you could pass on anything you liked, provided you took care not to marry the girl next door.'

After that the enthusiasm really got under way. Somebody or other, who was the greatest something or other of our time, had invented a method of testing intelligence that dispensed altogether with acquired knowledge and only tested natural aptitude. This had revealed the alarming fact that if you took children out of a slum and put them in decent surroundings their natural aptitude did not improve, so that the standard of human intelligence was steadily declining. One of the tests turned out to be a labyrinth problem, the second a picture of a heap of clothes on a strand, with a blank space in the middle of the clothes, which the unfortunate children were supposed to fill in with the name of the object that should have been represented. Being myself from a slum, I didn't like to admit that I didn't know from Adam what the appropriate object was, but curiosity compelled me to ask.

'Oh,' said Yeats, 'a dog. To guard the clothes.'

Intelligent or not, it struck me that the capacity of human beings for deluding themselves was practically infinite.

'By the way,' I asked, 'do you think you'd ever have passed an intelligence test?'

He thought about that for a while.

'No,' he admitted regretfully, 'I suppose I wouldn't.'

In the last letter[7] I received from him, written on his death-bed, he suggested that if I wanted his help I should wire and he would return and reorganise the entire Board of the theatre! I used to feel years younger after a visit to him. Disillusionment and cynicism simply dropped away from me when he was round.

NOTES

For a note on Frank O'Connor, see p. 270.

1. Lady Gregory.

2. In 1911 George Moore moved to London, where he wrote a long autobiography in three parts, *Ave* (1911), *Salve* (1912) and *Vale* (1914)—called collectively *Hail and Farewell*.

3. Yeats wrote in *On the Boiler*: 'Translate into modern Irish all that is most beautiful in old and middle Irish, what Frank O'Connor and Augusta Gregory, let us say, have translated into English.'

4. Frank O'Connor became a director of the Abbey Theatre in 1936. He resigned in 1939.

5. *Coriolanus* was first produced by the Abbey Theatre on 13 January 1936.

6. Yeats had been studying eugenics in Cattell's *Psychology and Social Progress* and from

material supplied by the secretary of the Eugenics Society; 'and he spoke much of the necessity of the unification of the State under a small aristocratic order which would prevent the materially and spiritually uncreative families or individuals from prevailing over the creative'—Joseph Hone, *W. B. Yeats, 1865–1939* (London: Macmillan, 1965) p. 468.

7. This letter is not included in *The Letters of W. B. Yeats*, ed. Allan Wade (London: Rupert Hart-Davis, 1954).

W. B. Yeats: Chameleon of Genius*

CLIFFORD BAX

He was difficult (perhaps impossible) to know well. If we were merely 'willing ears' to Æ, we were even fainter apparitions to Yeats, as when, having talked to a lady for an hour, he politely peered forward and asked, 'Am I speaking to Mrs Podmore or Mrs Dryhurst?' He must have surprised many acquaintances. For instance, one evening at Edmund Dulac's he said that the *News of the World* was his favourite English newspaper 'because it reports the actions of men and women, not the babble of politicians'. A moment later he challenged his host (and me) to name any detective story which he had not read. He had also much more humour than most of his devotees would have expected. On the same evening he told us how once when he was walking down Grafton Street with James Stephens they passed a dog. 'After a few more steps,' said Yeats, 'Stephens exclaimed, "I'm sorry, Yeats. I must go back and pat that dog. You see, I am a sort of honorary dog."' And I have a letter[1] in which the poet records that in a Paris hotel George Moore, disturbed by the presence of a mouse, detected the creature's hiding-place, took up his shot-gun, and sat for a long time in front of the hole in the wainscot, hoping to fire at the mouse.

There were at least six personalities in Yeats, and he never managed to integrate them. There was the lyric poet with his extreme sensibility to verbal rhythm and music; the story-teller who, a little tediously, wrote as though 'beggars' and the Irish peasantry were more interesting than men with more culture; the 'sixty year old smiling public man', a 'mask' which he created for important occasions; the uneager politician who, external-ized by Maud Gonne, floundered in the rough sea of Irish affairs; the courteous gentleman who extolled the aristocracy and liked to fancy that he belonged to that order; and the occultist, always trying to construct a metaphysical system. Few men apply every part of their minds to each matter with which they are engaged, and so difficult is it to attain

* Extracted from *Some I Knew Well* (London: Phoenix House, 1951) pp. 98–100.

sovereignty over our conflicting interests that even those few are usually suspected of hypocrisy. Gladstone tried hard to blend his religion with his politics, and that is why he remains as one of the noblest personalities of the nineteenth century. This, too, is the cause of Tolstoy's immense prestige. Gandhi attempted a similar synthesis but not with so much success. Indeed, it is always surprising that Hindu politicians make no reference to the law of *karma*, for presumably they believe in it as definitely as Western politicians believe in the law of gravity. Yeats never harmonized the complicated contents of his mind.

It is curious to read in Joseph Hone's biography[2] that the poet's friends were 'bored' by his occultism and, in Eglinton's Life[3] of Æ, that this other poet's friends took little interest in his theosophical convictions. People do not realize how deep was the influence upon both poets of Madame Blavatsky. Yeats was born in 1865, Æ in 1867, and when they were both in their early twenties the doctrines of theosophy were almost intellectually fashionable. Æ always revered the old lady, and Yeats declared that she was the most impressive person whom he had ever met. The so-called exposure of Madame, by the Society for Psychical Research, did not shake the belief of either poet that she had been a spiritual messenger of great importance in a materialistic age. They knew that the exposure was based upon the evidence of two servants who had been given notice; and they knew that many mediums indulge in trickery when they are not 'in form'. Moreover, H. P. Blavatsky had left her impressive and exciting interpretation of the universe. 'In any great system of thought,' said Æ, 'you must have a cosmogony, not just a set of moral rules.' Seeing, then, that after Blavatsky's downfall our intellectuals abandoned religion and adopted socialism, we should be surprised that two theosophical poets achieved so much success. At the turn of the century we had to look to Ireland if we wanted to find authors who assumed that men and women are spiritual beings involved in physical organisms. In England we had to find what nourishment there might be in Wells, with his confidence in nineteenth-century science; Bennett, with his matter-of-fact mind; Shaw, with his brain-spun socialism; and Galsworthy with his sentimental humanitarianism.

If only a few men could, like Blake, transcend the atmosphere of their period. . . . In 1900 agnosticism was 'the only wear' for our intellectuals. William Rothenstein says in *Men and Memories* that 'Stephen Phillips as well was a rising star. I asked Yeats and Phillips to lunch at Glebe Place. Yeats was in one of his best moods, and he and Phillips sat and talked for hour after hour until I, who had a dinner engagement, had to break up the party. In Phillips there was little of Yeats's nonsense, and but little of Yeats's poetic sense; but he had admirers, and his populairty made Yeats curious to meet him. Poor Phillips! There was always something pathetic about him. I suspected that, at heart, he did not think himself a great poet'. We should have been in debt to Rothenstein if, instead of these brash and

fashionable verdicts, he had troubled to record something of a conversation between the best poet-dramatist and the best lyric-poet of our
century.

NOTES

For a note on Clifford Bax see his previous article, 'Yeats at Woburn'.

1. This letter is not included in *The Letters of W. B. Yeats*, ed. Allan Wade (London: Rupert
Hart-Davis, 1954).
2. Joseph Hone, *W. B. Yeats 1865–1939* (London: Macmillan, 1943).
3. John Eglinton, *A Memoir of AE: George William Russell* (London: Macmillan, 1937).

Quarreling with Yeats:
A Friendly Recollection*

FRANK O'CONNOR

A few years before his death W. B. Yeats reconstituted the Abbey Theatre
Board by bringing on new members. The most important of these were
F. R. Higgins, the poet, and Brinsley MacNamara, the novelist. Because he
never forgot an obligation, he also appointed Ernest Blythe, who as
Minister of Finance had given the theatre a small subsidy of eight hundred
pounds a year,[1] in return for which the Government appointed one
director. It wasn't a very sensible board, for when one Government
representative retired, Yeats reappointed him; the Government appointed
a new representative, Richard Hayes, and, between Hayes and Blythe, it
would not be unfair to say that the Establishment had a more than
adequate voice in the running of the theatre.

*   *   *

I saw Yeats's original production of his own translation of *Oedipus Rex* in
which Oedipus hardly changed his position from beginning to end of the
play, and for the only time in my life I wanted to scream. Years later, I saw
Sir Laurence Olivier's production of the same version, and Sir Laurence,
remembering that 'Oedipus' means 'clubfoot,' demonstrated the fact by
jumping nimbly up and down boxes until I wanted to cry, 'Is there an
orthopedic surgeon in the house?' That, it seems to me, is the weakness of
the Shakespearean convention; it runs to irrelevant bits of business that

*   *Esquire* LXII, no. 6 (Dec 1964) 157, 221, 224–25, 232.

merely distract attention from the eternal words. Once, when we had a famous English actor playing in the theatre, he expressed intense intellectual effort by slowly picking up a match from the floor, and later in the crowded foyer, Yeats illustrated it for me. 'When he should have been calling down the thunderbolt,' he said, raising his right hand toward the ceiling, 'he was picking up matches,' and the tall figure bent and groped on the floor.

Now, Hugh Hunt[2] had been brought up in the Shakespearean convention, and later, when he produced the plays of Lady Gregory and Yeats, he did have a tendency to encourage the players to pick up matches, real or metaphorical. I had Lady Gregory's beautiful *Dervorgilla* revived, but at the dress rehearsal I found that the young actress who played the Queen sobbed through the whole last moving scene. All producers encourage sobbing, all actors love sobbing; sobbing is action, divorced from mere words. Later that evening when I went out to see Yeats I asked him, 'Is it *ever* permissible for an actor to sob on the stage?' 'Never!' said Yeats, and, as at that time he was writing a poem called *Lapis Lazuli*,[3] he embodied my Advice to the Players:

> Yet they, should the last scene be there,
> The great stage curtain about to drop,
> If worthy their prominent part in the play,
> Do not break up their lines to weep.

At the same time, though I was a Senecan as opposed to a Shakespearean, I was much more interested in cutting the throats of André Obey, William Shakespeare, Christopher Marlowe, and naturally, Henri Ghéon. I was not interested in foreign plays, which could be produced much better by the two young rascals across the road. I wanted new Irish plays, and I soon realized that nobody could produce them as Hugh Hunt could. In his productions of new plays, the peculiar clash of Shakespearean and Senecan resulted in an entirely new style and an entirely new type of actor—represented by Cyril Cusack—that suited perfectly the sort of theatre I wanted. As a result, I found that joining Yeats on the theatre board did not mean that he and I were to become better friends, but that I was to exchange casual disagreement for regular employment in which we would fight 'bitter and regular, like man and wife.'

*   *   *

Yeats, who really loved Robinson and knew how much I admired him, was forever probing me about him. 'What *is* wrong with Lennox?' he asked me one night point-blank, and, remembering that other conversation of a year or two before, I replied 'Dissatisfaction with his work.' Yeats looked at me over his glasses and said, 'I was afraid you were going to say dissatisfaction with something else.' By this time I think he knew what the something else was—old Mrs. Robinson had lived too long and had had too good a son.

*   *   *

When, soon afterward, Robinson's misbehavior[4] came to a head in a public outburst against myself and Hunt, the Government representative, Richard Hayes, tabled a resolution demanding his resignation from the Board. Before the Board meeting Yeats asked me to tea in his club. He began as only Yeats could begin. 'Richard Hayes has proposed a resolution demanding Robinson's resignation. I have personal reasons for opposing it, and I want you to understand that I shall have to oppose it.'

'We shan't quarrel about that,' I said. 'If you feel that way about it, I'll support you.'

It was the first time that I realized how attached I was becoming to that extraordinary man. We took a taxi to the theatre, and I paid the taximan before Yeats could get the money out of his pocket. Then he went mad and grabbed the taxi driver's arm.

'Give it back! Give it back!' he stammered. 'I have the money. Give it back!'

'Don't make a fuss, W.B.,' I said, and he turned on me.

'I wouldn't mind,' he said excitedly, 'But George[5]—George would never forgive me.'

I was touched again because I knew that when a man feels he must tell his wife who paid for the taxi, he must be very fond of her indeed.

It was a queer, agonizing evening, almost every detail of which I could still reproduce. There was the misery of the theatre back stairs, for instance. Yeats was obviously very ill and could climb only a step or two before pausing for breath. If it had been Russell, I should have taken his arm and lifted him up, but I knew Yeats wouldn't tolerate that from me. I could have run ahead and chattered from the top of the stairs, but I had been trying, without much success, to get the other members of the Board to stand up when he came into the room, and that didn't seem right either. At last we got up and he fell into a chair close to Robinson. Heyes's motion came up, and he spoke to it stingingly. Yeats began his reply and I have not forgotten the first words. 'Every member of this Board knows that Lennox Robinson is no longer responsible for his actions.' He ended with, 'Robinson will apologize for his behavior and his apology will be published in the Dublin newspapers.' Robinson sat through it all, showing no emotion. His very despondency was his greatest strength in obstructing business. When he was challenged, he merely relapsed into silence and pain. And yet I knew he worshiped Yeats and that it must have been agony for him to endure that humiliating apologia, as it was for Yeats to offer it. We were all glad when it ended. Then Yeats got up and went out without a word to Robinson.

Tragic, but comedy returned when Robinson wrote an apology that was a repetition of everything he had said about Hunt and myself. Yeats took it back, rewrote it and sent for Robinson. 'Now sign that,' he said. 'And he signed it,' Yeats added wearily when he told me the story later. I knew then that this had been Robinson's real offense in Yeats's eyes. One flash of defiance and Yeats would have stuck by him to the end.

*   *   *

I wanted to produce *The Player Queen*, my favorite Yeats play. As Hunt wanted occasionally to work with an English actress, I suggested that we should try Jean Forbes-Robertson, who had the unearthly, coloratura quality that the Player Queen must have. Yeats had promised the part to an actress friend of whom I had heard no favorable accounts and refused to accept. After that, all he would give us was *Deirdre*, a play I dislike, and which anyway was quite unsuitable for Jean Forbes-Robertson. It was like asking the perfect Zerlina to play Isolde. I felt even more unhappy when I took Jean out to lunch and she said gaily, 'Well, I don't understand a word of the part but I've made up a little story of my own that covers it pretty well.'

So, on the first night I gave up my seats to friends from the country and went to the theatre only to check the takings. I was in the box office when Yeats came staggering up the stairs from the stalls, clutching his head. 'Terrible! Terrible! Terrible!' was all I could get out of him. I was certain he was exaggerating, but when I saw the play myself next night, I felt he was optimistic, because he only disliked Jean Forbes-Robertson while I hated everybody on the stage. I felt they must all have heard Jean Forbes-Robertson's 'little story.' None of them could keep still; none of them could remain within the few notes that are all a real literary actor needs to produce any effect he pleases. 'Porthery,' as Higgins called it, simply couldn't exist in that Shakespearean atmosphere.

So, after a year or so, I became convinced that I couldn't keep Hunt on over the opposition of Yeats and Higgins, which was usually unreasonable and often ungenerous. One night Yeats asked me point-blank, 'Why do you insist on Hunt?' and I replied, 'Because I must have a competent man in the theatre.' Yeats gathered up his forces, and again referred the cause to an absent judge. 'As my crazy brother once said to me, "What business has an artist with competence?"'

*   *   *

He was the easiest man in the world for me to quarrel with, but it was hard to stay angry with him. One evening, after I had been a Director for a year or so, we attended a Board meeting and the Secretary said, 'Gentlemen, I have some good news for you. The Society now has a credit balance of three and sixpense.' I shall not swear to the exact figure, but it was somewhere in the neighborhood of seventy-five cents. After the usual letters from the bank manager, regretting that he would have to close the theatre down, it was a relief and we applauded. As we were leaving, Yeats asked me to walk with him to his bus. When we reached O'Connell Bridge he stopped and made one of his little formal speeches. These, like his reminiscences of people he hadn't met for twenty years, were part of his dramatic stock-in-trade, and had the same childlike quality. I wish I could recall its perfection of phrasing, but it had obviously been thought out, because, as so often with that strange, romantic man, self-accusation blended with congratulation.

'There's something I wanted to say to you, O'Connor. You may not have realized that I was watching what you did, because I have had to oppose so many of the things you have done, but all the same, I knew they had to be done. Thirty years ago, I should have done them myself, but now I am an old man and have too many emotional associations. Thank you.'

That made up for a great deal of squabbling, but, of course, it did not mean that the squabbling stopped. On the contrary, it went on worse than ever, and it never dawned on me that every squabble seemed to begin and end with Higgins.

There was that matter of *The Herne's Egg* for instance. Yeats had read it to me as he wrote it, and I thought it magnificent. When it came before the Board of the theatre only Ernest Blythe supported me, and he did so on the ground that the play was so obscure that no one would notice it was obscene. This was not what I felt at all, but I was glad of any support, because my friend, Hayes, the Government representative, threatened to resign if the play were produced, and I was voted down. I challenged Hayes about it afterwards, and he told me that Yeats had admitted to Higgins that the seven men who rape the priestess were intended to represent the seven sacraments. Now, the play isn't very difficult. Any reader of Yeats can test that argument for himself. I feel sure that the seven men represent the sciences and the priestess revealed religion, while the rape is merely a stylization of the nineteenth-century attack on religion, and, from the point of view of Catholic orthodoxy, you could produce *The Herne's Egg* in any ecclesiastical seminary—indeed, it might well be the last place in which you could produce it. But Hayes was very certain about what Higgins had told him, and I knew that Yeats did get embarrassed and excited and say things he regretted next day, so I could only reply that he didn't seem to understand his own work very well.

Finally, in a fit of exasperation, I said I would produce the play myself at my own expense, with the woman I was proposing to marry as Attracta. When I told Yeats, he turned on me with real anger, and I saw that under all the good-humored detachment, he was bitterly hurt at the rejection of his beautiful play by a gang of nobodies. 'And why did you not insist on its being produced when you had a majority of the Board behind you?' he shouted. I didn't know what to say, because the meeting had taken place some months before, and I had forgotten the details, but I told him that Hayes had threatened to resign if the play were produced, because he was supposed to have said that the seven men represented the seven sacraments. Yeats blew up. 'How could I have said anything so silly?' he asked, which was precisely what I had wondered myself. It wasn't until I was in bed that night that I remembered that nobody but Blythe had supported me, and that Yeats's friend, Higgins, had not only been against the play but was the person who had told Hayes what Yeats was supposed to have said about it. And still, it never occurred to me but that the whole business was a misunderstanding. I still believed that 'the great majority of people did not intend much harm to others, for the greater part of the time.'

*   *   *

My last memories of Yeats would have been sadder than they are if it hadn't been for his sister, Elizabeth. Elizabeth was a handsome woman with the gift of calculated indiscretion which, for some reason, I associate with America rather than Ireland. I went to see her one day and she asked:
   'Been up to see W.B.?'
   'No,' I said.
   'Why? Having a fight with him or something?'
   'No, it's not that. It's just that I feel I bore him.'
   'I wouldn't say that,' she said thoughtfully. 'He usually comes in here to tell me who has been to see him. The reason I asked is he always mentions when you've been up. No, I wouldn't say you bored him. Ring him up.'
   I saw him for the last time shortly before he left for France, and then it was to offer my resignation as director. It was obvious that the annulment action could not go through without some publicity, and I was afraid of its effect on the theatre. He knew that as Managing Director I had been very straitlaced and threatened action against two of the company whose love affair became public. 'But this is quite different, O'Connor,' he said with his sly humor. 'A Protestant director and a Catholic actress—I should demand their resignation at once. A Catholic director and a Protestant actress—we are unassailable. . . . The case will have to go to Rome, of course,' he added, as though he were regretting that he couldn't dissolve the inconvenient marriage by his own episcopal power. Then, becoming emotional and remembering the cruel remark I had made about him twelve months before, he added: 'I know you think I listen to greenroom gossip, but you saved my theatre, and when I die I want to leave it to Higgins and you. I will not accept your resignation.' There, again, was the essential Yeats—the man who never ignored a rebuke or an obligation.
   He went on to say that at the next meeting of the Abbey Board he attended he wanted me to propose Lennox Robinson's dismissal from the Board. 'When you quarreled with him before I had to oppose you, but I

knew you were right. He is a danger to the theatre, and he must go.'

Then I went too far and begged, as I had begged before, for the appointment of Denis Johnston as Manager of the Theatre and struck on old Rocky-face. Because he was feeling fond of me, he let me down lightly. He had obviously noticed that I was fond of his wife, and when he wanted to compliment me quoted her as his authority. 'You and George think exactly the same about Denis Johnston. George made me listen to a radio program of his on the Siege of Derry, and it was a masterpiece. But Johnston is a young man who would want his own way.' Swallowing the gentle snub, I wondered bitterly what he thought Higgins and Blythe wanted.

And then, a couple of days later, what should have happened years before happened. Yeats had a furious quarrel with Higgins. All I knew of it was a reference in one of Higgins' letters. 'W.B. has left in a difficult temper, owing to a personal awkwardness.' Apparently 'personal awkwardness' was a mild description of Yeats's discovery of how Higgins had been playing fast and loose with him for years. After this, Higgins did not reply to Yeats's letters at all, and Yeats, knowing he had only a short time to live, dictated a letter to me. He asked that if I agreed with him about what was necessary, I should telegraph and he would take a plane home, dismiss the board of directors and start again with one chosen by ourselves. I had no notion that he was dying, nor—apart from that phrase in Higgins' letter—had I any idea of the gravity of his quarrel with Higgins, so I took my time over replying. I was in a hotel in Chester waiting to get married when I settled down to write him a long soothing reply to say that everything in the theatre was fine. (Within a few months of his death Higgins and Blythe had maneuvered me out of it.) I was taking the letter to the post office when I bought a *Daily Telegraph* and read of his death.

NOTES

For a note on Frank O'Connor see p. 270.

    1. At the end of the civil war the Abbey Theatre was virtually bankrupt. Time and time again Yeats and Lady Gregory had had to go to their rich friends, mostly English, to save the Irish dramatic movement. Then, when the Treaty was signed, both felt that it would no longer become Irish dignity to seek support outside Ireland. Though the new government could not afford to set up a state theatre, chiefly through the good offices of the Minister of Finance, Ernest Blythe, a connoisseur of dramatic art, it gave the little theatre an annual subsidy, in the first year (1925) £800, and in subsequent years £1000.

    2. Hugh Hunt, a young English producer, had already been imported by Hilton Edwards and Micheál MacLiammóir for their Dublin Gate Theatre. He joined the Abbey Theatre as producer in 1935.

    3. In *Last Poems and Plays* (London: Macmillan, 1940).

    4. Lennox Robinson was the nominal producer, but he was drinking too much; the players usually produced themselves and often even selected the plays.

    5. George Yeats (Mrs W. B. Yeats).

Encounters with Yeats*

V. S. PRITCHETT

When I was 22 I had my first encounter with literature in person. I met my first great man. Until then I had been safely in the shellac trade but now I suddenly found myself reporting the Irish Civil War in Dublin. One day I had the, to me, incredible experience of seeing Mrs W. B. Yeats riding a bicycle. Soon after, with the sensations of one who is attempting a breach of natural law, I was knocking the door of the famous house in Merrion Square, to have tea with Yeats himself.

It was a Georgian house, as unlike a hut of wattle in a bee-loud glade as one could imagine. To begin with, the door opened on a chain and the muzzle of a rifle stuck through the gap. A pink-faced Free State soldier asked me if I had an 'appointment'. I was shown in to what must have been a dining room but now it was a guard room with soldiers smoking among the Blake drawings on the wall. Yeats was a Senator and he had already been shot at by gunmen known, to Irish respectability, as the Irregulars. Upstairs I was to see the bullethole in the drawing-room window. Presently the poet came down the stairs to meet me.

It is a choking and confusing experience to meet one's first great man when one is young. These beings come from another world and Yeats studiously created that effect. Tall, with grey hair finely rumpled, a dandy with negligence in collar and tie and with the black ribbon dangling from the glasses on a short, pale and prescient nose—not long enough to be Roman yet not sharp enough to be a beak—Yeats came down the stairs towards me, and the nearer he came the further away he seemed. His air was bird-like, suggesting one of the milder swans of Coole and an exalted sort of blindness. I had been warned, in Dublin, that he would not shake hands. They said his manner was very English, and an Englishman, in those days, was thought to be a man who believed the most important thing in life was to know the difference between Sole Colbert and Sole Meunière. I have heard it said—but only by the snobbish Anglo-Irish—that Yeats was a snob. I would have said that he was a man who was transported into a higher world the moment his soft voice throbbed. He was the only man I have known who spoke naturally in verse. Cool but fervent verse.

* *New Statesman* (London) LXIX (4 June 1965) 879–80.

He sat me in the fine first floor of his house. After all these years all that remains with me is a memory of candles, books, woodcuts, the feeling that here was Art. And conversation. But what about? I cannot remember. The warm voice flowed over me. The tall figure, in uncommonly delicate tweed, walked up and down, the voice becoming more resonant, as if he were on a stage. At the climax of some point about the Celtic revival, he suddenly remembered he must make tea, in fact a new pot, because he had already been drinking tea. The problem was one of emptying out the old tea pot. It was a beautiful pot and he walked the room with the short aesthetes steps, carrying it in his hand. It came towards me. It receded to the bookcase. It swung round the sofa. Suddenly with Irish practicality he went straight to one of the two splendid Georgian windows of the room, opened it, and out went those barren leaves with a swoosh, into Merrion Square—for all I knew on to the heads of Lady Gregory, Oliver St John Gogarty, AE, and that gifted lady—whose name I forget—who did stained glass windows. It was a distinguished square. They were China tea-leaves.

I can remember only one thing he said. We had got on to Shaw, whom he disliked. I murmured—showing off—something about Shaw's socialist principles. The effect on Yeats was splendid. He stood now, with a tea-pot full of tea in his hands, saying in his beautiful voice that Shaw had no principles. He was a destroyer. Like lightning. Shaw flashed in hilarious indifference, like forked lightning, and what the lightning revealed was interesting, but it was not interesting in itself. This has always stuck in my mind; but of the rest I remember nothing except that with solemnity he pointed to the inner hall of the room and said that, sitting in this room, he had experimented in thought transference with Mrs Yeats in the room next door. As I say, I had seen her out on her bicycle and I have often wondered, as the fine mind expelled its thoughts to the wall, whether Mrs Yeats was always next door at the time. He was kind enough to walk with me to the Irish Senate, nearby, and I was overcome when he leant on my shoulder while he lifted a foot, took off his shoe and shook out a stone. I noticed he had a pretty, dull blue stone in a ring on one of his fingers. I left him, semiconscious.

Fifteen years passed before I spoke to Yeats again. I had seen that blue stone on his finger as he paced the floor of the Irish Senate—other Senators stayed stolidly in their seats—making utterances on behalf of freedom of conscience, denouncing censorship, speaking for divorce—all lost causes in Ireland—while irascible characters like Col Moore, George Moore's brother, went red with the silly old Irish rage. For the first time, by ear and eye, I understood that an artist is before all else a man of courage. I have always detested the Irish mockery of Yeats.

And then came one Sunday in London during the Thirties. I was having luncheon at the long table of a London club, the only member there. I was eating quickly because I was due to tread the peanuts in Trafalgar Square where one of those not very mass meetings about Spain was to take place.

Presently, in came Yeats and sat, aloof, with his blind look, nearly opposite to me.

To speak or not to speak? It is always the question with the very great. Perhaps they like to be alone. I had seen him sometimes walking in Leicester Square or Regent Street, tall, lonely, unconversible and with his lips moving as if he were going over lines of verse. In the end, I spoke. I told him I was going to the mass meeting. The effect was of having put a coin in a sublime juke box. He raised his head, gazed at some far away place and the exalted voice intoned dramatically words like these:

'I remember,' the Irish voice said, taking off, 'I remember,' he reverberated, 'marching down O'Connell Street with many thousands of Irishmen and,' he paused for an expression of supreme pleasure, 'we smashed £10,000-worth of plate glass.'

Smash, smash went the glass—with a short 'a'—and plate glass, not glass in general. The sound was like laughter yet the tone was that of the Book of Common Prayer.

Years pass. And then, one day into this same club comes rosy H. G. Wells. He sits down and looks with astonishment: 'Hullo Yeats! Haven't seen you for God knows how many years. Good God. How are you? The last time we met must have been at Mrs X's. Must be 20 years ago. What a beautiful woman! I saw her last week. Have you seen her?'

'No,' comes the exalted Celtic voice, pained, mournful, withdrawing.

'Oh don't, Yeats!' says Wells. 'Don't. The years! Paralysed all down one side, Yeats, twisted, terrible, can't speak. She was so beautiful. Ah Yeats. Old Age. It gets us all. The stairs—that's where you notice it. Did you pant as you came up the stairs today? Ha! Ha—that's where it gets us. The heart. You get breathless, pant. Terrible. Then it comes. Death! Don't let's think of it. Yeats. Let's forget it. What are you eating? Mince? I'll have lobster and a pint of bitter.'

A few months pass. Yeats is dead. My last encounter is like my very first; the first time I was thinking of clay and wattle on his doorstep. The last, I visit an elementary school off Tottenham Court Road, the usual class of 40 children, boys and girls, to see how English was being taught in the Thirties. It was the done thing for writers then to get in touch with 'the people'. The radio is switched on and a refined Cityfied voice succinctly utters in neutralised English the well-known lines, done to death. The children sniffle, fidget and listen. The schoolmaster takes a bit of chalk and writes. 'Children remember this: The Lone Isle of Innisfree, by W. B. Yeats.'

I hear a smash of plate glass, the end of a great man.

NOTE

Victor Sawdon Pritchett (1900–) is an English novelist and critic. After working as a commercial traveller and shop assistant he became a journalist and was for two years literary editor of the *New Statesman*. He wrote novels, *Claire Drummer* (1929), *Nothing like Leather*

(1935), *Dead Man Leading* (1937) and *Mr. Beluncle* (1951); short stories *You Make Your Own Life* (1938) and *It May Never Happen* (1947); criticism, *In My Good Books, The Living Novel* (1947) and *Books in General* (1953); and *A Cab at the Door: An Autobiography—Early Years* (1968).

Glimpses of W. B. Yeats*

AUSTIN CLARKE

During the early thirties, when I was earning my livelihood in London as a reviewer, I was asked by a publisher to write a biographical study of Yeats. Despite the reputation of the poet as a Nobel Prize-winner, only three studies of his work had appeared, the first, a short one, by an American writer,[1] the other two by Irishmen, J. M. Hone,[2] and the novelist, Forrest Reid.[3] The alert young director who interviewed me in the great office of the firm asked me whether the love affair between Maud Gonne and Yeats had been platonic or not, as this would give interest to the book. I said that I would question the poet himself and the director looked at me with such surprise that I realised at once the rashness of my promise. When I got back to Bricket Wood, a wooded corner of Herts near St. Albans, where I lived, I took down from the shelf *The Wind among the Reeds* and read it carefully in order to see if I could find out the truth from the poems themselves. These lyrics have the languorous, sensuous quality which the poets of the Nineties borrowed from Rossetti and his school. Certainly in some of them there were indications that the poet's relations with Maud Gonne had been immoral! He speaks of—

> Passion-dimmed eyes and long heavy hair
> That was shaken out over my breast.[4]

And again—

> White woman that passion has worn
> As the tide wears the dove-grey sands.[5]

And in one of the later poems, 'The Lover Speaks to the Hearers of his Songs in Coming Days.' I was among those hearers as I read the line—

> Bend down and pray for all that sin I wove in song.

I sat for a long time wondering over the character of Yeats and recalling various occasions on which I had met him.

When I was seventeen, I went frequently to the Abbey Theatre and sometimes saw Yeats sitting in the stalls beside Lady Gregory. When one of

---

* Extracted from *Shenandoah* (Lexington, Virginia) XVI, no. 4 (Summer 1965) 25–36.

his verse plays was performed, he came always on to the stage afterwards and talked about it to the audience, a black lock falling over his brow, the long black ribbon of his pince-nez dangling. Tall and shadowy in a Celtic Twilight of his own, he would wave his arms as he chanted his chosen words. I met him some years later in a romantic way. I had gone down to Co. Sligo to see the Lake Isle of Innisfree, the cairn of Maeve between the town and the ocean, the little waterfall at Glencar and other places associated with his early poems. After that, I cycled down to Co. Galway and, on a sunny morning, stood outside the gates of Coole. I went into a field, climbed over a loose stone-wall and dropped into the Seven Woods. As I trespassed among them, I came after some time to the edge of the trees and, looking from my hiding place, saw, to my astonishment, the poet stalking across the lawn to Lady Gregory's mansion with fishing rod, basket and net, looking like one of the gentry. Shortly afterwards I was lunching with him in a small house outside the gate of Coole where he was staying after his marriage. He spoke to me at length of Donne, Vaughan, Herbert, Dryden and then of Landor, his voice rising and falling as he urged me to study their works and follow their austere example. As I was a lecturer in English Literature at the time in University College, Dublin, and still immersed in Gaelic mythology and poetry, his severe lecture chilled me and, like Joyce, I felt that I had met him a generation too late.

When Yeats returned to Dublin, I saw him every Thursday evening during the following winter at the house of Joseph O'Neill,[6] Secretary to the Department of Education and a very original novelist. Yeats was then writing *A Vision*. Women crowded around him in that drawing-room, listening eagerly as he discussed the book with them. Across the room I could hear his monotonous tones: 'One may regard the subjective phases as forming a separate wheel. Its phase 8 between phases 11 and 12 . . . of the larger wheel, its phase 22 between phases 19 and 20 . . .' I turned to talk to others, but I could still hear that chanting voice: 'The true *Creative Mind* of phase 27 I described as super sensual receptivity and it is derived from phase 3 as that phase is modified by its *Body of Fate*.' I disliked astrology, horoscope casting and other follies of the past and so during that winter I carefully avoided the poet on these occasions. One night, however, I found myself walking home after midnight with him and Iseult, the beautiful daughter of Maud Gonne. They talked happily together and I felt an intruder as I kept up with their rapid pace for both were long-legged. As we were passing Harcourt Street Railway Station, I glanced at both of them furtively and they seemed so much alike that I could not help wondering whether the rumor that they were father and daughter were correct. Later I learned that this literary legend of Dublin was completely false.

I wrote to Yeats asking whether he would approve of my wish to write a biographical study of him and asked if he would be kind enough to see me some time at his convenience, when I was over in Dublin. While I waited for a reply from him, I started to collect material for the work and went to the Reading Room of the British Museum three or four times a week.

*   *   *

One happy morning, I received a note from the great man to tell me that he would be in London during the following week and would meet me in the Saville Club at four o'clock on the Tuesday afternoon of that week.

In the sedate, gloomy lounge of the Saville Club, W. B. Yeats was seated alone at a small tea-table, already waiting for me. He got up at once, shook hands with me, and spoke at once.

'I am over in London for a few days to arrange about the publication of my new book, *A Vision*,[7] which has taken me many years to write. I have no doubt that the critics and philosophers will not agree with what I have said in it, but I am sure that I am right in my theory of the universe.'

He remained standing for a few moments, his head bowed in humility, looking so absurd that I could not help smiling secretly to myself. Somehow I could not believe in this new pose but I have no doubt that he felt a little anxious about the reception which the book would get because of its strange admixture of philosophy, astrology and abracadabra. He could not have guessed that in later years his theories would be analysed respectfully by professors and students with scant knowledge of the follies of the past. When he sat down, a waiter appeared immediately and the poet ordered tea. Then, much to my surprise, in a stern reproachful tone, he said:

'This is not an interview and on no account must anything I say be given to the press.' He added, however, in a milder tone and with a smile, 'When I was a younger writer, I frequently attacked the journalists, but since then I have learnt to tolerate them.'

As I was only a book reviewer and much too impracticable to be a Fleet Street journalist, his suspicions made me uneasy—all the more so as I had before me the difficult problem of asking him about his relations with Maud Gonne.

We had scarcely begun to talk when, much to my alarm, I saw Sir John Squire,[8] poet, critic, former editor of the *London Mercury*, and literary dictator, coming into the lounge. He hurried over to Yeats and began talking to him. After a minute or so he turned to me and asked agreeably, 'How is your Celtic Empire getting on, Clarke?' For a moment I was puzzled and then I remembered the evening I had spent with him some years previously at his house in Chiswick. As we sat in his small, book-lined study upstairs drinking beer, he spoke unsympathetically of the Irish struggle for freedom. Provoked by his attitude and slightly intoxicated by the mild-and-bitter, to which I was not accustomed, I described rapidly a great Celtic Empire spreading to England, the Colonies and the United States of America. I had forgotten long since my horrible vision of a corrupting, powerful Tammany Hall—our contribution to modern civilisation. Fortunately, Yeats remained aloof and, seeing that he was not wanted, Sir John left us and strolled into the bar room.

We returned to our conversation and I mentioned Forrest Reid's book.

'I have forgotten it,' intoned Yeats, gently waving away that invisible volume with his right hand, on which gleamed a large signet ring of silver made for him by Edmund Dulac. No doubt my own study would be forgotten as quickly, I thought, and my depression increased. He became cheerful again and said to me, as if by rote, 'There are portraits of me in the National Gallery in Merrion Square, and also in the Dublin Municipal Art Gallery. There are others in the galleries of Liverpool, Birmingham, Bristol, Leicester and Edinburgh.'

This was not very helpful but he mentioned soon afterwards that few critics had written about his plays and it was clear that he wished me to deal specially with them. As I had always admired his plays very much, I agreed with him about the critics. I would have liked to have told him of those early years when I had seen them at the Abbey Theatre, but I hesitated and the opportunity passed. There was a lull in our conversation and I knew the dire moment had come when I must ask about Maud Gonne. Carefully wrapping up my question in as many vague words as was possible, I said, 'Mr. Yeats, I would like to discuss with you *The Wind among the Reeds*, a book which I have always liked immensely. It would help me very much in writing my study to have a general idea of your inclinations in those love-poems. Would it be too much to ask if there is any basis in actual fact for them?'

Yeats caught my implication at once. His manner changed and, looking down at me like an eminent Victorian, he exclaimed: 'Sir, are you trying to pry into my private life?' Then, seeing my startled expression, he must have felt that he had gone too far for, in a trice, he had become confidential and, smiling pleasantly, continued with a vague wave of the hand. 'Of course, if you wish to suggest something in your biography, you may do so, provided that you do not write anything that would give offense to any persons living.'

As a Victorian, he wanted to have it both ways. Unfortunately, during this interview, I was sitting close to Yeats on the inner side of the small table and occasionally, as I turned to him, I could see behind the thick lens of his glasses a brown eye straining at its tiny muscles as if trying to peep into my very thoughts. It was the acute eye of a Sligo man and yet it seemed, somehow, to have an existence of its own. Every time I saw that small watcher, I turned away in embarrassment. About five o'clock he appeared fatigued and said the time had come for him to lie down and rest before dinner. He stood gazing into space as I put on my overcoat, took my hat and stick, and then said farewell to me at the entrance of the lounge.

I never wrote the book.

NOTES

Austin Clarke (1896–1974) was an Irish poet who won the Tailtean Award for poetry in 1932 and who, since Yeats's death, has been regarded as Ireland's greatest poet. He was a foundation member of the Irish Academy of Letters and became its President from 1952 to 1954. His latest volumes of poetry include *Later Poems* (1961) and *Flights to Africa* (1963). He has also written novels, *The Bright Temptation* (1932) and *The Singing Men at Cashel* (1936); and an autobiography, *Twice Around the Black Church* (1960). His *Collected Plays* were published in 1963. Clarke has written extensively on Yeats.

1. H. S. Krans, *William Butler Yeats and the Irish Literary Revival* (New York: McClure Phillips, 1904; London: Heinemann, 1905).

2. Joseph M. Hone, *William Butler Yeats: The Poet in Contemporary Ireland* (London and Dublin: Maunsel and Roberts, [1915]).

3. Forrest Reid. *W. B. Yeats: A Critical Study* (London: Secker; New York: Dodd, Mead, 1915).

4. W. B. Yeats, 'He Reproves the Curlew', *The Wind among the Reeds* (1899).

5. W. B. Yeats, 'A Poet to His Beloved', *The Wind among the Reeds* (1899).

6. Joseph O'Neill (1886–1953), Irish novelist and member of the Irish Academy of Letters. His novels include *Wind from the North* (1934), *Land under England* (1935), *Day of Wrath* (1936), *Philip* (1940) and *Chosen by the Queen* (1947). Yeats gained much of his knowledge of the Irish educational system from his friend Joseph O'Neill.

7. W. B. Yeats, *A Vision: An Explanation of Life Founded upon the Writings of Giraldus and upon Certain Doctrines Attributed to Kusta Ben Luka* (London: T. Werner Laurie, 1925) (privately printed).

8. Sir John Collins Squire (1884–1958) became literary editor of the *New Statesman* in 1913, and from 1919 to 1934 was editor of the *London Mercury*, in which he wrote under the name of Solomon Eagle.

Visions of Yeats*

WALTER STARKIE

I discovered in my talks with Yeats that his own antagonism to Ibsen—'the chosen author of very clever journalists'—and Bernard Shaw—the 'sewing-machine,' as he once called him—was deep-rooted. He himself longed to create a form that would be the direct antithesis to naturalistic drama, a remote, spiritual and ideal form which at the same time should embody energy and noble speech. 'I wished,' he said, 'to leave the drama of every day to Lady Gregory and Lennox Robinson. I know that beneath the surface of modern middle-class life in Ireland there existed a primitive peasant culture possessing racy living speech and deep human qualities.' When he used to invite me to discuss these problems with him he would stride up and down the rooms, gesticulating with his hands and soliloquizing rhythmically. 'One has,' he chanted, 'a thousand idea, but only

* Extracted from 'Yeats and Company', *New York Times Book Review*, 14 Nov 1965, pp. 90–2.

one or two are carried out. One cannot understand the Odyssey if one has not sailed in a trireme.'

At times when he was depressed, he wished to abandon Dublin and obtain respite from what Verlaine had called '*Tout cet ail de basse cuisine.*' 'It is time,' he said, 'for Lennox Robinson to shoulder the burdens. He has been tested in the fire and he will show his mettle. Lady Gregory comes up from Coole regularly, but she is getting old.' How often Yeats had gone away from Dublin for long periods, knowing that Lady Gregory from her watchtower in Coole would never fail to keep the theater under her protective care.

The rejection of 'The Silver Tassie' by Yeats sprang from his rooted antagonism to the dramatic form common to Ibsen, Shakespeare and Sophocles—the drama that consisted of a moral analysis of character within a more or less logical framework. Ever since Yeats's mentor, Ezra Pound, had introduced him to the Noh plays of Japan, he had dreamed of creating 'an unpopular theater.' 'I want,' he said, 'not a theater but the theater's antiself.'

During the years when he had abandoned writing for the theater he had been schooling himself in theater practice and meditations on drama, and now in his old age, he emerged with a series of new plays combining music and the dance. The forerunner of the series was 'The Player Queen,' which he had begun to write as far back as 1909 but did not terminate until 1922, when it was played by Ninette de Valois at the Cambridge Art Theater.

During those last years I noticed in Yeats an increasing interest in music, and so fascinated was he by ancient Irish songs that he published many broadsides which contained verses of his own, engravings by his brother Jack and melodies from the treasure-store of Irish folk-music. He used to boast that he had no sense of pitch, but a perfect sense of rhythm. This explains his attitude towards music, which was partly friendly and partly hostile. He was highly suspicious of professional musicians and maintained that a poem should not be set to a musical accompaniment, for then the words are sacrificed and become distorted by the rhythm of the music. 'Any musician,' he asserted, 'who claims to translate the emotion of a poet into another vehicle is a liar.'

To judge by the music he selected for his plays for dancers, we should infer that all he really wanted was rhythm, hence his preference for drums, knucklebones and gongs and his rejection of piano and strings. Nevertheless, on many occasions he used to invite me to his house in Riversdale, where he was alone. He would read aloud poem after poem, asking me to improvise on my fiddle rhythmic tunes between the stanzas, adapting my music to the character of the poem. He would also ask me to tell him of the young poet-dramatist Federico Garcia Lorca, whom I had recently seen directing his caravan-players in Spain, and I would translate passages from the latter's plays which combined poetry, music and the dance.

My last vision of W. B. Yeats was in August, 1938, during the Abbey
Theater Festival, when he produced his 'Purgatory,' a one-act play based
on the idea that a family can never purge itself of a crime inherited with its
blood, but repeats its transgression again and again until the last evil
consequences to itself are purged away. The play, as well as dealing with a
favorite theme of Yeats, the remorse of the dead which chains them to the
spot where they lived, reflects also the poet's deep sadness at the
government's wanton pulling-down of Coole, which he had loved above
all other houses. As he said to the press after the performance: 'In my play a
spirit suffers because of its share, when alive, in the destruction of an
honored house. The destruction is taking place all over Ireland today.'

NOTE

Walter FitzWilliam Starkie (1894–   ) was a Director of the Abbey Theatre from 1926 to
1942 and a Professor-in-Residence at the University of California in Los Angeles from 1961 to
1967. As a young man he had studied music and played the violin all over Europe, using his
skill to acquire friendship of the gipsies and to study their music and folklore. From this came
Raggle Taggle (1933), an account of his adventures in the Balkans. *Spanish Raggle Taggle*
(1934), *Gypsy Folklore & Music* (1935), *The Waveless Plain* (an Italian memoir; 1938), *In Sara's
Tents* (1953), *The Road to Santiago* (1957) and *Scholars & Gypsies* (autobiography; 1963)—all
reflect this lifelong interest. In a letter to Lady Gerald Wellesley dated 30 June 1936, Yeats
described Starkie as a 'fat man . . . who most years spends a couple of months among gypsies
in Spain, Austria, etc., playing his fiddle and escaping among the gypsy women, according to
one of the reviewers, "a fate worse than death" . . .' Starkie's writings on Yeats include an
'Introduction' to *The Celtic Twilight and a Selection of Early Poems by W. B. Yeats* (New York:
Signet Classics, 1962) and 'W. B. Yeats, premio Nobel, 1924', *Nuova Antologia*, series 6,
ccxxxiv (1 Apr 1924) 238–45.

Some Memories of
W. B. Yeats*

BRIGIT PATMORE

Yeats—the sound of the name pulls one up short—it is imperative or
questioning. He was unique: How write about him? True, D. H. Lawrence
was unique, Ezra Pound is unique, but one can gather up the golden
strands around them and weave a small pattern, but Yeats's darkly
sportive imagination is awe inspiring.

I cannot remember ever having seen a smile on Yeats's face: it was
difficult to see what expression passed in his eyes, for the thick lenses of his

* *Texas Quarterly* (Austin, Texas: University of Texas) VIII (Winter 1965) 152–9.

spectacles hid them completely. I feel that his rapt enjoyment of beauty did not allow itself to be shown by shining teeth and jovial, mobile lips; indeed his desire for style in behavior demanded gravity on his dreamer's face and besides, the Celts often hide their laughter, and how cruel that laughter can be! Not that I ever saw any cruelty in Yeats, and his courtesy was unfailing. What gave me confidence in him was the unconscious pride that pierced to his very bones. The kind of pride noble animals have and *they* never fail one.

Quite early in my friendship with Ezra Pound he took me to Yeats's rooms in Woburn Place, which is one of those strange quiet little courts in the middle of busy districts. I remember blue curtains and candlelight and a tall, dark, gracious host, but all else was lost in the bewilderment of a dumb child in Heaven. Even Ezra was a little subdued—except for, at times, an explosive question, such as: 'Do you think Stendhal was wrong in his descriptions of Italy?'

And Yeats's cryptic answer: 'Ah! He was a man of many masks!'

The great poet had in him what I love and have found only in a few people—something I can simply call an ambience of being at home with the saints, and this has nothing to do with religion or churches.

I knew three of the women who were important in Yeats's life. Olivia Shakespear,[1] who was beautiful, full of charm and sympathy, highly intelligent and most kind, but she seemed worldly compared with the other two, Maud and Iseult Gonne, for they lured one into an heroic age. After Yeats married George (called this instead of Geo*rgie*, which both husband and wife disliked) Hyde-Lees in 1917, Yeats loaned 10 Woburn Place to Maud and Iseult and I saw them both there, but I would prefer to write about that later, and jump ahead to Rapallo in 1928–29.

Our hotel was on the left of the bay. Ezra had engaged rooms for us, R.[2] and myself, and welcomed us enthusiastically, which was very good, but took us at once to have tea at the English Tennis Club, which was odd, for we had come to Italy to be with him away from England, both climate and people. To my great joy he told us that Yeats and his wife were expected in a few days. As Yeats had been ill and ordered to rest, he was to be allowed some days to recover from the journey, and then we would have permission to see him. One wondered how long Yeats would allow Ezra to arrange his life.

It must have been about two days after the Yeatses' arrival that, whilst I was writing in my sitting room, R. was standing at the window, watching the parade of people by the seashore—for the sun was brilliant. Suddenly he said eagerly: 'There's Yeats walking by the sea. He's so tall . . . in his black coat and large black hat . . . obviously a disguised god visiting these short bumbling Italians. He stops to gaze at something on the beach: his hands behind his back he ponders long. Wonder what it *could* be . . . it's such a treasureless strand. He moves on. He would never stop to stare, but is clearly interested in a girl . . . she's very brightly colored . . . probably too much dazzle on his glasses. Ah! there's George. She comes up to W. B. who hasn't seen her. She takes his arm, he seems surprised and a little startled. Who is this stranger? Can it be? . . . It is! It's my wife! Relieved, he allows her to lead him to the Savoia for the *café Belge* he loves. Let's go and join them.'

Two days after this Mr. Yeats telephoned to the hotel and asked us to tea on that same day.

Yeats never seemed to be troubled about his background: he did not, apparently, wish for luxury, although I'm sure he loved beautiful houses and the finely imagined living they were made for. The flat that George and he had in the Via Americhe 12−8 was in a modern block of flats and was plainly furnished by English people—it had not an Italian look. The Yeatses had brought books and a few engravings: the sitting room had a large bookcase, a round table, and an upright armchair in three corners, the door was next to the fourth corner.

We had tea in the dining room, and Yeats led us into the sitting room. He placed us in the armchairs, seating himself in the one at the apex of the triangle.

He had a sheet of paper in his hand.

'I'd like to read you a poem I've just written—if I may. It is called "Three Things." '[3]

We said we would be honored. He began:

"'O cruel death, give me three things back"
Sang a bone upon the shore;
"A child found all a child can lack,
Whether of pleasure or of rest,
Upon the abundance of my breast:"
A bone wave-whitened and dried in the wind.'

He chanted the words, as he always did while reading poetry, but accented the rhythm so that it was not monotonous. R. and I exchanged a quick glance at 'Sang a bone on the shore.' So *that* was what he looked at so long the other day!

But after every two lines he raised his head a little and over his spectacles, looked at me and then after the next two lines, at R. This continued during all the three verses. Somehow it was very disconcerting, and I saw R's throat move as if he were swallowing and knew that nervous laughter was tormenting him. This strange birdlike glancing first to one corner and then to the other, was quite hard to endure, and I could only gaze bright-eyed at Yeats, hoping I looked intelligent and would not giggle like a silly schoolgirl.

Fortunately R. could say the right thing as one poet to another and I murmured reverently words of praise.

Yeats repeated what he often said:
'We always strove for the effect of the spoken word.'

Two days later Mrs. Yeats rang me up on the telephone to ask if I could come to tea that same afternoon—'But by yourself. Willie says that you hardly speak at all when R. is with you.'

I accepted but protested that I never spoke much—especially before anyone I respected as much as Yeats.

George said, very matter-of-factly, 'Oh nonsense!'

But she did not know. Yeats was used to women who were—not aggressive—but strong and full of confidence, like herself and Maud and Iseult Gonne, but in me, apparent ease and calm covered an absurd diffidence and shyness. However, I went to the Via Americhe excited, but with teeth chattering, for had not the great man written in *Per Amica Silentia Lunae:*

'How shall I forgive that woman who sat next to me at dinner last night and repeated the common-places of the newspapers.'
And then again in a letter: 'Every thought made in some manufactory and with the mark upon it of its wholesale origin.' You see? These sentences are a little like plaster over one's mouth. Had it been Lawrence, who was also a great man, one could be sad or cheeky or intense and he would quickly talk some sense into one.

Anyway Yeats was welcoming, genial, and seemed happy. When George was going out of the room to get tea, Yeats asked her:

'Have you heard from Ireland about the visitor we're expecting? You'd better write again, George.' In explanation to me: 'We have invited a gunman to come here and are anxious he should make no mistake, or think we do not want him. They're so sensitive, these gunmen.'

It was a new aspect of gunmen to most people, but very typical of Yeats.

'It is surely a long time since I saw you. Do you ever see those energetic, eager young American girls who came over to study with Freud?'

'They went back to their American homes after a few months.'

'One rather emphatic young lady I remember. Why . . . why she talked about the phallus as if it were no more than a carrot.'

I allowed myself a smile, wishing that somehow the adorable man would give one a cue for laughter, but said: 'She was of German origin and called Rosel Armata. She wanted to know about your adventures—may I call them that—with spirits when you were in Paris with—it was Macgregor, wasn't it?—I tried to tell her about the elemental in your room, and how you only got rid of him by getting him one side of the table and pushing the table to the window and him *out* of the window.'

'Did I tell you that?' Yeats said, a little remorseful it seemed to me. 'But I wouldn't have called "it" him. He was evidently a bad spirit.'

In order to change the mood Yeats showed me the William Morris volumes he had arranged by themselves, and some reproductions of—I think—illustrations to *The Earthly Paradise*.

Bookcases are irresistible: I had to look at the one in this room. The books were mostly memoirs, autobiographies or volumes of letters. I saw Horace Walpole's letters, and saying: 'May I?' took them down and read a few lines. Putting them back I said:

'How I should love to read those. But you wouldn't trust me. You'd think I'd never bring them back!'

But W.B. took them out again, and put them in my arms saying: 'You won't, I know. You'll forget, but take them.' His accent becoming slightly more Irish—'Ye will Ye won't!'

'See how we trifle! But one can't pass one's youth too amusingly; for one must grow old, and that in England; two most serious circumstances, either of which makes people grey in the twinkling of a bed-staff; for know you, there is not a country upon earth where there so many old fools and so few young ones.'

HORACE WALPOLE

The above-written extract from Horace Walpole's letters I showed to R., and he decided to use it as a suitable quotation after the title page of his novel *Death of a Hero*.[4]

From Eire came Lennox Robinson, so tall and thin, his height resembled the mysterious elongation of a giraffe, his large spectacles making a half mask, effectively hiding his constant vision of the humor of things, or perhaps it was the ludicrous. At the same time came also a roundheaded little man who looked as if he might be a merchant but he was a senator from Dublin—his name I have forgotten.

The Yeatses gave a dinner party at the Savoia and I was more than pleased to be seated by Lennox, for his wistful, unsmiling laughter-making enchanted me, particularly as no bitter lines distorted his smooth youthful face.

He was staring at Mr. Blank, the senator, who was seated on the opposite side of the table: then he murmured: 'It *can't* be true!'

'What can't be true,' I asked anxiously.

'It couldn't have been a chambermaid.'

'What on earth . . .?'

'The most unbeguiling females one has ever seen. The manager must have staffed the hotel with all the bewhiskered great-aunts of a horde of mountain bandits. No, *not* a chambermaid . . . I know he hasn't been out all day.'

Amazement kept me silent.

'Don't you see?' lowering his voice, 'Those marks on his forehead, his poor, bald high forehead—scratches, fresh ones—not healed, congealed—and those lower down on his cheeks. No razorblade marks a face like that, not even after a hangover after four Stregas and five Grappas.'

He was talking so like a detective in a Who-done-it that I gazed open-mouthed at the victim, while Lennox went on with his analysis.

'My first thought naturally was an amorous adventure begun mildly and then going far too far—there was some talk about a pretty waitress—fifteen years ago, it's true—but one thinks, one hopes, the fires have died down, and then freedom, a new country. . . . *You* tell me—how did he get them?'

'Mosquito bites, then scratching them, or walking into a cactus hedge?'

'Summer sports, me dear, and it's January. No. I see it! Remember the woman of a certain age we saw here wearing so much jewelry on her magnificent bosom, so many diamond medals for bad conduct that—oh the glass mountain it was! Well, he goes into her room, by mistake—or on the leer of invitation, as Shakespeare puts it. Just when he is on his knees, declaring himself—to use a euphemism—the door bursts open, her latest gigolo rushes in, flaming eyes, whirling arms! She clasps the poor senator to that glittering mountain—and his face is ruined on other men's tokens of approval. Sad, sad! But how clearly one sees it!'

This broke me down into laughter, and Lennox turned his head to look very seriously at me.

'Tell me,' I said, 'someone told me that when Yeats engaged you, or rather, chose you, for the Abbey Theatre, that he said afterwards . . .'

'I know,' Lennox interrupted, raising his hand in a characteristic gesture of Yeats, 'there's something about that young man's back . . .'

'I wonder what he meant. Does he always form his opinions from unusual aspects of people?'

'As to meaning, perhaps he thought troubles would slide off my back, because he couldn't have thought it would bear any burden, or could he? And no one knows for certain how he decides anything—though sometimes he might be not unlike a theatre man in Dublin who has, according to a stagehand "words to fit every occasion and guaranteed to blister asbestos." '

Having enjoyed Lennox's conversation for too long, I turned away and heard George's voice describing to R. an encounter with 'rebels' in Eire. People belonging to a conquering race usually speak of their conquered unconquerable victims with fury or the condescending amusement sometimes shown before the antics of a clever naughty child: this latter attitude was what George adopted.

'They came,' she was saying, 'three or four men, and were going to blow up the bridge by our house. As we have to use it I asked them if they couldn't blow up the little one further down the stream. They had a short confabulation and then said the little one would do, but to me they said, "Please ma'am, put your tooth on this an' never breathe it again." '

R. must have asked something about her son Michael,[5] for she said:

'He likes his school in Switzerland and doesn't want to come here very much, although his attitude to his father is kinder than the time he was a small boy, when his opinion was—"I don't like the man [meaning Willie] the man I pass on the stairs"!'

R. and I dined with Yeats and George, when the heavy snow of the 1928 – 29 winter suddenly fell on Rapallo. We were afraid that this awkward weather would chain Yeats to their flat, but he felt well and accepted our invitation to dine at our hotel. The manager and staff were excited because *Il senatore* was honoring their house: it seemed they thought it much finer to be a senator in the Dail than one of the world's finest poets. They insisted on serving our dinner in a separate room divided from the big general dining room by the entrance hall. A fiesta was being held: colored streamers of paper, Japanese lanterns and baloons hung from every available peg and chandelier, with mimosa and carnations on every table.

In order to prevent any delay in bringing them into the warmth, we waited near the door for our guests. Whilst R. was helping George with her galoshes and furs, Yeats held out, like a confiding child, what seemed to be two stumps, but they were his gloved hands with a thick woollen sock drawn over each one. Most people would have joked about this rather strange equipment, but Yeats never excused, explained or bothered about trifles, and yet, as I drew the socks off and then the gloves, it seemed to me that a fibre in him quivered with faint amusement. If he did not appear to be listening to his 'high amorous music,' Yeats often looked as if he were repeating to himself in pure surprise, the words of Empedocles:[6] 'From what height of bliss have I fallen to go about among mortals here on earth!' Perhaps that look expressed the sense of wonder he so often said we lacked nowadays. He spoke of the loss that night.

'We have lost the sense of wonder,' including himself with generosity but not with truth. 'We neither see nor hear.'

Italians are not quiet during their meals or amusements and this does not help conversation, especially in this case, for children began to play games and run round our table, enchanted because George laughed and caught at them as they rushed past. Yeats, completely unaffected by all this movement, hung his head down in a meditation, then, raising it, he suddenly questioned us:

'How do you account for Ezra?' We looked at him in astonishment, and he explained:

'Here we have in him one of the finest poets of our time, some erudition and a high intelligence and yet he is sometimes so . . . amazingly clumsy, so tactless, and does what one might call outrageous things.'

We made no attempt to account for Ezra, and Yeats murmured: 'And those little books of poetry by new writers he shows me.' He slanted his head back and said firmly: 'They are just shell-shocked Walt Whitmans!' Then down sank the noble head: 'But we are all just pebbles on the beach in the backwash of eternity.'

George had acquired the habit of bending her head over her plate and, with her eyes fixed on some ice pudding, she said in a low voice, 'Willie talking poppycock?'

I almost choked in horror. Had I really heard this irreverence? Yes, there was no doubt about it. I loved her courage.

Once Yeats and I were together in Edmund Dulac's studio. It interested the poet that the painter Charles Ricketts had been persuaded to have his horoscope cast. Dulac reported that it was most dull and uninteresting. Yeats said at once: 'Ah, the stars only affect passionate people. My daughter's horoscope shows a very passionate life.' And his voice was very proud.

On wonders what he really thought of women: he was chivalrous and ready with praise, but considerable reserve about them showed in many lines of his verse. For instance, in 'A Prayer for my Daughter' these lines:

> It is certain that fine women eat
> A crazy salad with their meat
> Whereby the Horn of Plenty is undone.

One can read a distrust and doubt. For anyone who has seen Maud and Iseult Gonne it is abundantly clear that their beauty had his worship, but beyond that such unimaginable grace had been laid on them that their power was indescribable, and to a man as perceptive of rare loveliness it must have been enthralling.

Towards the end of the 1914–1918 War, Iseult asked me to lunch with her and her mother at Woburn Place, which had been lent to them by Yeats. Maud could not have been old, but who knows what political passions and frustrations had lined her face and drained beauty from the chalice.

She paced up and down the room in a kind of distraught dream. With characteristic generous hospitality, Iseult had bought cutlets (not easy to find in those days) and the gnomelike old maid who was cooking them over the tiny glimmer of gas in the kitchen, wandered in now and then to wave her wrinkled hands in despair. Iseult and I did not mind: we huddled quite happily over the faint fire and talked of friends, books—anything. Once she turned to Maud and said: 'Take off your hat, darling.'

Her mother took it off absent-mindedly and Iseult said to me: 'The shape of her head is lovely, isn't it?'

A few weeks later Iseult was lunching with me at the hotel in Richmond where I was living. The date was November 11, 1918. We were mazed and choked with a great thankfulness and a terrible pity for those who were grieving. My husband rang up to ask us to go to town, meet him, and join the exulting crowds, but neither of us felt we could bear the hysteria, even when mixed with the joy of the young.

Iseult was a serene and lovely companion on such a day. We drank coffee in front of the fire in my sitting room. I had always thought that

Iseult did not realize how rare and astounding her beauty was, and received proof of this when I said, taking powder puff and lipstick from my handbag: 'It's too absurd, but my one burning desire is to look like a girl on a chocolate box.'

'Yes, but it's mine too. A pin-up chocolate box beauty—that's what one yearns for— . . .'

So of course! She had found out that loveliness is a handicap. She must have felt the angry jealousy of ignorant people who are never grateful. I wanted her to stay the night, fearing she, so noticeable, might be caught in wild crowds and not be able to reach home. She scorned the idea of danger, so I sent her off but very regretfully. She soon went over to Eire and married in order to devote herself to the struggles in our strange country, which is also Yeats's.

NOTES

Brigit Patmore (1882–1965) was born Ethel Morrison-Scott. When she married John Deighton Patmore, the grandson of the famous Victorian poet, Coventry Patmore, she was immediately welcomed into the London literary circles dominated by such personalities as the poetess Alice Meynell and the novelist Violet Hunt. Here she met many of the leading writers and artists of the day and she was an indefatigable sponsor of unknown talent. She remained energetic in the arts until her death. Her works include *This Impassioned Onlooker* (1926), *No Tomorrow* (1929) and *My Friends When Young: The Memoirs of Brigit Patmore*, ed. with an introduction by Derek Patmore (1968).

1. Yeats had been introduced to Mrs Olivia Shakespear by Lionel Johnson, her cousin, at some literary dinner. Hers is the 'lovely face' of his later poem 'Memory' (*The Wild Swans of Coole*). At the time Yeats met her Mrs Shakespear was a young woman of about his own age, well read in English, French and Italian literature. She sent him the manuscript of a novel, *Beauty's Hour*, and he criticised it for her very carefully. During the winter of 1911 Mrs Shakespear brought him to Brighton to see her brother, Mr Tucker, and his wife, formerly Mrs Hyde-Lees of Pickhill Hall, Wrexham. Some months later Yeats revisited the Tuckers at Lynton in Devonshire, and there made the acquaintance of Georgie Hyde-Lees, Mrs Tucker's daughter by her first marriage, a young girl with musical and literary interests, whom he met frequently during the next five years, and whom he married in 1917. Mrs Shakespear received several letters from Yeats.

2. Richard Aldington (1892–1962), the English poet and novelist.

3. W. B. Yeats, 'Three Things', *The Winding Stair and Other Poems* (1933).

4. *Death of a Hero*, published in 1929, was considered one of the most noteworthy novels produced by the war.

5. Michael Butler Yeats, now Senator Michael Yeats.

> Bid a strong ghost stand at the head
> That my Michael may sleep sound

> (W. B. Yeats, 'A Prayer for My Son', *The Tower (1929)*)

6. Empedocles, Greek philosopher and statesman of the fifth century BC

The Yeats I Knew*

FRANCIS STUART

During the years I knew Yeats I was so aware of him as the creator of poems that haunted me that I gave little thought to what kind of person he was, beyond a recognition of his generosity towards younger writers, which he showed by never failing to praise those of us with whom he felt some kinship, however slight. I was aware of a strange, contradictory person, whose every sentence and mannerism seemed controlled and formalised, a being not capable of spontaneity except perhaps when roused to defend a cherished principle, somebody whose studied humour I didn't find comic and for whom I had awe, admiration and a certain respect, but never, that I can recall, a sense of friendship or even the affection that a much older man can sometimes inspire in a young one. At the time this didn't strike me as particularly strange. I looked on Yeats as living in a world of his own, the dream world of his poetry, and being beyond ordinary human relationships. It was only long afterwards that I began to see him differently, and to suspect how unfulfilled and lonely he had been in the latter years.

My first contact with Yeats was a slight and indirect one but it has remained in my mind. I was a boy at Rugby School and our English master with whom we were reading 'The Countess Kathleen' wrote to him to elucidate some point in the play. A note came back from the poet in the spiky script I was to become so familiar with later, and was pinned on the notice board where I contemplated it with a kind of awe.

During the next few years my life was coloured by Yeats's poems. He himself seemed almost as remote and legendary as those other stirrers of my youthful imagination, Shelley, Wordsworth and Blake. So when, at eighteen, I married Maud Gonne's daughter, Iseult, and found myself in the circle of his friends it appeared to me as an extraordinary turn of events.

Before I actually met him, my wife told me stories about him, some from the time just before the 1914 war when he had stayed with her mother in their villa at Colville on the Normandy coast. It was there, she told me, that he had written her the poem 'To a Child Playing on the Shore [sic]'.[1]

But the tone of most of her memories came as a shock to me. They seemed to show Yeats in a somewhat ridiculous light. It took me a time to realise that to a child, as Iseult had been at this period, Yeats would be a very queer phenomenon. Nobody had a less easy or spontaneous manner

* *The Yeats We Knew*, ed. Francis MacManus (Cork: Mercier Press, 1965) pp. 27–40.

and to the not-always deep-seeing eye of a child he was bound to appear to give himself airs and certainly be a bore. So that Iseult had been pleased at his discomfitures such as when he had sat on a tarry breakwater in some new flannel trousers on which he'd set great store. And even more so when after listening to him relating one of his psychic experiences of the night before in which the scent of violets had been wafted across his bed, her mother interrupted to tell him she had broken a bottle of perfume in her room and for a time the whole house had smelt like a beauty parlour.

Even when Iseult told me how, a few years later, he had proposed to her, it was impossible for her to treat the episode seriously and she related it in a tone of banter.[2] She never got over her early impressions. To her, and I think to Maud Gonne herself, Uncle Willie, as my wife called him, was an enigma with his deliberate ways, his carefulness about his clothes and about money on the one hand, and his passionate, romantic poems on the other.

My own first meetings with Yeats were after my release from internment during the Civil War in 1923.[3] I had had a small book of poems, 'We Have Kept the Faith', privately printed and published, and I remember the shock it was to me when I realised that this strange and rather chilling figure with his eagle glance was talking about this little book. And not only talking about it, but telling us that the Royal Irish Academy had selected it to give a prize to. Of course I guessed that it was Yeats who had been the cause of this unexpected move on their part. I realised then, and later this was often borne out again, that behind the forbidding and pompous seeming air there was a great generosity of spirit.

He spoke to us (to Iseult rather than to me, sensing, I think, the depths of confusion he'd have put me in by addressing me directly) of one or two of the poems with that enthusiasm that could change his whole manner, giving it naturalness and warmth.

Later, at the ceremony at the Mansion House, I felt little of that touch of the ridiculous that Yeats's solemnity could so easily evoke, in having to go up to a dais and kneel while he placed a laurel crown on my head. My mother-in-law had impressed on me not to refer to Yeats as Senator in my short speech of thanks, and this I refrained from doing, not out of nationalist reasons though, but because there seemed to me to be no greater honour than being plain W. B. Yeats.

Afterwards Yeats, Major Bryan Cooper[4] (both in top hats and morning suits), G. K. Chesterton (why he was there I don't remember), Iseult and I, walked down Dawson Street to a restaurant called the Bonne Bouche for tea. Yet once at our table Yeats seems to have retreated (as he could when the atmosphere was unpropitious) into shadowy silence and all I recollect are a string of humourous anecdotes told by Chesterton and chuckled over by the almost equally enormous Major Cooper, while I, in loyalty to Yeats, tried to reflect his own absorbed and oblivious expression.

Being in his company (no matter how great an honour I may have felt it) was not a relaxation. In later years when he stayed with us at Laragh I avoided, if I could, being left alone with him. I could never be sure of finding the right responses to the kind of speculative talk he was given to. Sometimes, almost in desperation, I managed to say something that he would seem to find profound and enlarge on. But I always had the fear that I couldn't keep it up.[5]

'Willie thinks you're a genious,' my wife told me, and this made me more than ever anxious to hit on the right conversational tone. For the truth was that I never found the company of Yeats anything but a strain as, I believe, did most if not all of his friends. There was little or no ease or lightness in the talk, his humour seemed studied and ponderous, the atmosphere had something formal about it. Not that I wasn't aware of being with somebody full of intellectual passion, whose great mental energy had no real outlet except in his work, and which, socially, scared off more people than it attracted. Of course there were always some literary snobs and sycophants who hung around him for the reflected prestige, but his real friends were few because few could breathe the strange, rarified atmosphere.

I recall remarking how scant the gatherings were at his Monday evenings (I think it was Mondays he and Georgie set aside to receive friends when they lived in Merrion Square). And Yeats himself complained of this lack of society in Dublin, though I imagine it was not much different when he lived in England.

Yeats himself wasn't unaware of the effect he often produced on his admirers. He told me of how Sean O'Casey had come to see him and had sat on and on after the six o'clock drinks and through the dinner to which he'd not been invited, too petrified to get up and go. He also knew the effect he produced—aloof, severe, romantic—on women. I remember how he pulled down the waistcoat of the beautiful fawn suit which is the one I always see him in, smoothing it over a belly that was becoming portly and remarking that the ladies set great store on his appearance. And this shrewd awareness of the reactions of those around him went with a genuine obliviousness and absentmindedness in many other ways. So that when we stayed with the Yeats in the Merrion Square house, Georgie had to pin a notice on the door of our room to remind him that it was no longer his.

It was on one of our visits there that I told him about a periodical that Cecil Salkeld, Con Leventhal, Fred Higgins and myself were bringing out. I had got a rough lay-out of the paper from the printers and I showed him the rather amateurish-looking sheets.

The idea attracted Yeats and to our surprise and delight he offered to give us a new and unpublished poem of his to print in the first number. It was the poem 'Leda'[6] and when I read it I realised that because of this poem our paper, which we called 'To-Morrow',[7] would be of importance. But Yeats's interest in the project went even further. He wrote an editorial for us (not, of course, to appear above his signature though there was no mistaking the rounded, sonorous prose). In it he deplored the lack of any cultural standards in the new Irish State and in the Church in Ireland, and criticised the Bishops for what he called the 'rancid' style of their Pastorals. He went on to argue that had their faith been of anything but a timid and conventional sort it would have inspired their language and saved it from staleness and cliché. He contrasted them to Pope Alexander who had commissioned Michael Angelo to decorate the Sistine Chapel and thus manifested a vigour and wisdom now completely lacking.

I don't think we realised what a bombshell we were exploding when we printed this article, to say nothing of the poem with its strange, perverse eroticism. I know *I* didn't. 'To-Morrow', of which we had envisaged selling a very limited number in Leventhal's bookshop, was soon sold out. It was discussed and denounced, and was seen being read in such unlikely places as the dining-room of a hotel in Athlone and a country pub in Donegal. This delighted Yeats, who loved controversy and pitting himself against the less imaginative and daring. He was naturally opposed to what he saw as conformist and accepted attitudes, believing in what he called the 'aristocrat principle' by which he meant, I think, an original and speculative way of thinking as opposed to what was then the incoming tide of popular and democratic concepts. Or, as he put it:

> 'Not a fool can call me friend,
> And I shall dine at journey's end
> With Landor and with Donne.'[8]

He saw in these writers the aesthetic and intellectual qualities he admired, and this caused him, I believe, to exaggerate their real merits. He sent us at about this time the complete works of Walter Savage Landor in something like a dozen volumes. Not having managed to work my way through even the first of them, I was a little apprehensive of our next meeting what I should say if Yeats launched out on one of his enthusiastic appraisals. But for some reason he hardly referred to Landor again, possibly because, having got all out of him that was grist to the mill, he dropped him, as was his way when something had served its purpose.

Yeats was not only opposed to a good deal in the new Irish State but he equally disliked the left-wing liberalism and rationalism that flourished in England between the wars. He told me that he had been asked to join in a petition signed by almost all the writers in England protesting against the Reichstag Fire Trial[9] then being conducted in Berlin, and said that he had refused. Not that, as I knew, he had any sympathy at all for totalitarianism but because he carried his love of individual freedom further than most of the signatories; to the point, in fact, where he became suspicious of the smugness and collective self-righteousness which they seemed to him to embody.

Out of the same instinct he talked with admiration of d'Annunzio[10] who was much in the news at about that time, fascinated by a writer who was also a man indulging in dramatic and individual exploits.[11] He quoted with approval d'Annunzio's dictum that it is necessary to live dangerously.

It was about this time too (in the middle thirties I think) that he came and stayed alone at the Royal Hotel, Glendalough, not far from where my wife and I were living. He wrote several poems there in the little back room built out over the stream from the lake, and sometimes read one to us when we visited him on an evening. His work was now becoming more erotic and concrete, just as his obsessions, as shown in his conversation, were more and more with physical attributes: courage and sensuality. One of the poems was that about the bone that cried out on the shore.[12]

He often surprised me by taking in small facts that I thought he would be bound to ignore. Unimportant coincidences would take his fancy in a way that I couldn't foresee. At dinner one evening we mentioned that the roast chicken was no doubt one of ours, as we had a contract to supply the hotel with poultry. And only a year or two ago, on looking through a volume of his letters, I came on one of them in which he had related this.[13]

When we mentioned a writer we held in esteem he would hear what we had to say with that air of grave attention of his that made him a good if somewhat disturbing listener (making me always fear that what I had to say wouldn't come up to his obvious expectations). Then sometime later he would refer to the poet or novelist in question with a sentence usually begining: 'My friends tell me . . .' and repeat the judgment of somebody whom I imagined as Edith Sitwell or another of the small circle of literary arbiters to whose taste he seemed, always to my surprise and irritation, to defer.

But I had an inkling that this was more of a defensive measure. Like many great artists Yeats was only really interested in, or absorbed by, what was of use to his own work, what could, in often strange and oblique ways, stimulate and inspire him. He had little interest in writers who, however good, were too far away from him to have this effect.

He garnered his harvest from many strange fields. From such unlikely experiences as playing the Senator and hobnobbing with Lord X and Z. And from public controversy he got a stimulation which intensified his life and indirectly his work.

I think the founding of the Irish Academy of Letters[14] was something he undertook out of this instinct. As a weapon to wield against the Censorship laws it promised to involve him in the kind of passionate debates he thrived on. I still see him looming large and threatening on the small stage of the Peacock Theatre on the night of the Academy's inauguration, a glowering presence, one hand in the pocket of his fawn jacket, the other raised to stress what he was saying or to brush back the lock of dark-grey hair falling over the eagle brow, as he denounced what he looked on as the frightened and narrow attitude of the New State to literature. As one or two members of the audience got up and walked out (journalists from the more nationalist or pious section of the press) Yeats burnt with an even more intense indignation; and it was at such moments that, as a man, he was most admirable.

This was the nearest, perhaps, Yeats could come to the adventures of somebody like d'Annunzio, to that life of danger and violence that was the only kind (aestheticism having failed) that he could now reconcile with art. I sensed that Yeats wanted a life purged of its vulgar, trivial, coarse or even everyday qualities in order to bridge the gulf between it and his work. As he got older one could see this separation of art from life leading him into lonelier and lonelier paths. He tried to explain this by his phases of the moon and his theory of the antithetical self, but I couldn't help feeling, as he expounded it, that his semi-mystical philosophy had no real roots and was even sterile as a further impetus to his work. I think he was aware of this growing threat and in his conversation he lauded those qualities or vices which he lacked, using words like 'wild', 'violent', 'passionate', 'filthy', 'riotous', and so on. Just as in the conscious content of his work he tried to bridge the widening chasm by more and more 'realist' or 'brutal' images such as:

> 'Now that my ladder's gone,
> I must lie down where all the ladders start
> In the four rag-and-bone shop of the heart.'[15]

But the impression one received was that, far from his ladder having gone, he was constructing ever longer and longer ones.

I think this sense of discord weighed on him and drove him to try such solutions as his undergoing of the rejuveneration operation, and his seeking out the company of extroverts, who naturally, while being flattered, found him more than they had bargained for.

All my most vivid recollections of Yeats are either the earliest ones of his visits to my mother-in-law's house in St. Stephen's Green in the early 1920s, or during the period he lived in Merrion Square or from the times he came to Laragh and Glendalough. Those belonging to the latter years, when he had a flat in Fitzwilliam Square and, even more, at the house in Rathfarnham are fainter.

Whether this is because the inner fire was dying down in him or because my own life and development was taking me out of his strong and peculiar spell, I don't know. The talk was as intense and intellectually stimulating as ever.

Indeed I remember one evening in the Fitzwilliam Square flat Georgie saying that if we kept him up talking beyond a certain hour he wouldn't sleep till morning. But for me a lot of the old, rare magic had gone out of it and I was aware of somebody more and more isolated and with less and less to fall back on except the insubstantial consolation of world recognition.

He was more than ever concerned with the psychic. Like the magicians of old searching for the philosopher's stone, he seemed to be looking for concrete proofs of the supernatural. And apropos of the indication of such that he came across, he told a story of two interlocked rings made out of different kinds of wood that a woman friend of his had shown him. Then with the upward jerk of the head and the searching glance focussed so keenly on his listener, he announced like an ultimatum: 'That's your tangible, concrete miracle!'

Phrases of his, ennunciated in that sonorous chant, remain in my mind even when the argument and the context has faded. A typical sentence, for instance, beginning: 'The contemplative nun in her cell and the great lady in her boudoir . . .'

And side by side with what struck me as the growing desperation within, there were the indications of a physical crumbling. He lived in latter years in a hothouse degree of warmth. I recall him extricating his feet out of the enormous fur-lined slippers he wore in his study, coming with us to the door of his house at Rathfarnham and, although it was a warm summer day, shivering as he said good-bye.

He would sometimes talk with nostalgia to Iseult about the far-off days in France. He questioned her about her mother and at last came out with what I had a feeling had been on his mind. Would Iseult find out from her if she would care to see him again? I don't think they had met for many years. In fact there had been a certain rift and coolness between them, especially on Maud Gonne's side. She violently disapproved of his acceptance of the Free State status and his becoming a Senator. But even earlier I had heard her criticise him for what, now that he was married to a wealthy wife and had received the Nobel Prize, she looked on as his meanness. She had told me how, when she was in Holloway Prison in 1918, he had rented her Stephen's Green house and not only taken advantage of her circumstances to get it for a very low rent but allowed the pet rabbits he kept in the garden to eat all the plants!

However this might be, and Maud Gonne was a woman capable of much prejudice and unjust judgments, we knew the unlikelihood of her agreeing to see Yeats. But in the end Iseult managed to persuade her. They met at the Kildare Street club of which Yeats was a member, an arrangement that showed how completely out of touch Yeats was with his early love.

The reunion was not a success. My mother-in-law returned to Roebuck House in Clonskeagh with an ironic account of the meeting. By then Yeats appeared to her more ridiculous than ever. What Yeats thought of the haggard woman to whom remnants of great beauty still clung I don't know. She probably harassed him with the extreme politics that obsessed her as did his by now far-different preoccupations him. For she was not one to attune her talk to the company any more than could be. She told us they had tea in a gloomy room (in the hall, I think, because perhaps women were not admitted further) under a painting of some former viceroy, and that Yeats had had the insensitivity to introduce her to an Anglo-Irish peer of his acquaintance.

When, as I sometimes do, I look back and try to formulate an abiding impression of Yeats, I find I cannot do so by remembering him apart from his work. For what wasn't clear at the time was that the clue to much that was mystifying lies in the fact that his life and his poetry never merged. Or to put it another way, in spite of his interest in philosophy and mysticism (indeed I think this was an instinctive attempt to impose a meaning on his poems from outside) his work was not the expression of a deep, personal faith as it was say, for Rilke, Wordsworth or Blake.

In this, if in no other way, he was like Joyce. And in asking why it was that these two of our greatest artists were both, towards the end of their lives, deeply unhappy, it strikes me that it was just because of this; that in both their cases their work, so wonderful in texture, detail and artifice, lacks an inherent unifying vision of man.

NOTES

Francis Stuart (1902–   ) is an Irish novelist who was born in Queensland, Australia. In 1920 he married Iseult Gonne, Maude Gonne's daughter. His early poetry won him critical praise in America and Ireland and the patronage of Yeats, who hailed him as one of the great new names of Irish poetry and writing. His volume of poetry *We Have Kept the Faith* (1923) was awarded a prize by the Royal Irish Academy. He has also written plays, *Men Crowd Me Round* (1933) and *Strange Guest* (1940), both produced by the Abbey Theatre. However, his fame was secured by his novels, which include *Women and God* (1930), *Pigeon Irish* (1932), *The Coloured Dome* (1932), *Try the Sky* (1933), *Glory* (1933), *In Search of Love* (1935), *White Hare* (1936), *Julie* (1938), *The Great Squire* (1939), *The Silver Ship* (1940), *The Pillar of Cloud* (1948), *Redemption* (1949), *The Flowering Cross* (1950), *The Wild Wings* (1951), *The Chariot* (1953), *The Pilgrimage* (1955), *Victors and Vanquished* (1958) and *Angels and Providence* (1959). *Things We Live For* (1935) is autobiographical, as is *Black List, Section H* (1971), his latest novel.

1. W. B. Yeats, 'To a Child Dancing in the Wind', *Responsibilities* (1914).
2. 'That he should have been in love with the mother, and then wished, years later, to marry the daughter, has almost the tang of a Maupassant story. And, by a further coincidence, the drama was staged in Maupassant's native Normandy.'—Monk Gibbon, *The Masterpiece and the Man: Yeats As I Knew Him* (London: Hart-Davis, 1959) p. 33. Of Iseult's marriage to Francis Stuart, Yeats wrote of having known

> . . . A girl that knew all Dante once
> Live to bear children to a dunce

('Why Should Not Old Men Be Mad?', *Last Poems*)

3. Francis Stuart fought in the Irish Civil War and was interned from 1922 to 1923, and then settled in Wicklow.
4. Major Bryan Ricco Cooper (1884–1930), a strong Unionist and supporter of Carson. Appointed Press Censor in Dublin, he was sickened by the Black and Tan excesses and swung over to support Sinn Fein and the Republicans. However, in the civil war disputes he accepted the Treaty and the Free State, becoming a member of the Dail Eireann in 1923. In 1920 he had published his interesting *A Rebel's Diary*. Cooper became a friend and political colleague of Yeats in post-Treaty Ireland (1922–30).
5. Yeats wrote to Lady Gregory: 'Her [Iseult's] husband is silent unless one brings the conversation round to St. John of the Cross or a kindred theme.' Quoted by Joseph Hone in *W. B. Yeats 1865–1939* (London: Macmillan, 1965) p. 409.
6. W. B. Yeats, 'Leda and the Swan', *The Tower* (1928).

7. *Tomorrow* was published from Roebuck House, Clonskeagh, County Dublin. Only two issues appeared in August and September 1924.

8. W. B. Yeats, 'To a Young Beauty', *The Wild Swans at Coole* (1919).

9. On 27 February 1933 the Reichstag (lower house of parliament in Germany) building was destroyed by fire. On the pretext of a Communist plot to seize power the constitutional guarantees of individual liberty were suspended and the Reich government given emergency powers. It was in this atmosphere of fear and insecurity that the elections were held a week later.

10. Gabriele d'Annunzio (1863–1938), Italian author and soldier.

11. D'Annunzio's colourful career, the scandal of his amours, his daring in wartime, his eloquence and his political leadership in two national crises, all contributed to make him one of the most striking personalities of his day.

12. W. B. Yeats, 'Words for Music Perhaps: xv. Three Things', *The Winding Stair and Other Poems* (1933).

13. 'They dined with me here and are convinced that they ate one of their own chickens.' Quoted by Joseph Hone in *W. B. Yeats 1865–1939* (London: Macmillan, 1965) p. 409.

14. Francis Stuart was a founder member of the Irish Academy of Letters, which was inaugurated in 1932. For an account of the Academy see Stephen Gwynn, *Irish Literature and Drama in the English Language: A Short History* (London: Thomas Nelson, 1936) pp. 232–6.

15. W. B. Yeats, 'The Circus Animal's Desertion', *Last Poems*.

The Yeats I Knew*

MONK GIBBON

Towards the end of the Second World War Mr. T.S. Eliot flew to Dublin to deliver the first Yeats Memorial Lecture. I was standing in the crowded foyer of the Abbey Theatre about five or ten minutes before the lecture was due to begin when Sean O'Faolain, who was taking the chair, approached me. 'You must propose the vote of thanks.' I was in no mood to miss Eliot's interesting lecture while making notes for an oration of my own, but I retired to my seat in the brass-railed gallery, and in the four or five minutes which remained to me I jotted down certain lines of approach. From that dominating position in the gallery, immediately behind Yeats's widow, his daughter and his son, I was subsequently able to harangue, not only the whole audience, but Eliot himself on the stage; to chant some of the earlier poetry to them; and—in a sudden burst of confidence, influenced a little by the adjacency of those three relatives just in front of me—to tell the audience that I had seldom been in Yeats's presence for five minutes without irritating him to maddening point.

Perhaps the same confession is a necessary introduction now. The Yeats's band-wagon is overcrowded. Research students of every nationality spring up almost daily, thesis[1] in hand. But those who knew Yeats

* *The Yeats We Knew*, ed. Francis MacManus (Cork: Mercier Press, 1965) pp. 43–57.

personally are a diminishing body, and the longer one lives the greater one's rarity value therefore becomes, even though to some people I have seemed to be a traitor within the ranks. For that reason I am here.[2]

But am I a traitor? Yeats's poetry, early, middle and late, must have given me as much pleasure as any man has ever received from it. He is the arch-magician in words of the era in which I have lived. The writers of real significance for us are those without whom we cannot even imagine life as we have known it. Cadences of theirs are woven into the very texture of our being. I find it impossible to envisage a world without *Innisfree*,[3] without *Though you are in your shining days*,[4] without *Outworn heart in a time outworn*,[5] *Prayer for my daughter*,[6] *What then, said Plato's ghost, What then?*;[7] without *The Wild Wicked Old Man*.[8] The man who wrote those poems was my relative. His sisters used to sign their letters to me 'your affectionate cousin Lily', 'your affectionate cousin Elizabeth'. There was a double relationship, a few generations back, a Terry one and a Butler one. As a young man my grandfather used to walk daily into Dublin with John Butler Yeats, the poet's father. They were both law students and once, when my grandfather had an exam, they departed from their usual route in order to avoid meeting a red-haired woman lest he should bring the candidate ill luck. A little later when William Butler Yeats made his appearance on the scene in Sandymount my grandfather, who lived nearby, must have been amongst the first to offer his congratulations and to bend over the cradle. As a schoolboy, I knew my grandfather as an ardent lover of horses and a reader—if at all—of yellow backs, *The Strand Magazine*, Sexton Blake and Kipling. He died in 1909 almost certainly without having read even so much as a line of his distinguished relative.

I, however, was converted to Yeats's poetry at an early age by the gift of *Innisfree* as a wall-card from one of his sisters. Elizabeth had printed it but it was Lily who gave it to me and it was Lily who used to take me to the Abbey sometimes on Saturday afternoons, when I longed to see the poet himself but was always unlucky. When I did see him, I was aged twelve or thereabouts. It was one morning in a street in Dublin when shopping with my father, and the man in the broad-brimmed hat and with the black ribbon dangling from his pince-nez seemed to me both a little too fat and a little too deliberately absent-minded. 'That was your cousin, William Butler Yeats,' said my father, after we had safely passed him. I was a little disappointed. I had no objection to a man looking the part of the poet but I had an uneasy feeling that Yeats felt that it was *his business* to look the part. That was a different matter altogether.

Yeats's relationship with his two sisters was a curious one. 'I have two sisters,' he told Sturge Moore. 'One is an angel, the other a demon.' Both played a very appreciable part in smoothing his path as a writer. But the one who did most in that respect was the one whom he found it hardest to get on with, not because she had a mind of her own—for every member of that remarkable family had a mind of his or her own—but possibly because anyone who co-operated with W.B. was expected to do so on his terms; he found it hard to brook opposition. Elizabeth Yeats ran the Cuala Press. It was the successor to the Dun Emer Press whose founder and owner, Miss Gleeson, Yeats had presumably found insufficiently tractable. Both hand-presses had come into existence to publish early limited editions of Yeats's own work and the work of a few of his friends. Elizabeth Yeats—or Lollie as she preferred to be called—has left her own memorial in these hand-printed volumes. She had no say in what was printed, and there were frictions, which may have grown more frequent as time went on, although actually both sisters were tied by bonds of the most undeviating loyalty to their famous relation. Yeats might say to his wife in later days, 'I'm meeting Lollie at the Shelbourne[9] this morning. We're going there, because then we won't be able to shout at each other.' But no amount of shouting could lessen Elizabeth's pride in her brother. The whole family had learnt at a very early stage—almost certainly from John Butler Yeats himself—to regard Willie as a genius, and their respect for him never faltered.

I said once to Jack Yeats, as we sat together in his studio, something about the arrogance which W.B. could display on occasions. And in his entirely gentle and oblique way Jack came immediately to his brother's defence, hinting that it was a result of the humiliations which the poet had had to share in his youth, when family cash was always short and fame still very far off. But the picture which Katherine Tynan draws is of a young man quite indifferent to material considerations. I think it would be true to say that the poet came into the world with a good deal of latent pugnacity in his composition. Lily Yeats told me how a governess of theirs used to say, 'Everything is all right in the nursery until Willie comes home and then the fighting begins immediately.' Yeats was a fighter. I can imagine him enjoying his participation in *The Playboy*. It was probably a sharp-relished moment in his life, rather than an infliction.

I had seen the poet once, but it was ten years or more before I was to see him again. Home on leave from serving with the 31st Division in France in 1917, I bought the eight vellum-backed volumes of Bullen's Stratford Head Press edition of his works out of my pay as a subaltern, and directed my father to leave the first volume with Lily Yeats who was to get her brother to sign it for me. She did so. In microscopic handwriting on the first page are to be read now his signature and the two lines

> I have heard the pigeons in the Seven Woods
> Make their faint thunder

an allusion possibly to the considerably greater din which I was then hearing from the 16 inch guns in front of Arras. Yeats was not the perfect quarry when it came to autographs. Years later I asked both him and A.E. to sign copies of photographs which the Irish Times had taken of them. Russell signed in friendly fashion on the mount immediately below the photograph; but W.B. wrote his name on the very darkest part of the print itself where there was no danger of anyone save its owner ever suspecting the existence of a signature.

After the war Yeats came for a time to live on Sydenham Road in my father's parish of Dundrum. One of Yeats's children—I think I am right in saying—was baptised by my father. The poet had only two topographical influences in his life, Sligo and Dublin. They were a part of his being, Sligo in childhood, Dublin as an art student with A.E. and afterwards in the early days of the Abbey and in old age. Nothing of London, where he lived for a number of years, nothing of Oxford, nothing certainly of Dundrum passed into him and became a part of him, as places become a part of ordinary individuals. To a greater degree than any other man in my experience, Yeats *created* his own environment, rather than took on colour from one already in existence. Even in the case of Coole Park I suspect that it became Yeatsland when he was there—a metamorphosis which no doubt had the full approval of Lady Gregory. And his stay in Dundrum though it brought him within a mile or so of his sisters, and, probably, while it lasted kept the poor Cuala Press in a state of very considerable tension, was, like so much else, a biographical irrelevance as far as the poet was concerned.

I was teaching[10] in Switzerland at this time but even had I been at home it is most unlikely that I would have made the poet's acquaintance. That did not happen until he was living in Merrion Square. Plunkett and others had founded the *Irish Statesman* and put A.E. in charge of it and a poem of mine published therein had met with Yeats's approval. 'Who is Monk Gibbon?' he had cried down the stairs to Lily one morning; and she had replied, 'He is your cousin, Willie Gibbon,' not a very satisfactory classification, seeing that family ramifications were something quite outside his cognizance. His approval of my poem however was passed on to me, via Lily and my father, and I was told to call upon him when I next returned to Ireland.

The Yeats whom I met then and whom I knew thereafter for a certain number of years was the penultimate Yeats, the Yeats of the mid-twenties, the senatorial Yeats, re-patriated, re-established in concord with A.E., happy in his role of a public figure, and leagues removed from the gawky art-student of his earlier Dublin period. I doubt if his friends in youth, if they had been able to peer forward into the future, could have recognised him as he was now. I knew from Katherine Tynan that he had undergone a sea-change, and one not altogether approved by her. His fashionable and titled London acquaintances, she implied, had meant that the gentle, shy and altogether humble neophyte of literature that she had once known had vanished altogether and left not a wrack behind. Certainly humility is hardly the word that one would associate with the later Yeats.

We are up against one of the more interesting problems of personality, and in an acute form. Philip Toynbee, commenting recently upon Sartre's excursion into autobiography and on the French writer's savage rejection of himself as child and as small boy, has said, 'Self-hatred is at least as damaging an emotion as self-love, and we owe, I think, a very definite loyalty to those fragmentary and remote beings who are at least the progenitors of our present selves. We owe them the loyalty of admitting that they were, in however strange a sense, ourselves; that what we experienced of them was from inside and not from outside; and that there is in a human life, an unspeakable continuity of identity.' Sartre has not conceded this loyalty, and I don't think that Yeats ever conceded it either. I think he had broken off the relationship with his past self. A.E. was the only person who ever gave me the impression that he was conscious of a continuity of identity in Yeats. To him the poet was still 'Willie Yeats', the boy who long ago shared his belief in fairies and who—so Miss Yeats once told me—had discussed with him over the ashes in their basement kitchen range the arcane forces which could perhaps explain a mushroom's rapid growth. Indeed one of the reasons why A.E. slightly irritated Yeats—and I think he did often slightly irritate him—may have been because he insisted on clinging to this earlier individual; whereas the poet himself wanted to discard him and to thrust him back into the past. This diversity of approach to his adolescence had various ramifications. I always suspected Yeats of being subconsciously jealous of A.E. It seemed to be that they had both set out together upon the road of mystical enlightenment, but that Yeats had very soon turned aside into the by-ways of magic and symbolism. Whereas A.E., shedding the extravagances of some of his earlier convictions and fortified by a stronger moral purpose, had continued steadfastly on the path of enlightenment and had become the sage. I can claim Mrs. Yeats's support here in her remark to her husband after A.E.'s death 'A.E. was the nearest you or I will ever know to a saint. You are a better poet than he was; but you are not a saint.' Indeed W.B. seemed to endorse that verdict himself by quoting it in a letter to a friend.[11]

But the cleavage in Yeats—which of course extended to his poetry and is regarded by so many critics as a sort of watershed separating the great later poetry from what they consider the relatively negligible, earlier work—may have had other causes besides this abandonment of the mystical quest on which he had once briefly embarked with his friend, Sex, and his attitude to women had something to say to it. Another reason is suggested for it in a very revealing remark which he once made to L. A. G. Strong. He said, 'In my youth I was shy and awkward and terrified of any gathering. Then I read in that book which I still think the wisest of all books, Wilhelm Meister of Goethe, the following words: "The poor are. The rich are but are also permitted to seem". Thereupon I set myself to acquire this necessary technique of seeming. I attended athomes and soirees and dinner parties and gatherings of every kind until I had lost my awkwardness, and had acquired the technique of seeming.'

This seems to me an astonishing confession for a great man to make. The technique of seeming. It is difficult for those who are untroubled by shyness to realise what an affliction it can be. I have noticed in a number of shy people a sort of angry resentment against anyone who came into the world with more assurance than they themselves possess. But to cure one's shyness by creating a deliberate façade, that seems to be tampering with the integrity of personality which one expects in the great artist.

Until I read this testimony of Strong, fairly recently, I had always imagined that Yeats's air of aloofness was a self-protective measure adopted mainly to defend the poetic consciousness and to keep the intrusive world at a safe distance. And, though I disliked it, it seemed justifiable and praiseworthy. It was a continual affirmation of the right of a poet to be solely himself. But now it appears that this was a measure to enable him to meet the world, rather than to escape from it, and this—if it was the case—would explain why one could not help being slightly irritated by what always savoured of pose, even though one might condone it as poetic pose. Strong tells us that he was an extremely shy man. If it is correct, one can only say that Yeats concealed it well from strangers behind a mask of slightly arrogant superiority. Even his geniality was a little too olympian.

To say this shows that I never penetrated—as others claim to have done—behind the poetic mask to the human individual. Again it is Leonard Strong who suggests a possible explanation. He says, 'Yeats could not abide reverence. It made him tongue-tied, it forced him at once into his official manner. Towards the end of his life his best friends were young men who treated him as an equal and told him unseemly stories. He had a relish for the unseemly and some of his own stories were Rabelaisian!' Could not abide reverence? If that was the case then I must have exercised the worst possible influence upon him, for I was an idolator of his poetry. And to me, even in his own home and amongst intimates like A.E., Lennox Robinson, Walter Starkie and Gogarty, Yeats always seemed tied to an official manner, instigated quite possibly by my own initial reverence and by the very fact that where both he and A.E. were concerned, I was unavowedly in search of a messiah. This didn't trouble A.E. in the least, because to some degree he was a messiah, a very human messiah, who would let drop a phrase of Patanjali and send you home fortified in spirit; but it was clearly not the way to win favour with W.B.

Though I did not immediately realise it and though I had started with a favouring wind behind me—a poem approved—an invitation to dinner—and an open invitation to his Monday evenings in Merrion Square the auspices were really all against me; I was reverent, which was unforgiveable, I was talkative which is always a grave disadvantage, and, in my search for truth and hunger for discussion—a hunger probably accentuated by residence abroad—I did not hesitate to cross-examine Yeats from time to time upon the logical sequence of his ideas. He was a bad subject for such cross-examination. He much preferred to throw out the striking phrase and leave it at that. The phrase could take care of itself. He was a poet and not a logician.

Nevertheless for a time I enjoyed his favour. I could go to his Monday salon whenever I wished. Salon is perhaps the wrong word for a gathering of four or five old friends together with an occasional young man, like Lyle Donaghy[12] or myself. A.E. was my hero and he was nearly always there on these occasions which was perhaps a disadvantage. Strong has said, 'Of all men and women I have met, A.E. met life with the greatest serenity.' It was difficult not to contrast A.E. the sage, with W.B., the newly-made senator and slightly unconvincing man of the world.

I realised my privilege, but I suppose I was opinionated then, as I am opinionated now; and to be opinionated in youth is not always the best way to win favour with the elderly. Nevertheless Yeats could be kindly. He advised me strongly not to go and sit at the feet of Gourdjieff,[13] in his institute at Fontainbleau, where Katherine Mansfield had died. 'Take the advice of an old man. I've seen a lot of that kind of thing—' and he went on to say that it tended to end in a sort of priestcraft. This was a big admission from the one-time Rosicrucian.[14] I took his advice, paying only a brief afternoon visit to Fontainbleau, where in any case Gourdjieff was incapacitated with a broken leg and busy writing a book which, one of his disciples told me, he proposed to call 'Beelzebub's talks to his Grand-children'.

The poet could give me his friendly advice, he could invite me to his house, he could write me kindly and thoughtful letters about two of my books which I had sent him but he could never overcome my awe of him or a certain prim tendency to compare him to his disfavour with A.E., and to disapprove his slightly bawdy man-of-the-world pose which came out most strongly when he was in Gogarty's company. Nor could he silence me or satisfy my ravenous hunger—the hunger of youth—for a doctrine, a theory, a creed which might throw a little light upon the mystery of existence. When one asked A.E. for bread he gave you bread, the bread of the Bhagavadgita or of Patanjali or of some nameless sage, like the one who had said—'All lost oil burns in the lamp of the King'—a wonderful all-embracing phrase in which to gather up life's failures and misfits and all the apparent wastage of human personality which would nevertheless one day be justified in the divine scheme. But when one asked Yeats for bread, he did not actually give you a stone, but he gave you a beautifully polished pebble of phraseology, striking in its originality, but not exactly the sustenance which the soul sought at that moment. Of course he could say most brilliant and courageous things. I was not there when he remarked to two English dons, 'I can't see what you think you are achieving. You seem to be busy with the propagation of second and third and fourth hand opinions upon literature. Culture does not consist in acquiring opinions but in getting rid of them.' If I had been there I hope I should have applauded. I would certainly have appreciated that other brilliant remark, to an Oxford undergraduate who had told Yeats that he was contemplating a change of faith, 'In religion never leave your father's house until you have been kicked down the stairs.'

I have told in my book *The Masterpiece and the Man or Yeats as I knew him*,[15] how our relationship went from bad to worse until I had become—as he said—'one of the three people in Dublin whom I dislike—Dunsany, because he's rude to his wife in front of the servants, Monk Gibbon because he is argumentative and Sarah Purser[16] because she's a petulant old woman.' Yeats had other personal reasons for disliking Dunsany and Sarah. They had stood up to him on occasion. But in my case it was a true bill. Lollie probably only made things worse by defending me to him and by begging me not to argue when I next saw him. 'W.B. doesn't like being argued with,' A.E. could say to me. 'You are the only person in Dublin who argues with Yeats. He ought to be grateful to you.' Did I ever argue with him I ask myself now, or did I just ask embarrassing leading questions in the manner of Rosa Dartle? I fell further and further from grace. If I kept silence in his company I was a bore. If I spoke I was maddening. Finally I toppled utterly from grace by publishing a book on the wrapper of which Jonathan Cape had printed a highly appreciative letter to me from A.E. This volume, unlike the others, was not acknowledged.

The effect of *The Masterpiece and the Man* upon Frank O'Connor was to make him feel that I was the typical individual with a grievance. But O'Connor is not quite fair to me. He has left out my one big grievance—the attempt to take from me what A.E. had himself entrusted to me, the posthumous editing of his journalism. Moreover O'Connor himself, in a lecture to the Yeats Summer School has admitted that Yeats could be, and often was, a bully. Even Strong, his ardent admirer says, 'In contention Yeats was unscrupulous and adroit.' I was to receive in full measure a striking illustration of both these qualities. I would have been less than human if I had not resented it.

There are very few disagreements in life which can be said to be inevitable, but I am not sure that mine with Yeats was not one. I placed him upon a pedestal as a poet, but he abhorred all such reverence. I subconsciously reproached him for not being a saint; but after all a man is free to choose his vocation. I challenged his philosophic statements with the earnestness of youth; and, if he could read my thoughts which I always very much hoped he could not, he must have realised that I was continually making comparisons to his disadvantage with the serene A.E. As Lily Yeats once said to me, 'You are afraid of him.' Yes, exactly, afraid of him; but by no means sufficiently afraid of him to keep my mouth shut when I considered one of his pronouncements illogical. When it came to opposition Yeats was at his worst. He lacked fundamental magnanimity and he was as ruthless as those who are sensitive themselves can often be. He has unveiled his mind, but not his personality to us in his writings. Did anyone know him really well, except possibly the members of his own household? I doubt if A.E. did. Perhaps Gogarty did. Perhaps Strong did. But he has left us a tireless memorial of himself in his poetry, and, before that, I uncover.

NOTES

Monk Gibbon (1896–   ) is an Irish poet and writer who won a silver medal for poetry at Tailteann Games in 1928. His volumes of poetry include *The Tremulous String* (1926), *The Branch of Hawthorn Tree* (1927), *For Daws to Peck at* (1929), *Seventeen Sonnets* (1932) and *Insubstantial Pageant* (collected poems; 1951). He has also written two remarkable autobiographical novels, *Mount Ida* (1948) and *The Climate of Love* (1961). His other works include *The Red Shoes Ballet: A Critical Study* (1948), *The Tales of Hoffmann: A Study of the Film* (1951), *An Intruder at the Ballet* (1952), *Austria* (1953), *Western Germany* (1955), *The Rhine and Its Castles* (1957), *Great Houses of Europe* (1962) and *Great Palaces of Europe* (1964). His writings on Yeats include *The Masterpiece and the Man: Yeats as I Knew Him* (1959), *The Living Torch* (ed.; 1937) and 'Literary Ideals in Ireland: A Comparison', *Irish Statesman*, v (Dec 1925) 399–400.

1. By the time Monk Gibbon wrote these reminiscences (1965), over 200 dissertations on Yeats had been written.

2. These reminiscences were originally prepared as a lecture broadcast on Radio Eireann to celebrate the centenary of Yeats's birth in 1965.

3. W. B. Yeats, 'The Lake Isle of Innisfree', *The Rose* (1893).

4. W. B. Yeats, 'The Lover Pleads with His Friend for Old Friends', *The Wind among the Reeds* (1899).

5. W. B. Yeats, 'Into the Twilight', *The Wind among the Reeds* (1899)

6. W. B. Yeats, 'A Prayer for My Daughter', *Michael Robartes and the Dancer* (1921).

7. W. B. Yeats, 'What Then?', *Last Poems*.

8. W. B. Yeats, 'The Wild Old Wicked Man', *Last Poems*.

9. The Shelbourne Hotel in Dublin.

10. Monk Gibbon studied farming but took up schoolteaching after World War I and taught in Switzerland, England and Ireland.

11. In a letter to Dorothy Wellesley sent from Riversdale on 26 July 1935 (*The Letters of W. B. Yeats*, p. 838).

12. John Lyle Donaghy (1902–47), Irish schoolmaster and poet. His volumes of poetry include *At Dawn above Aherlow* (1926) and *Into the Light* (1934).

13. Gurdjieff had founded an esoteric community in Fontainebleau. Katherine Mansfield had gone there towards the end of her life and professed to have found the peace she was seeking. See Monk Gibbon, *The Masterpiece and the Man; Yeats as I Knew Him* (London: Rupert Hart-Davis, 1959) pp. 87–92. On Gurdjieff see Margaret Anderson, *The Unknowable Gurdijeff* (London: Routledge and Kegan Paul, 1962).

14. Member of an order devoted to occult lore said to have been founded in 1484 by Christian Rosenkreuz.

15. Monik Gibbon, *The Masterpiece and the Man: Yeats As I Knew Him* (London: Rupert Hart-Davis, 1959).

16. Sarah Purser (1848–1943), Irish artist.

The Yeats I Knew*

AUSTIN CLARKE

*   *   *

But the Plays of Yeats were a deeply imaginative experience, and, as the poet put on his own plays as often as possible, the experience was a constant one. On such occasions the theatre was almost empty. There were a few people in the stalls, including Lady Gregory, and, just after the last gong had sounded, Yeats would appear, dramatically, at the top of the steps leading down into the auditorium. Perhaps the actors spoke the lyric lines in tones that had become hollow-sounding with time, borrowing the archaic voice which is normally reserved for religious services. It seemed right that the poetic mysteries should be celebrated reverently and with decorum. Moreover, the presence of the poet himself in the theatre was a clear proof that all was well.

Scarcely had the desultory clapping ceased, when Yeats would appear outside the stage curtain, a dim figure against the footlights. He swayed and waved rhythmically, telling humbly of his 'little play', how he had re-written it, and what he had meant to convey in its lines. As the twenty or thirty people in the pit were more or less scattered, I was isolated usually in one of the back seats. On such occasions, I felt like Ludwig of Bavaria, that eccentric monarch, who sat alone in his own theatre. I enjoyed the poet's curtain-lecture, almost as if it were a special benefit performance for myself.

One night, however, my youthful and romantic illusions were suddenly shattered, and in a trice the Celtic Twilight was gone. As the poet appeared punctually outside the curtain, a dazzling light shone around him. It might have been the light of his later fame! I glanced up and saw that the brilliant shaft of illumination came from the balcony. A spotlight must have been clamped to the rail and switched on as the poet appeared. But my conclusion may have been unjust, for in youth we do not understand the complexities of human motives. I did not realise at the time that poetic drama was slowly vanishing from the Abbey Theatre. It seems to me now that, consciously or not, the poet might have been making a last

* Extracted from *The Yeats We Knew*, ed. Francis MacManus (Cork: Mercier Press, 1965) pp. 79-94.

despairing gesture to call attention, not to his own picturesque person, but to the struggling cause of poetry on the stage.

*   *   *

The centenary of Thomas Davis in 1914[1] was to be held at Trinity College, Dublin, but the meeting was banned by the Provost, Dr. Mahaffy[2] and in scornful words, which caused much indignation to Republicans, he referred to 'a man called Pearse' who was to be one of the speakers. So the meeting was held in the Antient Concert Rooms in Brunswick Street, later to be re-named Pearse Street after the Insurrection.

The long dusty hall downstairs was almost filled when I arrived but I found a seat half way down. Already on the platform were W. B. Yeats, who was to deliver the oration, Pádraic Pearse and the young chairman, Denis Gwynn.[3] One chair was still empty. I scarcely recognised the poet of the Abbey Theatre whom I had seen so often coming before the dim footlights on the stage after one of his plays had been performed. Gone were the flowing tie and the disobedient black lock that fell over his brow as he talked and swung back into place whenever he lifted his head. He was in evening dress and his long hair had been oiled and brushed back. This gave a saturnine look to his olive features so that he seemed to be extraordinarily like Sir Edward Carson, who was then the fearsome Dublin-born leader of the Unionist party in the North. Scarcely had Yeats started to speak when, on the right-hand side of the hall, there was a sound of heavy footsteps on the bare boards. It was the missing poet, Captain Thomas Kettle, braving us in the uniform of a British Officer. He marched up the hall so firmly that we almost seemed to hear the clatter of his sword but it was obvious that he had his fill of Irish whiskey in order that he might defy more confidently this small group of Sinn Feiners.

When Yeats rose to speak, I wondered how he would deal with the poetic problem of the Young Ireland School of the 'Forties' the rhetoric of those political and historical ballads of Davis, D'Arcy Magee, Gavan Duffy and other poets whom he had attacked—the jingle of their double rhymes, of which perhaps the worst was the constant rhyming of 'Ireland' with 'Sireland'. But the poet had been wily enough to choose the one poem by Davis which could lend itself to his own thrilling sort of chanting: *The Lament for Owen Roe*. As he rose to his full height, swayed and, with waving hands, intoned the poem, his voice spread in rhythmic waves throughout the hushed hall. 'Did they dare, did they dare, to slay Eoghan Ruadh O'Neill? Yes, they slew with poison, him they feared to meet with steel.' 'May God wither up their hearts! May their blood cease to flow! May they walk in living death, who poisoned Eoghan Ruadh!' The audience was overcome with enthusiasm and when he sat down again there was great applause. But before that there had been as much clapping when, by a simple device which I noticed at the time, he brought in irrelevantly the

name of Nietzsche, for the German poet and philosopher of the Superman
was regarded with horror in all our pro-British press during the First Great
War. I felt annoyed for I had been reading with guilty delight *Thus spoke
Zarathustra, The Joyful Science* and *The Birth of Tragedy* with its fascinating
theory of Dionysiac and Apollonian moods.

*   *   *

When the meeting was over and I came out, I saw W. B. Yeats surrounded
by disciples and watched the group walking towards Westland Row. The
next morning the placards appeared with the startling announcement:
Dublin audience cheers Nietzsche.

*   *   *

"
When I came to the little town of Gort, the ancient royal stories of Guaire
and Maravan vanished from my mind as night fell. I can only remember
the empty market place that seemed to lie in wait for a fair, three
melancholy foreigners who had come there to sell native frieze, and a girl
who stared into nothingness with a brazen face.

The morning sun was still clouded when I saw for the first time the
Woods of Coole. I found a small unlocked gate and in a few minutes I stood
within a dark plantation that was lit only by the cold sharp silver of the
hollies. I wondered if it were the nameless 'wicked wood' of the poem or
shady Kyle-dortha. Hastening along a winding, foot-beaten track, I came
into a thinner wood, and as I waited there, I grew aware that there was
secret honey around me. This surely must be Pairc-na-carraig.

> Where the wild bees fling their sudden frangrances [sic]
> On the green air. [4]

I had only known those deeper woods of the south, in which the very dews
stir heavily from a footstep: but in those thin western woods every tiny
sound of the leaves was delicate. In great delight I moved softly there and
not without scruples, for I was trespassing in the solitude where the poet
had found so much of his inspiration. The trees had become darker, wilder
again, and, because I could see a sunnier wood beyond them, I stayed
under those boughs. If I remained here long enough the unexpected might
happen, for I was certain that I had come to that secret place—

> Dim Pairc-na-tarav, where enchanted eyes
> Have seen immortal, wild, proud shadows walk. [5]

I closed my eyes but nothing happened. Then, as I opened them again, I
thought I saw a rich blue gleam dart through the distant leaves. I could not
be mistaken and so I strode forward cautiously. A moment later I saw the
blue flash again. Perhaps it was only a peacock searching in the grasses, but
why was it moving so rapidly? Coming nearer, I peeped through the leaves

and saw, to my chagrin, that I had mistaken for bird or spirit a tall sportsman, wearing an unusual rain-coat of sky-blue watered silk, and carrying the rods and fierce tackle of his craft. Believing that I had strayed into the wrong demesne and that I had been dreaming foolishly in ordinary woods, I was about to turn away, when I noticed that the angler was crossing a wide lawn towards the portico of a Georgian mansion. To my complete astonishment, I saw that it was the poet himself.

Bewildered by that unexpected encounter, I hurried through the underwoods and, in a few minutes, had lost my way. I came to long paths, grass-grown, hedged with wild pale privet. I wandered up and down in confusion for, though I was at the end of the woods, I no longer wanted to count them. At last I escaped from these hedges, where wildness was only neglect, and found myself on grey ledges of rock that dwindled among a few rushes growing by a small lake. Across the water was another wood. This must be Shan-walla, but I saw with a pang that the wild swans had gone.

I sat down on a rock near the water's edge, but mocking thoughts midged me from every side. The week before, I had crossed Lough Gill and, with great persistence and guile, had asked the boatman the name of every island we passed. As we came to the far end of the lake, he pointed to a rocky islet with high tufts of heather, a few sloe bushes and a small patch of grass, and he had said:

'That's Innisfree'.

I could hear his voice again and it had become horribly confidential.

'Would you believe it now, two ladies came here last year all the way from London to see that rock. They said it must be Innisfree, and that there was a poem written about it, though, round here, it is known as Rat Island. They brought their lunch with them, and stayed there for two solid hours, writing postcards to their friends.'

Crude coloured postcards with fragments of scrawled exclamations danced before my sight and, like those cards that Alice saw in Wonderland, they became suddenly shrill and in a pack they ran against me and the woods grew harsh with magpies and, stumbling blindly through brambles, I hurried along the grass-grown paths again. I came at length to some outbuildings. A man was standing with a bucket and brush outside a stable door. He told me that Mr. Yeats was staying in a house on the opposite side of the road and that in a week or two he was going to Ballylee. I had heard that the poet had acquired an Old Norman keep there.

The sun hid suddenly, and a fairy wind blew me, hat in hand, across the road. But the eddy of dust was gone even while I hesitated before the knocker.

Somehow I found myself in a plain room timidly picking at a fish and wondering if the poet had caught it himself. His own lunch was over and so he leaned from a sofa opposite the table, wearing a brown velvet shooting-jacket. A pallid mask of his features stared blindly from a glass case in the corner of the room.

'The imagination must be disciplined, when it is young. Therefore study the Jacobean lyrics, Donne, the poems of Landor . . .'

His voice rose and fell in a lulling monotone, while secretly I cursed the fish. It might have come from the cauldron of the elder gods, might have held the very smelt of knowledge, for, despite my desperate efforts, it would not grow smaller, and its tiny stickles seemed to threaten my very existence.

'Verse should be ascetic, the beauty of bare words . . .'

While he was speaking I seized the opportunity of pushing away the bewitched plate very gently.

'Master,' I said to myself in youthful enthusiasm, for I felt in happier mood, 'must not poetry sow its wild oats?'

I could hear that inner voice, despite me, imitating his chanting tone. But aloud I asked some polite question, to which he replied:

'Poetry needs the symbolic, that which has been moulded by many minds. The Japanese, when they hold their sacred processions, are accustomed to disguise themselves in the grotesque masks and armour of their ancestors . . .'

'I want,' he said later on, 'to see a neo-Catholic school of young poets in this country.' He spoke of Jammes, [6] Peguy [7] and Claudel, [8] and said much that I could not follow at the time, for I had been cast into a mild trance by the gleam of the great signet upon his waving hand. I could not help watching that tremendous ring for I thought at the time that it had been fashioned by an artist of the Renaissance. But even in that trance I was trying to defend myself from the religious novelty which he was evolving. How could we learn to write the traditional songs of repentance before we had known those 'morry sins' of which Synge had spoken? I thought of the extravagant Gaelic poetry of the eighteenth century. Once more the strapping heroine of *The Midnight Court* was railing again aged bridegrooms, denouncing the celebacy of the clergy. She was proving to her own satisfaction that it was heretical for these tonsured young men to live in a state of single bliss. Once more the Mangaire Sugach was reeling from another parish with a satire on his tongue and, in a distant tavern, O Tuomy was filling his till with the fine words of his fellow craftsmen.

'I have to catch a train at four o'clock,' exclaimed the poet, hastily rising from the sofa.

The sun was shining again, here and there, among the seven woods when we came to the door. As I stood with downcast head upon the threshold he must have noticed my depression, despite his short sight. For suddenly he cried above me in majestic tones:

'You must come and see me again, when I am in my castle!'

NOTES

Austin Clarke (1896–1974), Irish poet and foundation member of the Irish Academy of Letters.

1. On Yeats at the centenary commemoration of Thomas Davis on 21 November 1914, see Austin Clarke, 'A Centenary Celebration', *Massachusetts Review*, v, no. 2 (Winter 1964) 307–10. The commemoration was organised by the Gaelic Society of Trinity College.

2. John Pentland Mahaffy (1839–1919) scorned the nationalists of his day as provincial, and was caustic about Patrick Pearse. In 1916 he directed the defence of Trinity College Dublin against the insurgents, but in 1917 proposed at the Irish Convention to which he and Trinity were host, that Ireland should have a Federal Constitution on the Swiss model, with Ulster as an autonomous province. See W. B. Stanford and R. B. McDowell, *Mahaffy; A Biography of an Anglo-Irishman* (London: Routledge and Kegan Paul, 1972).

3. Denis Rolleston Gwynn (1893–   ), son of Stephen Gwynn, is an Irish journalist and historian.

4. W. B. Yeats, 'I walked among the Seven Woods of Coole', *The Shadowy Waters* (1906).

5. Ibid.

6. Frances Jammes (1868–1938), French poet and novelist.

7. Charles Pierre Peguy (1873–1914), French writer.

8. Paul Louis Charles Claudel (1868–1955), French diplomat, poet and dramatist.

The Yeats I Knew*

EARNÁN DE BLAGHD

Although I often met Yeats, particularly at the Board-Room table in the Abbey Theatre, and although I took part in many discussions with him, I feel that perhaps I can offer only a worm's eye view of the man. Everyone who can read, may, according to his capacity, form an opinion of Yeats's work. But I do not know whether there were very many who knew him really well personally. He always seemed to me to be an aloof man, who, even when he was being genial and sociable, never fully unbent. His air of being withdrawn may have indicated no more than the abstraction of a dedicated writer, and, in certain kinds of select company, he may have inspired much affection as well as that admiration which, in not a few cases, verged upon awe. But I was often struck by the way in which people, who were obviously impressed by his genius, failed to show kindly personal feeling for him. When at Yeats's repeated invitation, I hesitantly joined the Abbey Board, knowing that as a consequence of becoming a member of it, I must relinquish the tenuous connection which I still had with active politics, I was visited at my home by the other new Directors, Fred Higgins and Brinsley Mac-Namara. They wanted to arrange that the three of us should act together on the Board. When I not only declined to be a member of any 'cave' but added that I regarded Yeats as the inspirer and

* *The Yeats We Knew*, ed. Francis MacManus (Cork: Mercier Press, 1965) pp. 61–75.

real founder of the Abbey and that, however I might argue as a member of the Board, I should never go the length of voting against him, they both proceeded to tell me that I was altogether too simple-minded to deal with a man like Yeats. They said that I obviously had no idea of his craftiness, of the complexity of his mind, or of his capacity for using people for his own ends. I was taken aback by the vehemence of their talk. But I did not think that, in the case of the men mentioned, anything like subconscious jealousy was at the bottom of their iconoclastic attitude towards my image of Yeats.

I remember, however, talking to another literary man who astonished me by seeming almost to hate Yeats, whom he compared to a great towering wide-spreading tree, which was stunting and obscuring everything around it by keeping the sunshine from it, and depriving it of attention. In his case, I judged that a somewhat lunatic jealousy was at work. My two new colleagues on the Abbey Board who wanted to create an organised opposition to Yeats's views and policy may not only have been free, as I believe, of jealousy, but must also have been free of any idea that they underestimated or impeded their work. I did not return to the subject later to inquire why they, who knew Yeats so much longer and better than I did and who acknowledged his greatness, appeared to have no feelings of cordial goodwill towards him, especially as he had shown confidence in them by putting them on the Board. Later on, however, it occurred to me that their attitude may have come as a reaction against a concentration, on his part, on his art and ideals which excluded true and close friendship from his relationship with most of those who were in his circle.

Dr. Richard Hayes,[1] who had been for a long time on the Board of the Abbey Theatre before I joined it, had a great but somewhat cynical admiration for Yeats's conduct in the chair. He told me that when he saw Yeats guiding and controlling the Board, he was reminded of a wily old Chairman of a Board of Guardians smoothing over differences, preventing splits and leading his fellow members to the conclusions which he thought best. I soon saw the resemblance which struck Dr. Hayes; but it was superficial. I think Yeats dominated the Board because he had clear well-considered views on practically every issue that could arise, because he argued every point equably and reasonably and because his prestige and air of lofty detachment gave his views added authority. He never allowed anything to deter him from doing what he thought necessary for the good of the Theatre, or, to rush him into precipitate action. The big split between Sean O'Casey and the Abbey Board, which followed the rejection of *The Silver Tassie*,[2] was still unhealed when Yeats heard that O'Casey was ill in hospital. He went to see him as if no hard words had ever passed between them. He came away having promised that the Abbey would now perform[3] *The Silver Tassie* and having got permission to do it as well as *Within the Gates*.[4]

Again, when Yeats made up his mind that Lennox Robinson's lengthy

period of distinguished service as producer in the Abbey should end, and a
new man be appointed, he did not allow years of friendship and comradely
co-operation to deflect him from his purpose. He first enlarged the Board,
taking advantage of a seasonal increase in the ordinary public criticism of
the Abbey to secure acceptance of his nominees, and agreeing that the new
Directors should be without shares, and therefore easy to let go at a
General Meeting of the Company. Once the new Directors, who had all
been calling for changes in Abbey policy, were in office, Yeats proposed
that a new producer with different experience and a fresh outlook should
be appointed for a period. Through the good offices of John Masefield,
Yeats found Hugh Hunt, a very young man who had produced for the
Oxford University Dramatic Society, and invited him over. Naturally
Lennox Robinson was deeply hurt by being ousted, on the advice of a
colleague with whom he had for many years been on the best of terms.

I felt that only a highly conscientious and devoted man and only a man
with a good deal of iron in him could have taken action so hard on a
colleague with whom he had no quarrel. Lennox Robinson was a master-
producer in some respects. No one could be better than he was in the
elucidation of character or in helping players, to convey temperament and
obsessions or to indicate hidden or subconscious motives. But the
establishment of the Gate Theatre and the work of Hilton Edwards and
Micheál MacLiammóir caused Dublin theatregoers to want productions
in which there was more stress on grouping and lighting and dressing than
had been usual in the Abbey. Hugh Hunt coming fresh to the Company
without preferences or prejudices got some of the results that are possible
for the new broom. He insisted on the installation of additional lighting
facilities and that the Abbey which had not previously had a full-time
designer and scene painter should appoint one. Yeats, of course, gave Mr.
Hunt any backing he needed.

A year or so later, Brinsley MacNamara, who had a strange irrational
dislike of O'Casey's plays, did a thing which aroused Yeats's fiercest
indignation. Encouraged, or led to forget himself, by some outside
criticism of *The Silver Tassie* which the Abbey had just put on, Brinsley
delivered himself of a diatribe[5] against the play. And of course, the
newspapers made the most of the intriguing situation thus created. Yeats
summoned a special meeting of the Abbey Board which, unfortunately, I
was unable to attend at short notice. Dr. Hayes, who told me about it
afterwards, relished the proceedings immensely. Yeats was at the top of his
form telling Brinsley that he had disgraced himself and thundering a
demand for his instant resignation from the Board. At the regular meeting
of the Directors held a day or two afterwards, Yeats was his usual calm self,
but was determined that Brinsley must go. He proposed that special
meetings of shareholders be summoned to dismiss him. When I suggested,
as an immediate measure, that for the next six months the Board should
delegate all its powers to a sub-committee consisting of six of its seven

members, thus depriving Brinsley at once of all opportunity to participate in the work of the Theatre, Yeats accepted the idea. Brinsley sent in his resignation next day. Yeats, in spite of his indignation against MacNamara, was so pleased to be relieved from the necessity for expelling him, that he designated me to preside at meetings of the Board thereafter if he should be absent.

I do not remember any great differences of opinion about plays during the years in which I sat with Yeats on the Abbey Board. He frequently talked about the very bad plays which had been produced in the Abbey in its early years. They were put on, he said, because nothing better was available at the time. Before I became a Director of the Abbey, I had found myself getting tired of George Shiels's[6] somewhat acid comedies, not realising that, for years, they had been an important factor in saving the Abbey from bankruptcy. I suggested that the Theatre should perform them much less frequently. Yeats promptly disagreed. He insisted that Shiels's plays were good: 'Rough work but good,' he said.

He was determined that no play should ever be produced in the Abbey which was likely to hurt the sincere religious feelings of anyone. Great as was his admiration for Synge, he had never permitted *The Tinker's Wedding* to be played in the Abbey because the representation of the priest in it would offend Catholics in the audiences.[7] Soon after I became a director, new Irish plays worth production were very scarce, and it was proposed to go outside for something to fill the gap. A play giving an unflattering picture of Mary Baker Eddy, Founder of the Christian Science movement, was recommended. It seemed suitable as a stop-gap and likely to bring in some revenue. Directors generally were willing to have it done, but Yeats voted against its production. He was not going to have a play performed in the Abbey which would offend the susceptibilities of Christian Scientists, however few of them might see it. The matter was discussed at some length by the Board and Yeats made it plain that in the earliest days of the Abbey he had decided on his attitude and resolved that no matter what his religion, no one, Catholic, Protestant, Jew or Mahommedan should ever have to sit in the Abbey and hear things which he held sacred being derided or insulted.

Yeats was always against plays embodying crude propaganda. Once, during his absence from the country, a play was rejected by the Board, partly on the ground that it contained too much anti-clerical propaganda. And an attempt was made on his return to Ireland to induce him to ask the Board to reconsider its decision—the play was *The White Steed*[8] by Paul Vincent Carroll. Yeats not only refused to disagree with the majority of the Board but gave a dissertation on how easily a literary work might be spoiled by the creeping effects of propaganda. I do not imagine that in this case Yeats was acting the part of the good senior colleague and throwing the protection of his mantle over the juniors on whom he had placed responsibility for carrying on in his absence. A matter of high importance was involved. A play by a major dramatist had been rejected. If Yeats had considered the Board mistaken he would not have hesitated to take steps to have the error rectified. However, when minor decisions were in question, it did appear to me that Yeats behaved, on occasion, as a good team-worker willing to support the action of the majority, by refusing to re-open a decided case.

In regard to plays generally, especially the work of new writers, his attitude was benign. Perhaps many years of often-disappointing search for a sufficiency of good work by Irish writers and of deferred hope for the appearance of another dramatic genius, had made him more eager than he had been in earlier years, to see signs of originality, of developing power or of instinct for the theatre in writers who, on the surface, did not appear so very promising. Consequently, there was not at Board meetings any appreciable difference of view-point between Yeats and other members of the Board, on the plays which came before us. Perhaps the only exception concerned the plays of his brother, Jack Yeats. These quaint rambling compositions had a strange charm and indeed reminded one of certain pictures which delight the eye and intrigue the mind, though it is with difficulty and some uncertainty that recognisable figures or objects can be discerned in them.

A couple of Jack Yeats's plays were performed, years later in the Peacock Theatre[9] or for a night or two in the main auditorium of the Abbey.[10] They were warmly received by somewhat atypical audiences, members of which saw or professed to see things in them that were hidden from ordinary theatregoers. When it was found that one of them was too long and would have to be cut, to let the final curtain come down before too many people had rushed from the auditorium to catch the last buses, an actor averred that cutting would be quite easy. All that was called for, he declared, was to determine roughly what number of words had to come out to bring the play down to a convenient length and then to calculate how many pages they would fill. Thereupon ten, twenty, or fifty pages, as might be appropriate, could be taken at random and simply torn out, without audiences either noticing the joins or being conscious of gaps in the narrative. Most Directors felt that Jack Yeats's plays had some sort of quality and were not indisposed to try one of them on the public, partly as a gimmick and partly in the hope that Jack Yeats's name and his fame as a painter might draw substantial audiences to the theatre for a week or so. When the proposal was made at a Board meeting, however, W. B. Yeats pronounced firmly and curtly against it. And nothing more was heard during W. B. Yeats's life-time about the production of either *In Sand* or *La-La-noo*.

I never heard Yeats talk about spiritualism or any form of mystical belief or give any indication of interest in phenomena of a supernatural kind such as, we are informed, fascinated him. As a member of the Abbey Board, he was always the cautious, cool-headed business man, the sober confident literary connoiseur with a tolerant appreciative outlook and occasional enthusiasms but with a magisterial distaste for the shoddy and vulgar.

National or political issues did not arise in discussions at Board meetings. Without anything being said, however, the atmosphere left no doubt that everything done was being offered for the honour and renown of Ireland. In all my encounters with Yeats it seemed to me that there was conscious patriotism behind his actions and attitudes. I think, however, we need not consider him very seriously as a practical politician. He was not capable, in public affairs of offering that firm resistance to a romantic personality or a romantic plan which is often the test of the politician who deserves to survive or to preserve his influence.

Though he professed to dislike personal involvement in controversy Yeats had no hesitation about coming out in opposition to the popular view or what he conceived to be the attitude of the mob. His stand for the freedom of the theatre from mob censorship was whole-hearted and uncompromising. I was in the Abbey on the night of the first performance of *The Playboy*. It was the first occasion on which I saw a queue outside the pit door awaiting its opening and it was the last time such a queue was seen for several years. Whatever kudos the *Playboy* row may have gained for the Abbey abroad, its effect at home was to drive away a great part of the following which had been gradually built up. That, however, was a small loss compared with what would have been suffered if a puritanical mob censorship had been made effective. Although Yeats had been associated, to some extent, with advanced nationalism and had been a friend and admirer of John O'Leary the Fenian leader, he did not hesitate to bring the police into the Theatre and to point out to them the disturbers whom they should arrest. After a week of arrests and fines the *Playboy* row was over, and there was no further attempt at communal censorship for a long time. On one occasion Yeats by a timely intervention averted a threatened disturbance. Norreys Connell's one act play *The Piper* got its first performance on Thursday 13th February 1908 when W. F. Casey's three-act piece *The Man Who Missed the Tide* was produced for the first time. There was no hostile reaction to *The Piper*[11] that night, but on Friday night it evoked a good deal of hissing as *The Playboy* had done on its first night a year previously. For the third performance of *The Piper* on Saturday afternoon, the auditorium was crowded, some people having come to see the play and others having come, as they would have said, to enjoy the fun. I was one of those who went both to see the play and to observe the disturbance which I believed would develop. Before the curtain went up, however, Yeats came out in front of it and made a very adroit speech. He would not attempt, he declared, to say what the author meant. The play was the author's own statement of that. But he would venture to tell us what he saw in the play. He saw the eternal heroic aspirations of the Irish people embodied in the character of The Piper. Then he came down to Black Mike whose cry 'God damn Father Hanningan' could well have been the spark which would start a blaze of anger in the auditorium. Yeats told us that he saw in Black Mike the embodiment of the men of burning sincerity, of the men who took action to achieve Irish freedom while others indulged in unending fruitless talk. In Black Mike he saw Robert Emmett and Parnell and all who had been willing to sacrifice themselves for Ireland. Having thus made his point, Yeats briefly left the play to the judgement of the audience without any sort of direct appeal. The performance proceeded and those who had come to hiss and hoot remained to applaud. Not only had the play been saved from attack by Yeats's beautifully balanced little speech but it had been helped to achieve popularity. With Yeats's interpretation in mind, audiences continued for years to receive it warmly every time it was revived and for a period it ranked almost equal, as a patriotic stimulant, with Yeats's own *Kathleen ni Houlihan* and Gregory's *The Rising of the Moon*.

That was the first time I felt the influence of Yeats's personality. I was full of admiration for the way he handled the situation, for his poise, for the phraseology in which he presented his argument and for the total effect of his brief statement, upon the audience.

I had, of course, frequently seen him in the front of the stalls. On my very first visit to the Abbey, when I was a couple of months over sixteen years of age, Yeats came to the rail which stood at the divide of the little stairs leading down to the stalls and leaned over it slowly scanning the audience as if he were looking for someone whom he expected to find in the auditorium. The man sitting next to me in the pit whispered that the poetic looking man who was running his eye over the audience was none other than Willie Yeats and that he was checking the box office returns by counting the number of people in each part of the house. So that even then, the story that the poet was a careful business man had become current.

I did not meet Yeats personally until he became a Senator. Because of a certain Gaelic League and Sinn Fein prejudice against him, because he did not esteem, or produce, straight practical political verse, I was inclined, in the beginning, to look upon him as something of a national backslider, a man who had been a thorough-going Nationalist, but who had excused himself from standing any longer in the front ranks in the struggle for Ireland's rights. But in 1913, I met Desmond Fitzgerald in Kerry. As an Irishman brought up in London, Desmond ascribed his national feelings and convictions to the influence of Yeats's poetry[12] and I began to read it without my old Gaelic League prejudice. From the moment proposals for a Senate took definite shape, Desmond Fitzgerald was determined that Yeats should be invited to become a member. His proposal encountered no opposition in the Cabinet and Yeats was enrolled as a Senator.

He allied himself with what has generally been described as the ex-Unionist group, though it included James Douglas, Mrs. Alice Stopford Green, the historian, and Sam Brown, K.C., none of them Unionists. Its leader, however, if it could rightly be said to have had a leader, was

Andrew Jameson. He had been head of the Irish Unionist Alliance and a redoubtable opponent of Home Rule, but he became a contented loyal citizen of the Free State on its establishment. It was natural that Yeats, back again for the first time for many years in active politics, should drift to this so-called ex-Unionist group. Most of its members were personally distinguished by reason of talent or influence and Yeats's romantic longing for aristocratic and authoritarian ways and standards made him feel at home in the circle which they formed. I should not say that his opinion carried great weight amongst them on general issues. But when he was on his ground he could, of course, bring the majority with him. For example, it was Yeats who secured the establishment of the Advisory Committee which recommended the designs for our coinage and it was he who guided its proceedings.

I do not think his contributions to the Senate debates on such questions as censorship and divorce influenced votes either in the House or amongst the electorate. In Matters of the kind, decisions depended on deep currents of opinion and only a combination of the most influential members of the Dail able to command wide Party allegiance, could have modified the ultimate result. I presume, however, that Yeats spoke not with the idea of influencing decisions or shaping convictions, but simply to satisfy himself and in the hope of gratifying certain special groups.

Yeats showed an interest in the Blueshirt movement when it was at the pinnacle of its strength and wrote a marching song[13] for it. But most of those associated with the movement disliked the song, with its refrain 'Hammer them Down' and Yeats, for his part, soon forgot about the organisation, which, in fact, had only a very brief period of vigour and began to feel itself superfluous when the Fianna Fail Government started to arrest members of the I.R.A. His move to help, or at least to encourage, the Blueshirts was, I think, Yeats's last political initiative. That he was an ardent unwavering patriot with the welfare and renown of Ireland constantly in his mind is beyond doubt. That he gave double service to his country is also clear. In the first place his high achievement as a writer glorified the land to which he was so obviously devoted. In the second place his treatment of Irish themes and his personal example of practical love of country inspired countless people with zeal for Irish nationality. He did more for Ireland working in his own way than he could have done by displaying the most consummate skill in organising voters, in drafting party programmes, and in conducting debates for the enlightenment of the electorate. His influence and the fruits of his labour spread very widely. That is exemplified in the theatre. While everyone knows of his responsibility for the founding and survival of the Abbey, not everyone knows that if the Abbey had not been established we should not have had the Gate Theatre either. And if we had not had the Gate, it is unlikely that we should have had the little theatres that are scattered over the city. Similarly in the higher national aspect of politics, Yeats has exercised and continues to exercise an indirect influence which extends far beyond the subjects and causes which he himself touched.

NOTES

Earnán de Blaghd was a member of the Irish Revolutionary Brotherhood, to which he was introduced by Sean O'Casey. He joined Sinn Fein and held many important government posts including the Ministry of Finance. At present he is a director of the Abbey Theatre.

1. Dr Richard Hayes, the government director on the Abbey Theatre Board. He wrote 'An Old Yeats Ballad', *Dublin Magazine*, II, no. 2 (Apr–June 1927) 59–61 and 'W. B. Yeats, a Catholic Poet', *Irish Monthly*, LVI, no. 4 (Apr 1928) 179–86.

2. Yeats's refusal of *The Silver Tassie* in 1928, with the concurrence of Lady Gregory and Lennox Robinson, created a sensation. See 'Mr. O'Casey's New Play. Why It Was Rejected. Mr. Yeats on the Dramatist's Job. The War and the Stage', *Observer* (London) 3 June 1928, p. 19. The play had its première at the Apollo Theatre, London, on 11 October 1929.

3. The play was presented at the Abbey Theatre on 12 August 1935.

4. *Within the Gates* opened at the Royalty Theatre, London, on 7 February 1934.

5. Brinsley MacNamara, 'Abbey Production of O'Casey Play: Revelations by a Director of the Theatre', *Irish Independent* (Dublin) (29 Aug 1935) p. 7. See also 'An Abbey Play: Views of Three Directors', *Irish Times* (Dublin) (29 Aug 1935) p. 7.

6. George Shiels's (1886–1949) real success was *Paul Twyning* (1922), and for more than twenty years he continued to write successfully for the Abbey. Lennox Robinson called him 'the Thomas Moore of the Irish Theatre', as his plays had the warm-hearted simplicity of Moore's poetry. Most of his plays are comedies and all of them have been revived many times: *Professor Tim, The Fort Field, The New Gossoon, Cartney and Kevney, The Summit* and *The Rugged Path*.

7. In the play, Sarah Casey and Michael Byrne, two tinkers whose morals and ways of life are highly irregular, appeal to a priest to marry them. At first he refuses, then agrees under their blandishments and the promise of 'a bit of gold and a tin can' as a fee. Old Mary Byrne, however, has exchanged the tin can for some ale, with which to celebrate the ceremony. When the priest finds that his can is gone he refuses to go through with the wedding and all three tinkers set upon him, bind him and threaten him with dire consequences. By the use of a Latin malediction he frightens the tinkers away. The play was first produced at His Majesty's Theatre, London on 11 November 1909.

8. In the play, Father Shaughnessy, an intolerant moralist, temporarily replaces Canon Matt Lavelle, whose legs have been paralysed by a stroke. He forms a vigilance committee to stamp out sin, which in his view includes drinking, courting and interfaith marriages. Through his committee he breaks up the engagement of schoolmaster Denis Dillon to a Protestant girl and discharges librarian Nora Fintry because she has been seen with a man. Denis is intimidated, but Nora is determined to fight the priest. She and Denis fall in love, and through her Denis finds the strength to stand up to the priest. Inspector Toomey, who has tried to protect the secular rights of those oppressed by the Vigilance committee, threatens to arrest the priest, and a mob gathers to prevent him from doing so. Then Canon Lavelle appears, miraculously walking. He calms his parishioners, sends them home, and rebukes Father Shaughnessy for his hotheadedness and 'spiritual snobbery'. The Canon's offer of reinstatement is rejected by Denis, who declares his independence and goes off to find his strength and love, Nora.

9. In 1925 the Peacock Theatre was constructed in a house adjoining the Abbey Theatre. With a very small stage and seats for only 102 persons in the auditorium it was designed to be used for experimental productions and for performances by pupils of the Abbey School of Acting.

10. *La La Noo*, a play in two acts by Jack B. Yeats, was produced at the Abbey Theatre on 3 May 1942.

11. The play deals with the rising in Wexford in 1798, and its chief character, Black Mike,

has some very unpalatable things to say about the Irish character. It is a rather obvious satire on Irish political tactics of the then recent past, and on Irish mentality generally, and it has some affinity with Bernard Shaw's *John Bull's Other Island*.

12. At the time that Desmond Fitzgerald and Arthur Griffith had been interned in Glouscester Jail, Griffith, knowing his ardent admiration for Yeats, said to him, 'What are you going to do about June 13?' Having drawn a confession of ignorance of the significance of that date, Griffith put on an air of pained surprise: 'Don't you know', he said, 'that June 13 is W. B. Yeats's birthday?' They went together to the Governor and told him that the Irish in Gloucester Jail would require special facilities on June 13th, as it was the birthday of their national poet. The Governor consented. See Joseph Hone, *W. B. Yeats 1865-1939* (London: Macmillan, 1965) p. 344.

13. W. B. Yeats, 'Three Songs to the Same Tune', *A Full Moon in March* (1935).

W. B. Yeats*

C. M. BOWRA

In the spring of 1917, when I was a cadet in London, the Crab asked me to lunch with him at the Savile Club, where, instead of sitting at small separate tables, the company sat at one long table. I was on the Crab's right, and on my right was a stranger to whom the Crab did not introduce me. He was tall and quite heavily built. His hair was turning grey; he had a fine straight nose, and dark eyes, which had that look of peering into infinity which is the privilege of the short-sighted. He carried his glasses on a black ribbon and manipulated them with a ceremonial care. He had no notion who I was, and did not ask, but began to talk freely. He spoke with a marked Irish brogue, and his choice of words was as striking as his sentences were well fashioned. He talked about the past, and, rather to my surprise, about Oscar Wilde, whom he had known and of whom he had much to say in praise and gratitude. I could not imagine who he could be, but did not dare ask the Crab until lunch was over, and the courteous stranger had disappeared. 'Oh', said the Crab, 'he's a poet called Yeats.' I found the Crab's nonchalance a little disturbing, especially since he was himself a cousin of J. M. Synge. I had read Yeats' early poems as far back as 1914 and thought them wonderful. Of the new poets he was the one I admired most and knew by heart, and I was not troubled by any nasty doubts that what I liked in them was their essentially romantic quality, their dream-laden themes and their caressing rhythms. I had also read quite recently a few of his later poems in *The Little Review* and *The New Statesman*, and though I saw how very different they were from the earlier, I was strangely moved by them, especially by *The Wild Swans of Coole*. The

* Extracted from *Memories, 1898-1939* (London : Weidenfeld and Nicolson, 1966) pp. 230-241.

moment I knew who the stranger was, everything fell into place. Later I understood why he talked about Wilde. He was at this time turning over in his mind the memories which were to appear later in *The Trembling of the Veil*. What he gave to me was the rough material for the remarkable passages on Wilde which he was shaping in his mind for this book.

After the war Yeats and his wife lived in Oxford, in Broad Street opposite Balliol in a house now demolished. I used to see him walking about, with a distant, abstracted air, wearing a grey, floppy hat and what was more a cravat than a tie. But I did not dare to approach him on the flimsy excuse of having met him once at the Savile Club, nor did any of my friends know him. But one evening A. P. Ryan of Balliol asked me to come to his rooms, where Yeats was going to read his poems. He was, as always, courteous in a stately, old-fashioned way and treated the small company of undergraduates with a fine consideration. He had with him a volume of his verse, which I cannot now identify. The pages were still uncut, and Yeats took out from his pocket a small paper-knife and cut them with careful gravity. He then read some poems, first from his earlier period, then from his latest, including *The Wild Swans of Coole, Easter 1916*, and *Solomon and the Witch*. The whole evening was a revelation. In reading Yeats emphasized the rhythm, which was of first importance, since it showed how the poems ought to sound and how far he had travelled from his earlier, easier and much slacker rhythms. But what I had not expected was the tone in which he read. It was not sing-song nor yet incantation, nor had it that rather too prophetic tone which he adopted in later years. Yeats stressed the rhythm as much as he could. His voice was very much the same in speed and volume as when he spoke, but different in pitch. He seemed to be carried away by his poems and to wish to convey as much of his feelings as possible. Yet the feelings were under full control, even in *Easter 1916*, when he began with a low, level voice and did not make it recognizably louder on reaching the end of the stanza, 'A terrible beauty is born'. His method was quite unlike the dry manner which was already becoming common in reading poetry and was to be popularized by T. S. Eliot. Nor was it like the public recitation favoured by young Russian poets today and intended to hold large audiences in a new communal art which has something of a dramatic performance. Having himself no ear for music, Yeats sought to put another kind of music into his reading. His method stressed what the poems had to say in all their depth and breadth, and though very few readers could take such risks as he did, there was no question of his being histrionic or trying to get more out of the poems than was in them. He was now at the height of his powers. He had perfected his new style and used it for matters of pressing urgency to all of us.

In the later twenties I met Yeats quite often, sometimes at Garsington,[1] where he liked to enunciate at their full value the words 'the Lady Ottoline Morrell', and where he could say what he pleased, even at the cost of shocking some of the more austere visitors. Then I met him in Ireland, when I was staying with my friend Pierce Synnott at Naas in Co Kildare. A guest in the house was Mrs Hinkson, who had in her youth been a friend of Yeats and won, under her maiden name of Katharine Tynan, a place for herself as a poet in the Irish literary revival. She was getting old and her eyesight was very bad, but she was full of life and comments on life. Like others of her countryfolk, she liked to put small pin-pricks into reputations, and though she had once liked Yeats and he had admired her, they had drifted a little apart. She had sold his letters to her, and that may have caused some slight chilliness. Still she recognized his greatness, even if she did not admire him as much as I did, and she sent Pierce, John Sparrow, and myself to Dublin armed with an introduction to George Russell, known as 'A.E.', who was one of Yeats' oldest and closest friends. We called on A.E. at his room in Merrion Square, and Yeats came in a little later. With A.E. he was more at his ease than at Garsington and talked freely on a number of matters, on the new Irish coins which he hoped would be as beautiful as the Greek, on the preposterous prohibition of divorce in Ireland, on the machinations of D. S. MacColl to prevent any of Hugh Lane's pictures from going to Dublin. He was beginning to find that politics, into which he had been lured after the establishment of the Free State, had its own faults and corruptions, and some man had incurred his displeasure, 'He may have been an honest man, but I have never seen anyone look less like an honest man.' He talked too of Edward Martyn, whom George Moore had guyed in *Hail and Farewell*, but who treated all Moore's gibes with complete disdain; of Maud Gonne, who was the great love of his life, watching a British battleship and hoping it would blow up; of how attractive Mrs Hinkson had been in her youth and how attached he then was to her.

With old friends, like A.E. and Lennox Robinson, Yeats, whose name A.E. pronounced to rhyme with 'Keats', was less elaborate and less formal in his talk than when he was among people more or less strange to him. He had then his noble set-pieces, which were too good to be unpremeditated, and no doubt he made use of them more than once. In particular there was the story of himself and a Persian poet, next to whom he was placed at an official banquet. Neither knew a word of the other's language; so the talk, as Yeats emphasized, was conducted decorously through an interpreter. It ran something like this, 'I asked the poet what poetry he wrote, and the Persian replied that he used to write love-poetry, which was so beautiful that it became a model of decorum and was studied in all the girls' schools of Persia, but that was a long time ago. So I asked him what he wrote now, and the Persian replied that now he wrote useful poetry.' (At this point Yeats' voice became indignant.) 'So I asked what might that be. And the Persian replied that he went as the representative of Persia on the League of Nations, and sent all his reports in rhyme.' A long and fascinating saga turned on George Moore, and much of it Yeats published later in *Dramatis Personae*, but I recall one small episode which he did not record. Speaking of 'the infinite malice of Moore', Yeats said that Moore would look for the weak point in everyone, but could not find one in A.E. He was much disappointed and complained that there must be a fault, and he would find it. Then one day he turned up triumphantly and said to Yeats: 'I have found out what is wrong with A.E. He neglects his wife', and with this he was content.

In these set-pieces Yeats may, more or less consciously, have followed Wilde, whom he had known in his youth and who liked to tell stories, though not quite of this kind. In his less formal talk Yeats was much freer and not at all above trivialities, though even these he managed to make dramatic by his presentation of them, as when he announced with indignation, 'I was so cold last night that I had to put the carpet on my bed.' As in his poetry he made a personal mythology out of people whom he had known and presented them as symbols of various ways of life, so in his talk he did something of the same kind. Hearing that I was going to be Proctor, he was reminded of his father's old friend, Frederick York Powell, who had been Regius Professor of History at Christ Church and on being asked to be Proctor said, 'No, no. The older I get the harder I find it to distinguish between right and wrong.' Yeats enjoyed telling how, when he went to Stockholm to receive the Nobel prize, Anatole France was also there 'with three mistresses and four parrots'. Yeats was not averse to general ideas but used them largely to give depth to particular episodes or to explain certain people. In the same way, when he read the Greek philosophers in the translations of Thomas Taylor, what he looked for in them was examples and images to confirm his own beliefs. Though his views on painting were what we used to call 'literary' and he thought that its subjects should be symbolical, he had been well instructed in its technique by his father. If something was on his mind because he was going to write about it, he would try the phrases out. Just as in 1917 I heard him describe how the harlots danced in the street at the conviction of Wilde, and he put it later into *The Trembling of the Veil*, so in the thirties when he was thinking about his Introduction to *The Oxford Book of Modern Verse* he said, 'I met Father Hopkins several times at my father's studio, but I don't remember a word of what he said', and in due course this became 'Fifty odd years ago I met him in my father's studio, on different occasions, but remember almost nothing. A boy of seventeen, Walt Whitman in his pocket, had little interest in a querulous, sensitive scholar.' Again, on Bridges he said, 'Every line a platitude, every poem a masterpiece', but wrote, 'Emptiness everywhere, the whole magnificent.' The strength of these final versions comes from long brooding on a single point and a resolve to enrich it beyond its first impact.

In 1931, when I was Proctor, I was entitled to put up a name for an honorary degree, and I put up Yeats for a Doctorate of Letters.[2] The older and less transient members of Hebdomadal Council, with whom the decision really lay, tried to persuade me to wait for some special occasion, but, since I had no trust in their willingness to go on with the matter once I was off Council, as I soon would be, I insisted on a vote being taken then and there. Rather to my surprise the degree was approved and was duly conferred in early June. The ceremony was in the Sheldonian Theatre, which had then not been restored to its present brilliance, but none the less appealed to Yeats, who said, 'What a beautiful building! The colour of ivory and of old books.' The ceremony was held at a meeting of Convocation, at which usually there is only a sparse attendance, but on this occasion several hundreds were present, for after the conferment of the degree there was to be a debate on the proposed abolition of Divinity Moderations, or 'Divvers', the absurd examination which had brought John Betjeman's career at Oxford to an untimely end. Yeats naturally thought that the crowd had come to see him, and was delighted. He looked magnificent in his scarlet gown, with his white hair, and his eyes, as Beazley said at the time, 'like an eagle's'. He did not stay for the debate, at which, I am glad to say, the young philosopher Gilbert Ryle united with Kenneth Kirk, soon to become Bishop of Oxford, to attack 'Divvers' and succeeded in getting it abolished.

That evening I gave a dinner for Yeats in our old Senior Common Room, which I thought he would like, since it is a fine panelled room of 1680 with carved swags by the school of Grinling Gibbons. I asked to meet him Kenneth and Jane Clark, John Livingston Lowes and his wife, who were visiting Oxford, Wade-Gery and his wife, Elizabeth Bowen, John Sparrow, and my young, beautiful and extremely lively friend, Nancy Mitford, who had somehow persuaded her ogre of a father to let her out for the evening. After dinner I made a very short speech in which I said that the University which had expelled Shelley had now tried to make amends by honouring the greatest poet of the age. When I said this, Yeats nodded. He did not make a formal reply, but from his chair said simply: 'A man may perhaps say a few words after a few minutes of warning but none after no warning at all', and this was agreed to be right. We then moved to my rooms, where Yeats read some of his poems. He began with some later ones, notably *In Memory of Eva Gore Booth and Con Markiewicz* and *A Dialogue of Self and Soul*. He introduced them with short explanations and comments, as if he thought that otherwise we might not fully understand them. He followed with some earlier pieces, beginning with *The Cap and Bells*, in which he said that he still delighted, but when he came to the words 'a flutter of flower-like hair', he interrupted himself and said, ' "Flower-like" is a *cliché*. I should not write it now.' Then Mrs Lowes, who was delightfully emotional and impulsive, asked him to read *The Man who Dreamed of Fairyland*, but met with a stern refusal, 'I will not read it . It is a bad poem.' Fortunately he proceeded with *The Happy Towland*, and all was well. He even read *The Lake Isle of Innisfree*, but explained that it was full of faults. When he went away, Yeats said to John Sparrow, 'No emperor does himself so well as an Oxford don', and I felt that the more material side of the evening had at least been a success.

A few days later I received the following letter,

> 42 Fitzwilliam Square
> Dublin
> June 10

Dear Mr Bowra,

I got back to Dublin last night and this morning have sat at my table and got out my letters and thought whom I should thank. You first of all certainly. That was a very charming evening at Wadham and especially charming to me, because you showed that you understood and valued poems that I like and that have not been much noticed. Henley told me once that he never knew if he had written well or ill until somebody told him that he had. I have not written verse for some months, and it may be owing to you and your friends that I am eager to write it. I thank you and thank them.

> Yours
>
> W. B. Yeats

In the uncertainty of his own judgement on his poems Yeats resembled other poets whom I have known. Though he took enormous trouble and was a ruthlessly exacting critic of himself, he was not sure how the result would appeal to others, and he felt that, if it did not, he had failed. He needed an approving audience to complete the process of creation, and in this he was like Boris Pasternak, who in his later years felt that he was writing in a vacuum, and was amazed when he found that I had written about him. The same was true of Edith Sitwell, who treated the foolish and frivolous things said against her as personal insults. She felt that she was being attacked in the most sacrosanct part of herself and deprived of that extension of personality which a right appreciation of her poems would give her.

I continued to see Yeats in the following years in London, Oxford, and Dublin. In London he made much use of the Athenaeum, of which I too was a member, where he would carry an attaché-case full of papers and spend much time in the library. I used sometimes to interrupt him, but he did not mind, since he would ask my opinion on whatever was in his mind at the moment. Often it was to do with the selection of poems for *The Oxford Book of Modern Verse*. Though he listened to what I said, he did not act upon it, and I could not persuade him to include either Wilfred Owen or Isaac Rosenberg. When the book came out, it reflected not so much his whimsical taste as a truth, which has long been clear to me, that poets are very seldom good judges of other poets. Just as Yeats said of Housman, 'I like only his humorous poetry', so Bridges, about 1923, said of Yeats 'Poor Yeats! He's finished.' Yeats was far too busy with his own creative problems to pay attention to the problems of others and their ways of solving them. His admiration for Lady Gerald Wellesley may have been largely due to his great affection for her, but there was some truth in his claim that she was trying to do the same kind of thing as himself.

Yeats was not in the least 'cosy'. His genius for words was an obstacle between you and any easy intimacy. They turned everything into a high occasion and encouraged you to ask for more of the same kind. He claimed, truthfully enough, that he was a shy man, and also that in company he adopted a mask which was not his real self, but this was not quite true. Rather, he made the most of his thoughts and feelings by adapting them to a public world, but the magnificent choice of words was the rough material from which he made his poetry. It had some of the same intensity and bore the marks of his creative personality. Nobody else spoke as he did, and it was impossible to imagine him speaking otherwise. He gave to his words an emphasis which hinted how carefully he chose them, and yet there was no hesitation in his flow. It could even have moments of singular charm. Once when a very pretty girl was leaving the room and standing for a moment by the door, he said, 'Stop! How sad it is to think of you standing there looking so beautiful—and yet I don't love you.' She was enchanted, and Yeats, who much admired good looks, meant exactly what he said.

Yeats' conversation sometimes turned to spiritualism, and he made no excuses for it. His attitude towards it has troubled some of his admirers, who cannot understand how a man of his sharp intelligence can have believed such twaddle or written so splendidly about it; for after all *All Souls' Night*, which is concerned with necromancy, is probably the finest poem ever written in Oxford. A way of escape is to claim that through séances and dreams Yeats found, as the spirits told him, images for poetry and that this was his way of exploiting his unconscious self. But this was not the impression he made on me. He talked freely about spirits and was convinced that No. 4 Staircase at Wadham, where I lived, was haunted, and he spent an evening on the roof of the New Buildings of Magdalen looking for elementals. The large structure which he made of spiritualism and developed with such eloquence in *Per amica silentia lunae* meant very much to him. It was his armoury against the scientific spirit and his alternative to the Christianity which had long lost all meaning for him. It may seem absurd today, but it was much in the air in his youth, notably in Paris, and he clung to it, just as Rainer Maria Rilke[3] felt the presence of ghosts as he laboured in solitude at his later poetry. Yeats' spiritualism may lack adherents, but that is because it was an essentially private religion. He made it for himself without reference to common creeds, which might seem equally absurd if they had fewer believers. Yet his credulity provided Yeats with ways of dealing with odd situations. Once, when he had muddled an engagement with me, he insisted on giving a party for me and was firm on his need to do so, 'I am laying a ghost and this requires an exact ritual.' This might be merely a manner of speaking, but it came from one to whom it meant much more than to most. Equally he was capable of using his spirits for what might be ironical purposes. Once on being asked if he liked a much praised man, he answered, 'I used to like him, till I saw that wherever he went he was followed by two small green elephants, and I knew that he was a bad man.' Was there a twinkle in his eye when he said it? Or did he believe that there was something so sinister about the man that it could be explained only by supernatural elements?

Another point on which Yeats has been increasingly criticized in recent years is his political views, and he has been accused of being a Fascist. The accusation is not preposterous, but it is wrong. His interest in politics was of a cosmic kind. He liked to discern vast movements in history and, though he was deeply involved in particular issues when he was an Irish Senator, he still saw them from a lofty detachment. This is why so much of his political poetry passes beyond politics into prophecy and vision. But his inability to fall into any ordinary party was dictated by his special position. As an Irishman he inherited a dislike of England, which, though he lived here for years, he never quite overcame. But as an Irish Protestant, a member of the old Ascendancy, he hated the idea of a new Ireland run by Roman Catholic priests. The first explained his condemnation of the First World War and his description of it as 'bloody frivolity'; the second explained his failure to find the place of honour which he would have liked in a liberated Ireland. If for a time he supported the ridiculous O'Duffy and his Blue Shirts, it was because he rejected equally the two parties which competed to govern Ireland, but he soon turned against O'Duffy, and towards the end of his life made fun of him, saying that his was the only contingent which went to fight for Franco and came home with more men than it went out with. Yeats, like others of his generation, was a romantic who dreamed of a world on which industrialism had not set its blight. He hoped to find it in Ireland, where its finest qualities would be embodied in a few country houses, like Lady Gregory's, and the arts and fine conversation would be practised in a way worthy of the Renaissance. In this search he naturally failed, and he was left with a grievance and a sense of defeat. He would have liked to be a national figure, as Stefan George[4] tried to be in Germany. Yeats more than once asked me about him, and saw in his cultivation of a few gifted friends something that he would himself like and which would revivify Ireland. But it was no more than a fancy, and he never took it very seriously. Indeed, when I told him that George's circle had disintegrated under the Nazis, who stole its slogans and set its members against one another, he said that he was not surprised.

*   *   *

A little before this I heard that Yeats was coming to Oxford to address some society, and wrote to him asking him to lunch. Rather to my surprise, I got a very formal and indeed curt note refusing. When I looked more closely at his not very legible writing, I found that the letter was addressed not to me but to a man whose name had the same number of letters and whom Yeats did not like. It looked as if he had misread my signature, which was more than forgivable, and confused me with the other man. I decided to do nothing, but I soon found that my surmise was right. Yeats had made a mistake, and when he discovered it, was much distressed. How deeply, I realized when a copy of his *Collected Poems* arrived with the following poem inscribed in his own hand on the front page,

> To Maurice Bowra
>
> Sound words from Yeats to Bowra: he
> Asks pardon for stupidity
> Committed in the month of June,
> Hand laid on heart declares the moon
> The Almighty and Devil know
> What made a sane man blunder so.

Nor was he satisfied with this. He insisted that he had been very discourteous and could make amends only by giving a lunch for me in Oxford, to which I must ask the guests. Unfortunately, circumstances were for a time against us. He fell ill, and I was in the United States, but in May 1938, we were able at last to arrange it. It took place in Wadham, and I asked a few of his admirers to meet him. Before we sat down he made movements with his hands to exorcise any ghosts who might still be lurking around to cause trouble. Though he had aged rapidly in the last year and stooped and walked slowly, he was as eloquent and as courteous as ever. He talked about the diatribes which he was writing in *On the Boiler*, deplored with irony his ignorance of Erse, explained how he wished to write poems which would catch the spontaneity of traditional ballads, and claimed that he could read nothing but boys' books about the Wild West. Before going away, he insisted on paying for luncheon, and was candidly pleased that it cost so little. He then departed for the Mitre Hotel and I never saw him again.

NOTES

Sir Cecil Maurice Bowra (1898–1971) was educated at Cheltenham and New College, Oxford. During World War I he served in France with the artillery. After it he became a Fellow of Wadham College and in 1938 was elected Warden. In 1946 he was appointed Professor of Poetry and in 1951 became Vice-Chancellor of Oxford and was knighted. An accomplished classical scholar, he had also a wide knowledge of modern works in many literatures. His works include *Tradition and Design in the Iliad* (1935), *Ancient Greek Literature* (1935), *The Heritage of Symbolism* (1943), *Sophoclean Tragedy* (1943), *From Virgil to Milton* (1945), *Edith Sitwell* (1947), *A Second Book of Russian Verse* (1948), *The Creative Experiment* (1949), *The Romantic Imagination* (1950), *Heroic Poetry* (1952), *Problems in Greek Poetry* (1953) and *Inspiration and Poetry* (1955).

  1. Garsington, the beautiful manor house of Lady Ottoline and Philip Morrell.
  2. Yeats received the Doctorate of Letters from Oxford University in May 1931.
  3. Rainer Maria Rilke (1875–1926), German lyric poet and writer.

4. Stefan George (1868–1933), German poet; associated with Baudelaire and Mallarmé in Paris and with the Pre-Raphaelite group in London; leader of 'art for art's sake' school of poetry in Germany.

W. B. Yeats—
A Generation Later*

THOMAS MACGREEVY

One of the things I most regret is that W. B. Yeats did not live for, at least, a year longer than he did. Had he lived through the autumn of 1939 he would have seen his divided fellow-countrymen re-uniting for the purpose of declaring Irish neutrality in regard to the second great war. Partition or no Partition, neutrality was a clinching re-affirmation of the Irish nationhood in which he believed and for the recognition of which he had helped to fight all his life long. He accepted the idea that a distinctive cultural heritage implies distinctive nationhood.

I cannot say whether W.B. would endorse a heartening remark Monsignor Paddy Browne[1] once made to me. It was to the effect that the civil war had left less bitterness between Irishmen than the Parnell split had left a generation earlier. But I incline to think that W.B., who lived through both crises, would have agreed. He knew that after the Parnell crisis and until the general election of 1918 there was disunion (as between Redmondites,[2] Healyites,[3] All for Irelanders, Independents and Sinn Feiners—not to speak of the less disinterested clique represented by Edward Carson).[4] He knew enough of human nature to realise that it is only in times of crisis that even the most serious minded and well intentioned men and women can overcome their inevitable, though ultimately perhaps minor, differences, and that the greater the crisis that has brought them together the greater for a certain length of time afterwards their differences will seem. His poem *The Road at My Door*[5] written, I think, at Ballylee in the early weeks of the civil war when he was 58 shows how complete was his understanding and his sympathy for the men on both sides.

> An affable Irregular,
> A heavily-built Falstaffian man,
> Comes cracking jokes of civil war
> As though to die by gunshot were
> The finest play under the sun.

* *University Review* (Dublin) III, no. 8 (1966) 3–14.

A brown Lieutenant and his men,
Half dressed in national uniform,
Stand at my door, and I complain
Of the foul weather, hail and rain,
A pear-tree broken by the storm.

I count those feathered balls of soot
The moor-hen guides upon the stream,
To silence the envy of my thought;
And turn towards my chamber, caught
In the cold snows of a dream.

Back in Dublin, later in 1922, he decided to accept a seat in the Senate from Mr. Cosgrave's government. He was a little put out when, daring to argue with him against his decision, I remarked that Leonardo da Vinci had remained utterly detached in regard to the unholy rivalries and wars that arose between the different claimants to the duchy of Milan. But in spite of much misunderstanding on the part of those who did not know him well, despite the occasional stubborn obstinacies on his part that could annoy even those close to him—myself, I would at times feel 'contrary' about what, until I could come to fuller understanding, seemed to be *his* 'contrarinesses'—I cannot, looking back, but think that W. B. Yeats was one of the most patient men I have known. He did not snub the young man that I was for disagreeing with a major decision he had made and I doubt whether his decision to enter the Senate cost him the regard of any serious minded Republican. Had he not written (in *The Celtic Twilight*) shortly after the Parnell tragedy: 'There is always something in our enemy that we like and something in our sweetheart that we dislike.' For him as for all Irishmen the evacuation of Dublin Castle by the English was a symbol and an event of the first magnitude in Irish history. After such a major achievement and taking the circumstances into account, a new disunion was not altogether unnatural. It happened. And the ranks did not close again until 1939. I think, however, that in spite of the civil war there was much understanding not only on the part of Yeats but amongst thinking men on both sides. I am sure that Republicans understood that W.B. made the decision he did make in order to see whether he could help to work constructively, in the new circumstances created by the unsatisfactory Treaty, for the cause of the Ireland he had always dreamed of and always written about. As was natural the Ireland he dreamed of was a cultural as well as a heroic Ireland deriving from its own past heritage adapted to present circumstances. It was to be the Ireland of *The King's Threshold* in which no mere man of power might, with impunity, dare to treat thinkers and poets, the men of mind and imagination, as inferior to himself. Ideally, the ambition for power should mean the ambition to be of service. The word 'minister' means 'servant' and 'to serve.' Has not the supreme Head of the Church to try to live up to his noblest title 'The servant of the servants of God'?

I have spoken of Yeats as a patient man. He had dreamed of a cultural panel in the Senate that would be a cultural panel in his sense of the word, a panel not of mere men of property and professional specialists but of all-round humanists. His dream was not realised but he did not make a fuss over his disappointment. He just left after a few years without complaining.

Again anyone who cared for his ideals in the theatre could not help but think that there, above all, he carried patience to excessive lengths. It was not from his Russian and French contemporaries, Stanislavsky and Lungé-Poe [sic],[6] that he got the idea of an art theatre for Ireland. He thought of it, he worked for it, he provided plays for it. Yet he allowed himself to be all but played out of that theatre by the realists and the defeatists. That he will yet be recognised as a great and inspiring dramatist I have no doubt whatever. Even I, who am growing old, hope that I may yet live to see Yeats's own plays—and Irish plays not unworthy to be played with them—being produced at the Peacock Theatre by a man or woman who has feeling for poetry; and, by God's providence, acted right through the year for Irish lovers of dramatic poetry, out of the tourist season as well as in it. The Abbey Theatre with its subsidy and its many more money-making plays should surely be able to act as guarantor!

I am quite aware that there are people who think that Yeats was not a dramatist at all. It seems to me that the poet who could present the miracle of the Resurrection of Our Lord convincingly in dramatic form was nothing short of a supreme dramatist. In any plays in which he collaborated with Augusta Gregory—they were both generous in acknowledging the debt they owed each other—we may take it that the heroic element was contributed by him, the passages of dialogue that made the heroic element easier for an audience to grasp, by her. He would have given her credit for that extraordinary prophetic play *The Unicorn from the Stars* in which the destroyer ends up with nothing to destroy except himself. But Lady Gregory would not have it that the play was hers. That play was written in 1908 twenty-five years before Adolf Hitler came to power in 1933, but when I saw it played in London in 1940 it seemed to me so cogent to the European situation of the day that (apart needless to say from the beauty of the treatment) it might have been commissioned from some Allied literary propagandist. Generous in her turn, Augusta Gregory, though she did allow herself to be treated as the author of *The Rising of the Moon*,[7] would insist that Yeats had an important part in the writing of it. (Incidentally, for those now living who saw Kerrigan's[8] performance as the man 'on the run' in that small masterpiece it must remain an imperishably inspiring memory).

There are a few of W.B.'s plays about which I have reserve. I once sat with him through a performance of *The Shadowy Waters*.[9] It was not, on that occasion, well produced but, reading it now, I incline to think that, heroic as is the idea and beautiful as is the poetry, it is not one of W.B.'s specifically dramatic successes. Again, *Calvary*,[10] which I have never seen played, though I am told that it is good 'theatre', is as unconvincing to me as the *Resurrection*[11] is convincing. Vis-à-vis Christian tradition it seems to derive, in the first place, perhaps, from the incipient scepticism of some of the dullest of the many dull lines in Tennyson's *In Memoriam*—

> Where wert thou brother, those four days?
> There lives no record of reply . . .

and in the second place from the over-clever English eighteen-nineties. And again, I think I see too much of that same English eighteen-nineties influence in *The King of the Great Clock Tower*.[12] I pay little attention to the influence of the so-called 'Celtic Twilight' in which, in his young days, even Yeats himself half-believed. The Celtic Twilight seems to have been a flapdoodle theory invented by Ernest Renan and propagated by his English disciple, Mathew Arnold. The Yeats who at 27 or 28 wrote

> Troy passed away in one high funeral gleam
> And Usna's children died

not only integrated Ireland's sorrow into the sorrow of all the world since European civilisation began with Homer but was more than ready for all that the Renaissance came to mean to him from the time of his first visit to Italy, which was not until 1907 when he was 42. Of the twenty four plays, from the *Countess Cathleen* (1892) down to *The Death of Cuchulain* (1939), and not counting the translations from Sophocles, most are masterpieces. For me *The Death of Cuchulain* which was the last of all, and which I saw acted by Mr. Austin Clarke's players (with scenery and costumes by Anne Yeats) some years since, is one of the greatest of all. The conversation between Aoife and Cuchulain in that play is surely one of the most moving dialogues any tragic dramatist has written.

Defeated in his hopes of seeing the cultural panel of all-round humanists, Gael and Gall, that he had dreamed of for the Senate, as he had been defeated in his hopes of seeing the art theatre he had dreamed of for the Abbey, W.B. still refused to lose patience.

In talk he would protest that he could not consider himself an educated man. Actually it is hardly to be questioned that all his life he went on educating himself to the extraordinary degree that was needed for the expression of his extraordinary gifts. In addition he had educated himself to the point of being able to say, simply and honestly, 'I don't know' in regard to subjects of which he sensed the importance but did not feel himself sufficiently equipped to express opinions. He despaired, however, of the type of modern man who, whether he owns fifty thousand acres or whether he be a specialist in some profession or other, will say, off-handedly 'I know nothing about art' and then insist on adding consequentially 'but I know what I like.' As if in regard to every aspect of living it did not take experience and study to know with some degree of certainty what one likes! Similarly W.B. despaired of the scientifically-minded amateurs who, whenever a new scientific discovery is made by technical experts, choose to assume that it justifies further disbelief in regard to the mysteries which, from the beginning of history, men of intelligence have pondered, the mysteries of God and of human existence.

Ostensibly the Yeatses were Church of Ireland Protestants but it would be difficult to say how far their upbringing encouraged them fully to conform to the teaching of any religion. Jack Yeats told me he had never been confirmed and in consequence had never 'taken the Sacrament' as, I gathered, would have been necessary if he was to be considered a full member of his church. How the girls and W.B. fared in that matter I do not know. But I think it could hardly be said that W.B. subscribed formally to any established religious belief—or for that matter, to any philosophical system. Yet those who knew him well often noticed that any reference to personal religious experience or to personal restatement of a philosophic position excited his eager interest. His confession in some essay of his—one referring to Rapallo if I remember rightly—that he liked to sit in empty churches may have been a characteristic reaction to his very nineteenth-century father's latitudinarian approach in such matters.

He was the reverse of anti-religious but he seemed to have met few clerics whose answers to his questions satisfied him. Yet when (again in *The Celtic Twilight*) he pointed out the contrast between the cruelty of the endings of many Scottish stories of the 'unseen', as compared with the good-natured and half humorous turn such stories take in Irish folk-lore as they reach their climax, he makes it quite clear that he was having a thrust at the pulpit-influence of Calvinist teaching and, on behalf of the Irish tradition, added 'the Catholic religion likes to keep on good terms with its neighbours.' I know that there was at least one Catholic cleric in whose conversation he took pleasure. That was Monsignor Browne. They met only rarely but I was myself present at one long evening session when the talk, whether serious or light, was of both men's best. I had been reading Duchesne[13] and I suggested that some remark of W.B.'s savoured of Gnosticism. W.B. was immediately interested and questioning. Monsignor Paddy, hiding his amusement at seeing me in the role of amateur theologian—though I heard about *that* as he drove me back from Rathfarnham to Dublin—was able to amplify satisfactorily on my suggestion as W.B. questioned further. Incidentally, I heard W.B. repeat, orally, at that session, the message which he had already had conveyed to Monsignor, that, on her deathbed, Augusta Gregory asked me to let Monsignor Browne know that the *Beatha Iosa Criost*, which Monsignor, in collaboration with Monsignor Boylan, had recently published, was the book that gave her most comfort in her last days.

Despite some far-back connection with the Butlers, who once wielded power in Kilkenny, the Yeats family were not what is known as 'big house' people. John Butler Yeats the Elder was a barrister turned artist. His father and grandfather were parsons. But one does not have to know much Irish history to know that in the nineteenth century 'the big house' rather took parsons for granted. It was more concerned with wooing Catholic priests, in the hope that they would discourage their parishioners from effectively participating in the ever-recurring rebellious political and social agitations of the times. The Yeatses, W.B., Jack and their sisters, could take pride in being Yeatses but they took just as much pride in being, on their mother's side, Pollexfens. The Pollexfens were millers and merchants and ship-owners. 'We had no gate lodges and no carriage drives,' Jack Yeats would say. As W.B.'s fame grew however, he inevitably had to rub shoulders with 'big house' people in England. At one stage he said to me that Ottoline Morell[14] was the only one of them he knew with whom he could talk his own kind of talk. I enquired of him about another group, socially but not intellectually of much the same world as Ottoline Morrell, with whom he had to do, when, on occasion, it suited their purpose to intrude on *his* world. 'Church-wardens,' said W.B. 'They are only fit to be church-wardens.' But, hopefully, he would make concessions. 'One is always making concessions,' he said to me once. At Coole and after he entered the Senate and the Kildare Street Club he had to meet more and more Irish 'big-house' people. In one case he went so far as to speak at an election meeting on behalf of one of them, an amiable enough man who had inherited a library and who could throw an occasional literary tag into his not very stimulating conversation. Again I dared to ask W.B. why. Patiently, and obviously in agreement with my estimate of the man concerned, he explained. 'For me, he represents the people who, in the eighteenth century, read their classics.' In retrospect, I think that that answer was a kind of preparation for the lecture he gave later at the Royal Dublin Society which startled many of his admirers, but which, again in retrospect, I incline to think was addressed rather more to the men of the 'big house' than to the Irish people. For W.B. knew quite well that in lore and song and story the Irish people had cherished undying affection for the memory of the professional men of the ascendency and the rare 'big house' men of the ascendency who, in the past, had deserted their own English provincial traditions and who, in such cases as those of Tone and Emmet—and Edward Fitzgerald too—had gone so far as to lay down their lives for the revolution it would have been had the people of the Irish nation won self-government. The Irish people knew also that Swift and Burke had on occasion been of some help. But, in his lecture, W.B. put forward these two, and George Berkeley with them, as reactionary (which to him, in his political innocence, meant merely orderly) counterblasts to the revolutionaries. Politically, W.B. was as innocent as most laymen. About 1923 or 1924 he told me he believed that Mussolini represented the rise of the individual man as against what he considered the anti-human party machine. I was most distrustful about 'Il Duce' but I did not know enough then to answer that Mussolini was believed to be in the hands of an economically, and therefore politically, powerful group of men in Italy. W.B. did know enough abstract history, to know that it is axiomatic that revolution has to be followed by reaction. The Irish ascendency as a whole had tended to be selfishly reactionary. In fact Irish landlordism had become a byword. W.B. would insist on trying now to provide the ascendency with a group of philosophic avatars, Swift and Berkeley and Burke, who were reactionary but not selfish. The question was whether, in the new order of things created in Ireland by the Treaty, ascendency people as a whole could be persuaded to play a constructive part. That could help towards the ultimate realisation of the unified and cultured Ireland of W.B.'s dreams. There is little evidence to show what influence his famous lecture has had on the ascendency, or how far any of its members has moved towards giving his or her first allegiance to Ireland.

Then, though now he was having to be careful of his health, W.B. began to plan something else. Myself, I had become *Lecteur d'Anglais* at the Ecole Normale in Paris. It would probably be an exaggeration to say that W.B. 'consulted' me about his newest scheme, that of founding an Irish Academy of letters. He could, and I have no doubt did consult men better qualified to advise him than I was. But, patiently again, he went into the question in some of his letters to me. I had no inner knowledge of the workings of the *Académie Française* and my first reaction was to point out that none of the modern French writers W.B. himself most admired, Balzac, Baudelaire, Villiers de l'Isle Adam, Stephane Mallarmé, had been elected to membership of it. Still W.B. persisted. Staying with him on my way home on holidays, I gathered a better impression of what his hope was—that in the matters of cultural values and style the standards set by his academy should constitute points of departure for Irish literary men in the future.

Perhaps they have already done so, perhaps they will do so yet. Perhaps there will one day be a permanent Irish art theatre. Perhaps there will one day be a cultural panel of humanists in the Senate. Perhaps one day the remnants of the ascendency—or for that matter their only too possible Commisar successors—will give their first allegiance to Ireland. It will not be the fault of W. B. Yeats if these things do not come about.

W.B.'s Irish Academy of Letters brings me to a subject which is seldom referred to—the *fun* that it was knowing W.B. He had endless humorous stories of people's oddities of behaviour and the 'contrarinesses' of individuals he had known. He could retail them lightheartedly and to effect. Thus he had at some time been involved in a London effort to establish an English equivalent of the *Académie Française*. The interested parties elected academicians and meetings were held. One of the members was an art authority and literary figure of some distinction named Selwyn Image.[15] Image, I gathered, was a slight little figure and mild of manner, but at every meeting he would, sooner or later, be heard protesting, gently but persistently, that there was no sense in calling themselves academicians unless they wore a uniform! Only thus arrayed could they, to his mind, rank in the world's eyes as the equals of the forty 'immortals' of the French *Académie* who, on official occasions, have to wear the famous *habit vert*.[16]

It may have been from the London academy also that a deputation of writers, which I think included W.B. himself, was chosen to convey to Doughty,[17] author of the famous but little-read *Arabia Deserta*, the information that the government wished to honour him; and to enquire whether he would accept the Order of Merit if it were offered to him. Doughty was a taciturn Olympian living a secluded life some distance from London. The deputation arrived at his house, was shown into the great man's presence and with all the courtesies and complimentary references to his work that the occasion called for, explained the purpose of the visit. Doughty listened in silence. When the visitors had each said his say, he gave his answer. Quite quietly and with the verbal economy that has become characteristic of him he spoke: 'I don't want the bloody thing' was all he said.

In the 1952 issue of *The Capuchin Annual* I referred[18] to the comic conspiracies of Dublin literary life as W.B. would tell how he found them over the years. One or two will perhaps bear retelling. *The Leader*, apparently, was liable to be unfriendly to his ideas on an Irish art theatre policy. But W.B. told me laughingly that if, in the old days, they had a play coming on which was likely to prove controversial he could call round to *The Leader* office, tell D. P. Moran, the editor and ostensible enemy, about it and ask that, if the play had to be attacked it should be on some, to W.B., unimportant, ground rather than on the one that might prove damaging to the theatre effort as a whole. Always D.P. would see what he could do about it and no harm would be done. Again, apropos of the controversy as to who it was who should be regarded as the real founder of the theatre which in time became known as the Abbey Theatre, I remember a night when W.B. had undertaken to give a lecture to a group of students at, I think, some place in Grafton Street. Apparently he had proposed a title for the lecture which allowed him some latitude. For he came back from the function full of glee. 'Frank Fay was in the front row' he told me, 'so I didn't give the lecture I meant to give.' Then he added with a mischievous smile, 'I told them instead that they should all read James Joyce.'

Actually, though he testified publicly that he thought Joyce had 'a heroic mind' I doubt whether he really felt sympathetic to the philosophic implications of Joyce's literary work. There was an afternoon in London when on my way back from Paris I had to get some heavy luggage registered through to Dublin in advance. Dolly Lennox Robinson came up to Euston with me. There we came on W.B. who was also out on some errand or other. 'We'll go to my club for tea,' he said. So in we got to a taxi and set off for Brook Street. But when we arrived at the club the hall porter pointed out that it was not a 'ladies' day, so Dolly could not come in. I proposed an alternative. 'Let us go to the Carlton instead and it will be my tea. It is the best three-an-sixpence worth in London.' Out we went, found another taxi and drove down Regent Street and Haymarket. Perhaps the Haymarket had already become a one-way street with a left turn at the end. At any rate I stopped the taxi at the side-door of the Carlton in Haymarket instead of going on to the main entrance which was in Pall Mall to the right. As I knew the way it was agreed that I should go first. But behind me W.B. whispered to Dolly. 'Look at the cool way MacGreevy walks into a place like this. I've always been afraid of grand hotels.' (Actually I had grown up more afraid of grand hotels than any Yeats but a short time as a young artillery officer in the first war had taught me not to be afraid of them and taught me too that you could often get better value in them than in less pretentious establishments). We did, in the event, have a very good tea and good service and I think we all enjoyed ourselves. Of the conversation, I remember particularly that W.B. said Joyce had been to see him early in the afternoon and that it had been a pleasant visit—though W.B. added 'There is still that element of pugnaciousness in Joyce's manner that one used to notice in Dublin long ago.'

Like most of the world and unlike the darkly resentful few, W.B. could have serious differences and even quarrels with people yet without final breaks resulting from them. He was young when he wrote 'There is always something in our enemy that we like' and I would say that, for himself, that remained true up to the end. He could make a mischievous joke but it was only a joke and I never heard him say anything really damaging about anyone. The verbal portrait of him that George Moore painted in *Hail and Farewell*[19] seems to me to be a piece of mocking mimicry rather than a portrait in the true sense of the word. Portrait painting after all is a noble art. As between Moore and Yeats there may or may not have been a final break but it was only when Moore Hall was burned down during the civil war that in my hearing Yeats bothered to invent a mischievous joke about Moore. 'At last people in London will believe that he was brought up as a gentleman,' he said. I never heard him refer to the story that Cardinal Logue had condemned *Countess Cathleen* without reading it and I never remembered to ask him about it.[20]

It was in London, where he introduced me to every friend of his who might be of interest to me or useful to me, that, at dinner one night, he said, 'You ought to know Arthur Waley[21] too. He is out with me at the moment but that won't last long.' On a night when, with Mrs. Yeats, he was passing through Paris I dined with them. My latest news was that one of the parties in a drama of personalities that was going on claimed to be a re-incarnation of Shelley. Gleefully W. B. commented, 'That makes four I have come across.'

When he was alone with A.E. I believe they talked contentedly like the life-long friends they were. But if they had an audience there was danger of argument. Once, in company with Eamon Curtis,[22] I heard them positively rage at each other about, of all thing, *The Playboy* row of years and years before. 'It's like a war of the gods and heroes,' Curtis whispered to me. I have friends who think that Yeats could be too cruel with A.E., as on a night in Merrion Square when A.E. rambled on for a while in praise of Walt Whitman. Yeats remained silent and then suddenly cut in with oracular finality, 'No, Russell! No!' he said firmly, 'Whitman is one of the errors of our youth.' But it could be that on such occasions Yeats was only getting his own back in his own forthright way. In the literary world, like all worlds, rumour circulates and Yeats must surely have known that A.E. wrote parodies of his work in both poetry and prose and at his home in Rathgar Avenue would read them to his cronies. I myself heard A.E. read a derisive extravaganza he had written on the head of W.B.'s literary heroics, with particular reference to the use of the word 'Homeric' in an article which W.B. had published on Lady Gregory's *Cuchulain of Muirthemne*. Except on the lips of some—and only some—of the characters in her plays, I, myself, have always found the Kiltartan dialect used by Augusta Gregory somewhat irksome. Still, looking back now, I incline to think that the account in the Gregory book of Cuchulain's interview with his mother before going out to what, he foresees, will be his death, may well be considered Homeric.

Both A.E. and W.B. were interested in psychic phenomena. Whether A.E. ever engaged in what is called 'psychical research' I don't know. W.B. did. So did people I occasionally came across, and in Paris and London as well as in Dublin. But it was W.B. who said to me, 'Practically every medium has to cheat at times, especially with people whose eagerness for results springs from the need of comfort.' I have never believed that knowledge of the inexplicable things that happen to all of us can be systematised. But, contrary to general belief, I know that, sooner or later, W.B. would come to laugh about occasions on which he had been ready to be over credulous. On the other hand, though he could laugh at the true comedy effects in Bernard Shaw's plays, he detested Shaw's tendency to dispose of the inexplicable with a smart phrase; as he detested the fact that Shaw's always too polemical plays tended to make actors speak like lawyers. W.B. would have them competent to speak like poets. It is to be feared that even in the Irish theatre the Shaw influence has gained ground at the expence of the Yeats influence.

Coming back to the fun it was knowing Yeats as a man, I would recall a letter he wrote to me about my monograph[23] on T. S. Eliot. I had some years experience of Eliot's phenomonal charm, but I came to think that there was a perennial though only faintly perceptible element of astuteness behind it. In conversation Eliot tended to be excessively flattering to his interlocutor. It was thinking of Eliot that I learned to advise people, especially young writers, to beware of charm. 'We can have charm ourselves,' I told them, 'when we want to.' After a kind reference to the 'momentum' he said he found in my 'crabbed, passionate and lucid' prose, W.B. went on to say—I quote from memory—'Eliot cannot write prose. Pound at his best writes finer prose than Eliot does. . . . Eliot is dancing among eggs.'

Finally, returning to the Yeatsian attitude to Shaw, I noticed recently that a paper-back edition of Shaw's *Androcles and The Lion* has been published. It is a very good serio-comic play about a mixed lot of early Christians. The prose preface to the play, however, is no more than an attempt by a good-natured but all too smart casuist to present Christ as a most estimable social reformer who was deluded into believing himself to be God. I am convinced that that preface has been a disturbing influence on intelligent youth ever since it was first published; and that it is responsible for much of the disturbed state of mind of the youth of to-day. W. B. Yeats tended to prefer belief to disbelief. In the two or three years before his death, however, I saw little of him and I do not know where he stood finally in regard to Christianity. The reappearance of the Shaw play and preface in the bookshops reminded me of something that could be cogent. Once W.B. asked me could I explain why Browning's poetry had intellectual quality when the work of most English poets had not. My answer excited him. 'Browning was a quarter Scots and a quarter Jewish.' If W.B. were alive now it is not an answer I would have to excite him with; but a seemingly outrageous question to put to him that, as things are to-day, he would, I dare to think, find exciting. It is a simple question for mature intelligences but one that the world we live in needs to consider: 'Would you agree that Saint John was a greater writer than Bernard Shaw?'

W.B. is dead over a quarter of a century. I think back on the excitement and fun that it was knowing him familiarly; and I miss him.

NOTES

Thomas MacGreevy (1893–1967) was an Irish poet and critic. He helped found the Irish Central Library for Students, lectured in Paris University (1926–33), and remained as a journalist of the arts there until the war. In 1941 he returned to Dublin and was made Director of the National Gallery in 1950. (When in 1926, on the resignation of Lucius O'Callaghan from the directorship of the Gallery, Dr Thomas Bodkin decided to stand for the post, Yeats put forward MacGreevy as candidate). His principal works include *Introduction to the Method of Leonardo da Vinci* (1929), *Jack B. Yeats* (1929), *Pictures in the Irish National Gallery* (1945) and *Nicolas Poussin* (1960).

  1. Patrick Browne, of Maynooth.
  2. Followers of John Edward Redmond (1856–1918), the Irish political leader who organised the home rule propaganda and led the Parnellite group on the death of Parnell in 1891.
  3. Followers of Timothy Michael Healy (1855–1931), the Irish Nationalist leader and statesman who vigorously advocated home rule and who became the first Governor-General of the Irish Free State (1922–7).
  4. Edward Henry Carson (1854–1935), British jurist and politician who became Solicitor-General for Ireland in 1892.

5. In *The Tower* (London: Macmillan, 1928).

6. Aurelien-Marie Lugne-Poe (1869–1940), French actor and manager who did much to encourage young playwrights, and at the same time helped forward the development of the modern French theatre by putting before it the best contemporary work of other countries.

7. *The Rising of the Moon* opened at the Abbey Theatre on 9 March 1907.

8. J. M. Kerrigan. According to the list as given in the original programme of the play, Kerrigan played the part of 'Policeman B'. See Lennox Robinson, *Ireland's Abbey Theatre* (London: Sidgwick and Jackson, 1951) p. 80.

9. *The Shadowy Waters* had its premiere at the Molesworth Hall on 14 January 1904; with it was produced *The Townland of Tamney* by Seumas MacManus.

10. In *Four Plays for Dancers* (London: Macmillan, 1921).

11. *The Resurrection*, a play in one act, was first presented at the Abbey Theatre on 30 July 1934. The first sketch of the play, more dialogue than play, and intended for drawing-room rather than theatre, dated from 1925, when it was read out at 82 Merrion Square to a few people.

12. The first night of *The King of the Great Clock Tower*, also a play in one act, was at the Abbey Theatre on 30 July 1934. Both *The Resurrection* and *The King* were presented together.

13. André Duchesne (1584–1640) was a French historian, known as the 'father of French history'.

14. Lady Ottoline Morrell, whose house and gardens at Garsington inspired the first section of Yeats's poem 'Meditations in Time of Civil War'.

15. Selwyn Image was a member of the Rhymers' Club, which was founded in 1891 and met in an upper room of the 'Cheshire Cheese'.

16. Green suit.

17. Charles Montagu Doughty (1843–1926), English poet and traveller.

18. 'Uileachan Dubh O', *The Capuchin Annual 1952*, ed. Fr Senan (Dublin, n.d.) pp. 211–42 [a tour of the Yeats country with reminiscences of the poet and an account of his reburial in Sligo].

19. George Moore, *Hail and Farewell* (London: Heinemann, 1911–14) vol. i: *Ave, passim*; vol. ii: *Salve*, pp. 69–107 *passim*; vol. iii: *Vale*, pp. 113–42 *passim*.

20. Yeats's play *The Countess Cathleen* provoked religious condemnation and Yeats and Lady Gregory had to consult ecclesiastical authorities who gave their approval of the play. George Moore, however, attacked Yeats for submitting a work of art to the criticisms of theologians. Yeats's old enemy F. H. O'Donnell wrote a pamphlet entitled *Souls for Gold*, which suggested that the selling of souls in the play was a slight upon the morality of the people of Ireland. A controversy arose in the public press: the play was condemned by Cardinal Michael Logue (1840–1924), who admitted that he had not read the text.

21. Arthur David Waley (1889–1966), Assistant Curator at the British Museum and translator of such Chinese and Japanese literary works as *170 Chinese Poems* (1919), *Japanese Poetry* (1919) and *The No-Plays of Japan* (1922).

22. Edmund Curtis (1881–1943), Professor of Modern History at the University of Dublin and the author of *A History of Ireland* (1936).

23. Thomas MacGreevy, *Thomas Sterns Eliot* (London: Chatto and Windus, 1931).

Appendix

Additional Bibliography

The references in this list—arranged alphabetically—comprise secondary material which may be of use in additional fields of biographical inquiry. A brief annotation has been supplied where necessary.

Aldington, Richard, *Life for Life's Sake: A Book of Reminiscences* (New York: Viking Press, 1941) pp. 107–9 [in London], 336–7 [in Rapallo].

Andrews, Irene D., 'A Glimpse of Yeats', *Reading and Collecting*, II, no. 3 (Feb–Mar 1938), 8–9 [at Dr Oliver St John Gogarty's Georgian mansion on Ely Place].

Cattaui, Georges, 'Rencontres avec W. B. Yeats', *Nouvelles littéraires* (Paris) 4 Feb 1939, pp. 1, 9.

Chesterton, G. K., 'Some Literary Celebrities I Have Known', *The Saturday Review Gallery*, sel. Jerome Beatty Jr *et al.* (New York: Simon and Schuster, 1959) pp. 156–61.

Curran, C. P., *Under the Receding Wave* (Dublin: Gill and Macmillan; London: Macmillan, 1970).

Daly, Dominic, *The Young Douglas Hyde; The Dawn of the Irish Revolution and Renaissance 1874–1893* (Dublin: Irish University Press, 1974).

de Blacam, Aodh, 'Memories of the Mighty', *Irish Bookman* (Dublin) I, no. 6 (Jan 1947) 15–18.

Eglinton, John, 'Apologia', *Confidential, or Take It or Leave It* [poems] (London: Fortune Press, 1951) pp. 5–10 [reminiscences of Yeats and his literary circle].

Ellmann, Richard, *Eminent Domain: Yeats among Wilde, Joyce, Pound, Eliot & Auden* (London and New York: Oxford University Press, 1967).

Esson, Louis, 'Irish Memories and Australian Hopes', *Union Recorder*, 24 Nov 1938, pp. 281–2. [some reminiscences of Yeats].

Gibbon, Monk, *The Masterpiece and the Man: Yeats As I Knew Him* (London: Rupert Hart-Davis, 1959).

Glenavy, Lady Beatrice, *Today We Will Only Gossip* (London: Constable, 1964) *passim* [personal reminiscences of Yeats].

Gogarty, Oliver St John, *As I Was Walking Down Sackville Street: A Phantasy in Fact* (London: Rich and Cowan; New York: Reynal and Hitchcock, 1937; Hardmondsworth, Middlesex: Penguin Books, 1954) *passim* [personal reminiscences of Yeats].

—, *Rolling Down the Lea* (London: Constable, 1950) pp. 108–11, 163, 219–21 [reminiscences of Yeats].

—, *It Isn't This Time of Year At All! An Unpremediated Autobiography* (London: MacGibbon and Kee, 1954) pp. 202–6 [on a performance of *At the Hawk's Well* held at Gogarty's house, and on Yeats's introductory speech].

—, *William Butler Yeats: A Memoir*, with a preface by Myles Dillon (Dublin: Dolmen Press, 1963).

Gregory, Lady, 'William Butler Yeats', *Lady Gregory's Journals, 1916–1930*, ed. Lennox Robinson (London: Putnam's 1946; New York: Macmillan, 1947) pp. 259–66.

Headlam, Maurice, *Irish Reminiscences* (London: Robert Hale, 1947) *passim*.

Holloway, Joseph, *Joseph Holloway's Abbey Theatre: A Selection from His Unpublished Journal*

'*Impressions of a Dublin Playgoer*', ed. Robert Hogan and Michael J. O'Neill (Carbondale and Edwardsville, Illinois: Southern Illinois University Press; London and Amsterdam: Feffer and Simons, 1967) pp. 61–250 *passim* [conversations].

—, *Joseph Holloway's Irish Theatre, 1926–1944*, 3 vols, ed. Robert Hogan and Michael J. O'Neill (Dixon, California: Proscenium Press, 1968–70) *passim*.

Jones, E. Aykroyd, 'The Sincerity of Yeats', *Focus* (Dublin) (June 1965) pp. 127–8 [recalls an evening spent with the poet in 1921].

MacBride, Maud Gonne, *A Servant of the Queen; Reminiscences* (London: Gollancz, 1938) *passim*.

MacGreevy, Thomas, 'Uileachan Dubg O', *The Capuchin Annual 1952*, ed. Fr Senan (Dublin, n.d.) pp. 211–42 [a tour of the Yeats country with reminiscences of the poet and an account of his reburial in Sligo].

Monroe, Harriet, *A Poet's Life: Seventy Years in a Changing World* (New York: Macmillan, 1938) *passim*.

Moore, George, *Hail and Farewell*, 3 vols (London: Heinemann; New York: Appleton, 1911–14; London: Heinemann, 1933; Ebury Edition, 1936–7) vol. I: *Ave, passim*; vol. II: *Salve*, pp. 69–107 *passim*; vol. III: *Vale*, pp. 113–42 *passim*.

O'Connor, Frank, 'The Old Age of a Poet', *Bell* (Dublin) I, no. 5 (Feb 1941) 7–18.

—, *My Father's Son* (London: Macmillan, 1968).

Ricketts, Charles, *Self-Portrait Taken from the Letters & Journals of Charles Ricketts*, collected and compiled by T. Sturge Moore, ed. Cecil Lewis (London: Peter Davies, 1939) *passim*.

Robinson, Lennox, 'W. B. Yeats', *I Sometimes Think* (Dublin: Talbot Press, 1956) pp. 101–4.

Rothenstein, William, *Men and Memories*, 2 vols (London: Faber & Faber; New York: Coward-McCann, 1931, 1935) vol. I: *Recollections 1872–1900*, pp. 282–3 *et passim*; vol. II: *Recollections 1900–1922, passim*.

—, 'Conversation of Yeats', *Since Fifty: Men and Memories, 1922–1938* (London: Faber and Faber, 1939) pp. 243–54.

Ryan, Desmond, *Remembering Sion; A Chronicle of Storm and Quiet* (London: Arthur Barker, 1934) pp. 86–7, 158, 164–5.

Sangu, Makoto, 'An Hour with Yeats', *Ieitsu Shiso* (Tokyo: Iwanami, 1946) pp. 153–63.

Strong, L. A. G., 'W. B. Yeats', *Personal Remarks* (London: Peter Nevill; New York: Liversight, 1953) pp. 13–33.

—, 'Memories of Yeats from 1919 to 1924', *Green Memory* (London: Methuen, 1961) pp. 242–63.

Tynan, Katharine, [Mrs H. A. Hinkson], *Twenty-Five Years: Reminiscences* (London: Smith, Elder; New York: Devin–Adair, 1913) *passim*.

—, *The Middle Years* (London: Constable, 1916; Boston: Houghton Mifflin, 1917) *passim*.

—, 'Personal Memories of John Butler Yeats', *The Double-Dealer*, IV (July 1922) 8–15 [on Yeats and his father].

White, Terence de Vere, 'Yeats as an Anglo-Irishman', *The Anglo-Irish* (London: Gollancz, 1972) pp. 39–51.

Yeats, W. B., *Letters on Poetry from W. B. Yeats to Dorothy Wellesley*, with a foreword by Dorothy Wellesley (London and New York: Oxford University Press, 1940) [includes comments and conversations].

Young, Ella, *Flowering Dusk: Things Remembered Accurately and Inaccurately* (New York and Toronto: Longmans, Green, 1945) *passim*.

Index

Page numbers followed by the letter n indicate that the reference is to a note.